T0178830

TORUS 1 – Toward an Open Resource Using Services

TORUS 1 – Toward an Open Resource Using Services

Cloud Computing for Environmental Data

Edited by

Dominique Laffly

WILEY

First published 2020 in Great Britain and the United States by ISTE Ltd and John Wiley & Sons, Inc.

ISTE Ltd
27-37 St George's Road
London SW19 4EU
UK

www.iste.co.uk

John Wiley & Sons, Inc.
111 River Street
Hoboken, NJ 07030
USA

www.wiley.com

Library of Congress Control Number: 2019956841

British Library Cataloguing-in-Publication Data
A CIP record for this book is available from the British Library
ISBN 978-1-78630-599-2

Contents

Chapter 17. Database for Cloud Computing   245

Peio LOUBIÈRE

**Chapter 18. WRF Performance Analysis and Scalability
on Multicore High Performance Computing Systems**   275

Didin Agustian PERMADI, Sebastiano Fabio SCHIFANO, Thi Kim Oanh NGUYEN,
Nhat Ha Chi NGUYEN, Eleonora LUPPI and Luca TOMASSETTI

Preface

Why TORUS? Toward an Open Resource Using Services, or How to Bring Environmental Science Closer to Cloud Computing

Geography, Ecology, Urbanism, Geology and Climatology – in short, all environmental disciplines are inspired by the great paradigms of Science: they were first descriptive before evolving toward systemic and complexity. The methods followed the same evolution, from the inductive of the initial observations one approached the deductive of models of prediction based on learning. For example, the Bayesian is the preferred approach in this book (see Volume 1, Chapter 5), but random trees, neural networks, classifications and data reductions could all be developed. In the end, all the methods of artificial intelligence (IA) are ubiquitous today in the era of Big Data. We are not unaware, however, that, forged in Dartmouth in 1956 by John McCarthy, Marvin Minsky, Nathaniel Rochester and Claude Shannon, the term artificial intelligence is, after a long period of neglect at the heart of the future issues of the exploitation of massive data (just like the functional and logical languages that accompanied the theory: LISP, 1958, PROLOG, 1977 and SCALA, today – see Chapter 8).

All the environmental disciplines are confronted with this reality of massive data, with the rule of the 3+2Vs: Volume, Speed (from the French translation, "Vitesse"), Variety, Veracity, Value. Every five days – or even less – and only for the optical remote sensing data of the Sentinel 2a and 2b satellites, do we have a complete coverage of the Earth at a spatial resolution of 10 m for a dozen wavelengths. How do we integrate all this, how do we rethink the environmental disciplines where we must now consider at the pixel scale (10 m) an overall analysis of 510 million km^2 or more than 5 billion pixels of which there are 1.53 billion for land only? And more important in fact, how do we validate automatic processes and accuracy of results?

Dartmouth Summer Research Project on Artificial Intelligence, 1956

A PROPOSAL FOR THE DARTMOUTH SUMMER
RESEARCH PROJECT ON ARTIFICIAL
INTELLIGENCE

J. McCarthy, Dartmouth College
M. L. Minsky, Harvard University
N. Rochester, I.B.M. Corporation
C.E. Shannon, Bell Telephone Laboratories

August 31, 1955

We propose that a 2 month, 10 man study of artificial intelligence be carried out during the summer of 1956 at Dartmouth College in Hanover, New Hampshire. The study is to proceed on the basis of the conjecture that every aspect of learning or any other feature of intelligence can in principle be so precisely described that a machine can be made to simulate it. An attempt will be made to find how to make machines use language, form abstractions and concepts, solve kinds of problems now reserved for humans, and improve themselves. We think that a significant advance can be made in one or more of these problems if a carefully selected group of scientists work on it together for a summer.

The following are some aspects of the artificial intelligence problem:

1. Automatic Computers

If a machine can do a job, then an automatic calculator can be programmed to simulate the machine. The speeds and memory capacities of present computers may be insufficient to simulate many of the higher functions of the human brain, but the major obstacle is not lack of machine capacity, but our inability to write programs taking full advantage of what we have.

2. How Can a Computer be Programmed to Use a Language

It may be speculated that a large part of human thought consists of manipulating words according to rules of reasoning and rules of conjecture. From this point of view, forming a generalization consists of admitting a new word and some rules whereby sentences containing it imply and are implied by others. This idea has never been very precisely formulated nor have examples been worked out.

3. Neuron Nets

How can a set of (hypothetical) neurons be arranged so as to form concepts. Considerable theoretical and experimental work has been done on this problem by Uttley, Rashevsky and his group, Farley and Clark, Pitts and McCulloch, Minsky, Rochester and Holland, and others. Partial results have been obtained but the problem needs more theoretical work.

Marvin Minksy, MIT
1927-2016

Claude Shannon, Bell
1916-2001

John McCarthy, MIT
1927-2011

Nathaniel Rochester, IBM
1919-2001

Figure P.1. *At the beginnig of AI, Dartmouth Summer Research Project, 1956. Source: http://www.oezratty.net/wordpress/2017/semantique-intelligence-artificielle/*

Including social network data, Internet of Things (IoT) and archive data, for many topics such as *Smart Cities*, it is not surprising that environmental disciplines are interested in cloud computing.

Before understanding the technique (why this shape, why a cloud?), it would seem that to represent a node of connection of a network, we have, as of the last 50 years, drawn a *potatoid* freehand, which, drawn took the form of a cloud. Figure P.2 gives a perfect illustration on the left, while on the right we see that the cloud is now the norm (screenshot offered by a search engine in relation to the keywords: Internet and network).

What is cloud computing? Let us remember that, even before the term was dedicated to it, cloud computing was based on networks (see Chapter 4), the Internet and this is: "*since the 50s when users accessed, from their terminals, applications running on central systems*" (Wikipedia). The cloud, as we understand it today, has evolved considerably since the 2000s; it consists of the mutualization of remote computing resources to store data and use services dynamically – to understand software – dedicated via browser interfaces.

The earlier US Patent US_5485455 linked above was filed Jan 28, 1994 by Cabletron Systems Inc. and includes the following diagram:

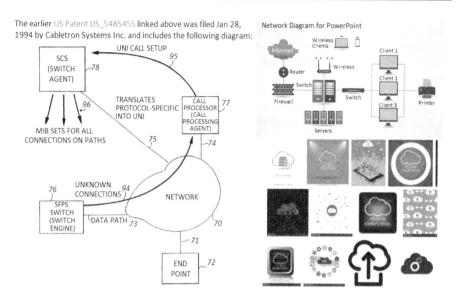

Figure P.2. *From freehand potatoid to the cloud icon. The first figure is a schematic illustration of a distributed SFPS switch. For a color version of this figure, see www.iste.co.uk/laffly/torus1.zip*

This answers the needs of the environmental sciences overwhelmed by the massive data flows: everything is stored in the cloud, everything is processed in the cloud, even the results expected by the end-users recover them according to their needs. It is no wonder that, one after the other, Google and NASA offered in December 2016 – mid-term of TORUS! – cloud-based solutions for the management and processing of satellite data: Google Earth Engine and NASA Earth Exchange.

But how do you do it? Why is it preferable – or not – for HPC (High Performance Computing) and GRIDS? How do we evaluate *"Cloud & High Scalability Computing"* versus *"Grid & High-Performance Computing"*? What are the costs? How do you transfer the applications commonly used by environmental science to the cloud? What is the added value for environmental sciences? In short, how does it work?

All these questions and more are at the heart of the TORUS program developed to learn from each other, understand each other and communicate with a common language mastered: geoscience, computer science and information science; and the geosciences between them; computer science and information sciences. TORUS is not a research program. It is an action that aims to bring together too (often) remote scientific communities, in order to bridge the gap that now separates contemporary computing from environmental disciplines for the most part. One evolving at speeds that cannot be followed by others, one that is greedy for data that others provide, one that can offer technical solutions to scientific questioning that is being developed by others and so on.

TORUS is also the result of multiple scientific collaborations initiated in 2008–2010: between the geographer and the computer scientist, between France and Vietnam with an increasing diversity of specialties involved (e.g. remote sensing and image processing, mathematics and statistics, optimization and modeling, erosion and geochemistry, temporal dynamics and social surveys) all within various scientific and university structures (universities, engineering schools, research institutes – IRD, SFRI and IAE Vietnam, central administrations: the Midi-Pyrénées region and Son La district, France–Vietnam partnership) and between research and higher education through national and international PhDs.

Naturally, I would like to say, the *Erasmus+ capacity building* program of the European Union appeared to be a solution adapted to our project:

> "*The objectives of the Capacity Building projects are: to support the modernization, accessibility and internationalization of higher education in partner countries; improve the quality, relevance and governance of higher education in partner countries; strengthen the capacity of higher education institutions in partner countries and in the EU, in terms of international cooperation and the process of permanent modernization in particular; and to help them open up to society at large and to the world of work in order to reinforce the interdisciplinary and transdisciplinary nature of higher education, to improve the employability of university graduates, to give the European higher education more visibility and attractiveness in the world, foster the reciprocal development of human resources, promote a better understanding between the peoples and cultures of the EU and partner countries.*"[1]

In 2015, TORUS – funded to the tune of 1 million euros for three years – was part of the projects selected in a pool of more than 575 applications and only 120 retentions. The partnership brings together (Figure P.3) the University of Toulouse 2 Jean Jaurès (coordinator – FR), the International School of Information Processing Sciences (EISTI – FR), the University of Ferrara in Italy, the Vrije University of Brussels, the National University from Vietnam to Hanoi, Nong Lam University in Ho Chi Minh City and two Thai institutions: Pathumthani's Asian Institute of Technology (AIT) and Walaikak University in Nakhon Si Thammarat.

---

1 http://www.agence-erasmus.fr/page/developpement-des-capacites.

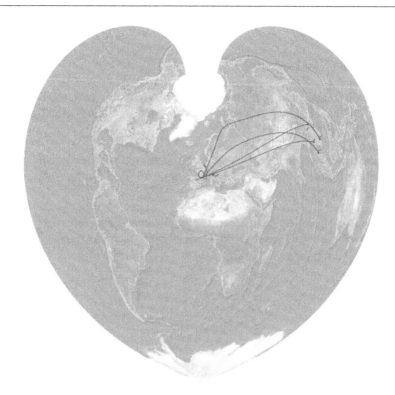

Figure P.3. *The heart of TORUS, partnership between Asia and Europe.*
For a color version of this figure, see www.iste.co.uk/laffly/torus1.zip

With an equal share between Europe and Asia, 30 researchers, teachers-researchers and engineers are involved in learning from each other during these three years, which will be punctuated by eight workshops between France, Vietnam, Italy, Thailand and Belgium. Finally, after the installation of the two servers in Asia (Asian Institute of Technology – Thailand; and Vietnam National University Hanoi – Vietnam), more than 400 cores will fight in unison with TORUS to bring cloud computing closer to environmental sciences. More than 400 computer hearts beat in unison for TORUS, as well as those of Nathalie, Astrid, Eleonora, Ann, Imeshi, Thanh, Sukhuma, Janitra, Kim, Daniel, Yannick, Florent, Peio, Alex, Lucca, Stefano, Hichem, Hung(s), Thuy, Huy, Le Quoc, Kim Loi, Agustian, Hong, Sothea, Tongchai, Stephane, Simone, Marco, Mario, Trinh, Thiet, Massimiliano, Nikolaos, Minh Tu, Vincent and Dominique.

To all of you, a big thank you.

Structure of the book

This book is divided into three volumes.

Volume 1 raises the problem of voluminous data in geosciences before presenting the main methods of analysis and computer solutions mobilized to meet them.

Volume 2 presents remote sensing, geographic information systems (GIS) and spatial data infrastructures (SDI) that are central to all disciplines that deal with geographic space.

Volume 3 is a collection of thematic application cases representative of the specificities of the teams involved in TORUS and which motivated their needs in terms of cloud computing.

Dominique LAFFLY
January 2020

Integrated Analysis in Geography:
The Way to Cloud Computing

Introduction to Part 1

What is Geography? Literally *"writing of the Earth"*, the Larousse dictionary gives the following definition:

"Science which has for object the description and the explanation of the current aspect, natural and human, of the surface of the Earth."

And Robert dictionary *"Science that studies and describes the Earth, as a habitat of the human being and all living organisms."*

It is therefore a Science, one that has its roots in China, Egypt, the Inca Empire and Greece for thousands of years because *"all societies have constructed an idea of their situation in the world and present a cosmogony that is at the same time, a great account of the origins"* (*ibid.*). The map was always a central element to accompany the thought of the representation of the world, and to manage and act on the territory. All the thinkers and scientists of the time were geographers or at least were geographers at the same time as they were philosophers, anthropologists, mathematicians, biologists or astronomers – Herodotus, Eratosthenes, Qian, Polo, Ptolemy, Al Idrisi, Al-Khuwarizmi, Mercator, Cassini, Van Humboldt, Darwin. Today, perhaps, are we all still geographers? Maybe most of us do not know it or do not (especially) want to claim it. Hence the initial question – what is Geography? Geography is a Geoscience. It is one of the Geosciences that is interested in the interactions of human societies with the geographical space – *"the environment"*, one that does not go without the other to build the landscapes – visible manifestations of interacting forces. For Geography, thinking about space without the social is an aberration just as the social is thinking while denying space. The spatialization of information is at the heart of Geography; the map – to put it simply – is the bedrock of geographic synthesis: concepts, methods and information to answer the central question *"why here and now but not elsewhere?"*. It is not enough to superimpose tracks, calculate an index and color shapes to make this cartographic synthesis and

Introduction written by Dominique LAFFLY.

get a *"good"* map. We will see that, like all Geosciences, today's Geography with the concepts and methods they mobilize are confronted with having to integrate massive data – Big Data. For this, it must not only evolve in its own paradigms but also in the control of analytical methods – artificial intelligence – and computer techniques dedicated to massive data – cloud computing.

> *"Is it permissible to assimilate the world to what we have seen and experienced? The common claim, as reprehensible as the refusal to dream – at least (for want of something better) – on the future! First: the question of recognizing the order of what is in the elements that the senses (or the tools that arm the senses) grasp is perhaps the very one of Philosophy in all its nobility. It has been said in Latin [...] that all knowledge begins with what is sensible in the objects of nature: 'Omnis cognito initium habet a naturalibus... vel: a sensibilibus.' Beyond this knowledge, there is only mystery; and the very revelation given by God is meditated on the example of what we have known by the natural play of reason. It is necessary here that the statistician, the surveyor and the sociologist are modest! In seeking what we have always had to look for, each generation cannot have done more than its share: the question remains."*[1]

Introduction: the landscape as a system

Protean word, a little magic in the geographical discourse – as Jean-Claude Wieber (1984)[2] liked to say – the landscape is dear to geographers although they have not truly defined a real status of the landscape within the discipline. Is it reasonable after all when a word has so many different meanings? The same author proposes that we refine the content:

> *"Is the use of the word Landscape in this case an abuse of language? Probably not completely. No one would think of denying relief a fundamental role in the differentiation of landscapes [...] by the influence it exerts on the aptitudes of the soils and the adaptations made of them by people and vegetation. In the same way, the examination of the Roman cadastres [...] of an ancient organization of space which one can sometimes perceive or guess [is called] 'landscape analysis'. In these two cases, we study directly, by the measurement of the processes, or indirectly, through the resulting traces, how work sets of forces produce the Landscape."*

---

1 Benzécri J.-P., "In memoriam... Pierre Bourdieu – L'@nalyse des données : histoire, bilan, projets, ..., perspective", *Revue MODULAD*, no. 35, 2006.
2 Wieber J.-C., "Étude du paysage et/ou analyse écologique ?", *Travaux de l'institut géographique de Reims*, nos 45–46, 1981.

The geographical envelope would therefore be the place of expression for all the landscapes themselves considered as a whole that can be approached by the instrumentalization under the constraint of the data available to describe it; the consideration of the landscape is then partial and biased, and the information and the protocols of collection and analysis are at the heart of the analysis of the landscapes considered as a system. E. Schwarz (1988)[3] gives a concise definition of systemic analysis that complements the Cartesian analytic approach:

> *"The systemic approach is a state of mind, a way of seeing the world [...] looking for regularities (invariant), to identify structures, functions, processes, evolution, organization. [It] is characterized above all by taking into account the global nature of phenomena, their structure, their interactions, their organization and their own dynamics. [...] The systemic brings together the theoretical, practical and methodological approaches to the study of what is recognized as too complex to be approached in a reductionist manner and which poses problems of borders, internal and external relations, structure, emerging laws or properties characterizing the system as such or problems of mode of observation, representation, modeling or simulation of a complex totality."*

Brossard and Wieber[4] propose a conceptual diagram of a systemic definition of landscape (Figure I.1). Between production – the *"physical"* producing system – and consumption – the *"social"* user system – the landscape is expressed by what is visible and non-reducible – the *"visible landscape"* system – to one or the other previous subsystems. This specificity of the geographer to understand the landscape so as to make sense of space places it at the crossroads of multidisciplinary scientific paths:

> *"The specialists of other disciplines now know that 'nature' is never quite 'natural', or, conversely, that the analysis of social systems can no longer be considered detached from the environments in which they are located. Also, they very often want the intervention of geographers, in the field as in the processing of data provided by satellites; one cannot go without the other."*[5]

---

3 Schwarz É. (ed.), *La révolution des systèmes. Une introduction à l'approche systémique*, Editions DelVal, 1988.

4 Brossard T. and Wieber J.-C., "Essai de formalisation systémique d'un mode d'approche du paysage", *Bulletin de l'association des géographes français 468*, pp. 103–111, 1981.

5 Frémont A., "La télédétection spatiale et la géographie en France aujourd'hui", *L'Espace géographique*, no. 3, pp. 285–287, 1984.

In fact, the satellite images mentioned by the author are not sufficient to describe landscapes. Other information is also available, their collection is essential, as is the methodological and technical mastery to ensure their analysis.

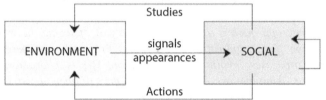

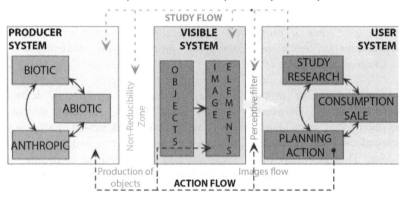

Figure I.1. *In the early days of the "Systemic Landscape" (modified from Brossard and Wieber). For a color version of this figure, see www.iste.co.uk/laffly/torus1.zip*

Thus chosen as a key concept, the landscape is an entry point for themes that have a practical impact. This concept is linked to an analysis method specific to the geographer and their needs to spatialize – in the sense of continuously covering the space. The landscape's *"signs"* – information – allow for a quantitative approach that relies on the use of statistical and computer tools in search of the fundamental structures to, in a way, *"replace the 'visible complicated' perceived landscapes by 'the invisible simple' spatial structure."*[6]

---

6 Perrin F., *Les atomes : présentation et complément*, Gallimard, Paris, 1970.

Geographical Information and Landscape, Elements of Formalization

"Using measures, observations and systems of knowledge inevitably means introducing the notion of representativity in various ways. It includes questions about sampling strategies, the nature of the data, their disaggregation and aggregation, the equations used to model, extrapolate or interpolate information (the same mathematical function can be used for one or the other of these methods)... Any reasoned approach in information analysis tries to integrate at best these different aspects of the measurement and their spatiotemporal representability."[1]

The analysis of the landscape thus formulated implies four principles:

– the mastery of space and time and the direct implications on scales and themes;

– the semantic control of the content of information between the *"knowledge"* of the specialist and the *"reality"* of the landscapes;

– the mastery of the constitution of information put at the heart of the process;

– the mastery of methods and instrumentalization.

In geography, we are also confronted with the difficulty of linking thematically specialized (endogenous punctual information) specific descriptions with general ones (exogenous areal information), the only ones that are amenable to taking into account the spatial *continuum* (Figure 1.1). To do this, in the framework

Chapter written by Dominique LAFFLY.
1 Laffly D., "Approche numérique du paysage : formalisation, enjeux et pratiques de recherche", *Editions Publibook*, 2009.

of the systemic formulation of the landscape and the mode of analysis related to it, we present a formalization based on four key elements: point, trace, order and inference.

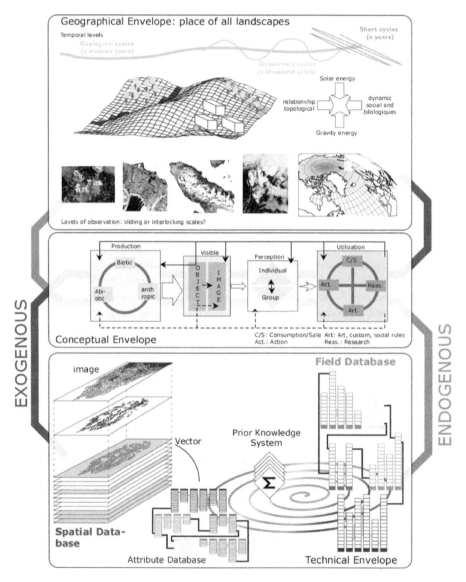

Figure 1.1. *Elements of formalization of the landscape system. For a color version of this figure, see www.iste.co.uk/laffly/torus1.zip*

Point: the basic spatial unit of endogenous observations made *in situ*. It is the subject of a precise location (differential GNNS and/or geocoding of addresses) and a standard description. Surveys are conducted according to a cybernetic logic and a systematic protocol, so as to lend themselves to quantitative analyses that describe and parameterize information structures. Sampling strategies are based on thematic and spatial criteria. For example, for biogeographic facies surveys, stratified non-aligned systematic sampling is commonly used at two levels[2]: the first to define the overall sampling plan of the points to observe in the field and the second to stop the *in situ* observation strategy for each previously defined entity[3]. Here, we find the notion of integrated or holistic analysis.

Trace: this is the message or sign that reflects the links between the structures identified from the analysis of endogenous data and the exogenous information that will serve as a reference for spatialization. This element includes images of satellites and other geographical information, such as altitude, slope, orientation, age of surfaces, distance to objects and any information likely to describe the landscapes and available under the continuous blanket form of space. It is the extension, via the geographical coordinates, of the description of the point in the exogenous information base. Beyond the pixels of images that are ideally suited to our approach, it can nevertheless be generalized to socio-economic data identified by a reference administrative unit, i.e. the most detailed level available: IRIS[4] in France, NUTS[5] for GADM[6]. It is still necessary that these data exist and that they are validated, updated and accessible. The point data observed *in situ* will first be summarized (pivot table) by a reference administrative unit and then confronted with the potential identification of links, here, the trace.

Order: this essentially refers to the spatial structuring of data, the arrangement of landscape elements relative to each other that induces differentiated spatial constraints and practices. In image analysis, order refers to the notions of textures and texture mosaics and spatial autocorrelation, and opens the perspective of the

---

2 de Keersmaecker M.-L, "Stratégie d'échantillonnage des données de terrain intégrées dans l'analyse des images satellitaires", *L'Espace géographique*, vol. 16–3, pp. 195–205, 1987.
3 Laffly D. and Mercier D., "Global change and paraglacial morphodynamic modification in Svalbard", *International Journal of Remote Sensing*, vol. 23, no. 21, 2002; Moreau M., Mercier D., Laffly D., "Un siècle de dynamiques paraglaciaires et végétales au Svalbard (Midre Lovénbreen, Spitsberg nord-occidental)", *Géomorphologie*, vol. 2, pp. 157–168, 2004.
4 "In order to prepare for the dissemination of the 1999 population census, INSEE has developed a division of the homogeneous size territory called IRIS2000. This acronym stands for 'Grouped Islands for Statistical Information' (*Ilots regroupés pour l'Information Statistique*) and refers to the target size of 2000 inhabitants per elementary mesh" (quote from https://www.insee.fr/fr/metadonnees/definition/c1523, translated into English from French).
5 Nomenclature of Territorial Units for Statistics (*Nomenclature des unités territoriales statistiques*), 6 levels, see https://gadm.org/metadata.html.
6 See https://gadm.org.

frequency analysis of Fourier transforms and wavelets. From vector objects – typically reference administrative entities – the analysis of spatial structuring uses topological operators of graph theory: shape descriptors (perimeter, surface, width, length, etc.); contiguity; inclusion; neighborhood; connection of smaller distances and so on (see landscape ecology).

Inference: this is inference in the statistical sense of the term, i.e. the application of the rules developed in the previous steps to ensure the link between endogenous and exogenous information. It is an ergodic approach – *"which makes it possible to statistically determine all the achievements of a random process from an isolated realization of this process"* – based on probabilistic models, which makes it possible to restore the continuity of geographical space from partial knowledge. We think in particular of Bayesian probability models (Bayes, the way!) as well as the Metropolis–Hastings algorithm:

> *"It is today the whole field of MCMCs, the Monte-Carlo Markow-Chain, whose unreasonable effectiveness in physics, chemistry and biology [...] has still not been explained. It is not a deterministic exploration, nor is it a completely random exploration; it is a random walk exploration. But deep down, it's not new; it's the same in life: by going a little randomly from one situation to another, we explore so many more possibilities, like a researcher who changes scientific continents with the passing of time."*[7]

From an operational point of view, the proposed formalization consists of measuring the degrees of connection between endogenous and exogenous information. When they are significant, we use them to generalize all of the space and all or part of the data observed punctually. It is important to distinguish now between the analysis methods we propose and the interpolation calculation procedures that also contribute to spatializing information. These last ones consist of filling the gaps in data of the same nature contained in the same grid of description as a phenomenon. For this we choose a calculation method inspired by the cases encountered, equation [1.1] which are binary, linear, quadratic, polynomial, exponential, cyclic and so on.

$$X_{lat,\ long} = f\left(X_{lat}i,\ longj\right) \tag{1.1}$$

where: X: variable to explain AND explanatory,

lat, long: latitude and longitude in the reference grid.

---

7 Villani C., *Théorème vivant*, Éditions Grasset at Fasquelle, Paris, 2013.

While relying on the same mathematical functions, the spatialization of endogenous data via exogenous information consists of developing a function, integrating different elements of the system taken into account:

$$X_{lat,\ long} = f\ (f_0(Y_{lat}i,\ _{long}j),\ Z_{lat}i,\ _{long}j),\ f_1(X_{lat}i,\ _{long}j),\ f_2(V_{lat}i,\ _{long}j),\ ...) \qquad [1.2]$$

where: X: variable to explain;

$Y,\ Z$: explanatory variables;

lat, long: latitude and longitude in the reference grid;

f_0, f_1, f_2...: functions on the explanatory variables.

The formalization, in time and space, of the interactions and dynamics of endogenous and exogenous data mobilize both the methods and the fundamental questions of nesting scales and resolutions or even scale invariants. Limit the term scale to the computational ratio between a field dimension and the map dimension, and instead use the term resolution to describe the basic level of description, observation and sampling of information[8]. In remote sensing (see below), we are talking about spatial resolution (pixel size) and radiometric resolution (characteristics of the bands), in no case of scale!

What about the problem that concerns us here, that of landscape?

---

8 Spatial, temporal and radiometric resolutions.... The very high spatial resolution – in the order of 50 cm – satellite images, such as those provided by GeoEye, Quickbird or Pléïades, versus the low spatial resolutions of Terra MODIS data (250 m to 500 m) or Spot VEGETATION and NOAA AVHRR (in the order of one kilometer), for example.

2

Sampling Strategies

Sampling geographical space is a delicate operation. The constraints are multiple and integrate into a nesting of levels to anticipate. Ideally – by which I mean statistically – the "*perfect*" sample is one that relies on a double probabilistic procedure to ensure the spatial and thematic representativeness calculated on the basis of *a priori* knowledge of the studied system, a census. This is a non-aligned stratified systematic random sampling, based on the initial assumption of the statistics of large number theory – a random variable is distributed according to a normal distribution, or even lower – where the geographical distribution of the points minimizes spatial autocorrelation. Figure 2.1 simply illustrates this type of sample, the space is divided into as many windows, within which the position of the point is randomly drawn, as one increments the size of the sample until the average value tends to a degree of near-average acceptance of the whole population a number of times in a row. Most often, the size of the sample will be set by quotas, more than from a probabilistic distribution law considering the nature of the available data (see ground occupation below) but the spatial reasoning remains the same.

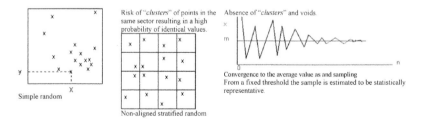

Figure 2.1. *Sampling the geographical area*

Chapter written by Dominique LAFFLY.

Endogenous and exogenous data are based on different observation levels that correspond to many interlocking geographical scales which, while failing to represent the continuous dynamics of local to global, offer thresholds of description that should orchestrate with the most melodious music. In sample terms, this means that there are as many samples to implement as there are observation levels. All these levels cannot be apprehended with the best of probabilistic wills. If we can consider the digital images of the altitude – from which are deduced the slope, the orientation, the complexity of the forms and indirectly the global radiation, the shading and so on – even a classification of the occupation of the ground resulting from remote sensing – as a comprehensive census of space, we never have such a repository for the more detailed observation levels (Figure 2.2).

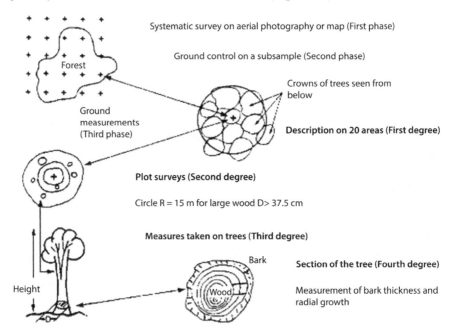

Figure 2.2. *Illustration of a survey based on a four-level survey (modified from IFN National Forest Inventory: https://inventaire-forestier.ign.fr)*

It will therefore be illusory to imagine a probabilistic sampling procedure, especially since feasibility constraints – in the sense of the humanly possible, or reasonable, on the ground – still counteract the law of numbers (hence polls by the transect method – Figure 2.3). The so-called reasoned sample, according, in a way, to the knowledge of the researcher, is very often the chosen solution and it will only be *a posteriori* that representativeness is calculated when it is possible.

Finally, the nature of the information collected *in situ* at the most detailed level mobilizes different methods of collecting information.

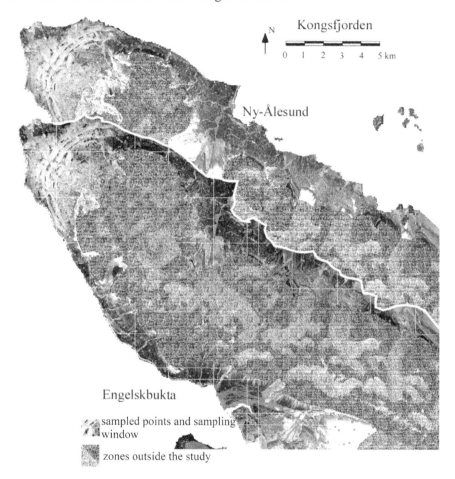

Figure 2.3. *Sampling the terrain, a probabilistic procedure (bottom) is not always adapted to the physical constraints of the field and the mission (here, in the Arctic, only a few weeks) where we prefer a transect track (at the top) (modified from Laffly D.,* Approche numérique du paysage : formalisation, enjeux et applications, Éditions Publibook, 2009). For a color version of this figure, see www.iste.co.uk/laffly/torus1.zip*

The vegetation component is measured by observation of the species present in the different strata of the vegetation. The observation may be of the presence/absence or estimation of occurrences per unit area. Several methods are used that rely on counts along transects at regular intervals (linear method) or with surface grids, within which the surface is estimated visually. In the 1960s, ecologists Braun and Blanquet made a significant contribution to defining this methodology (Figure 2.4), which also fit into the definition of minimum areas.

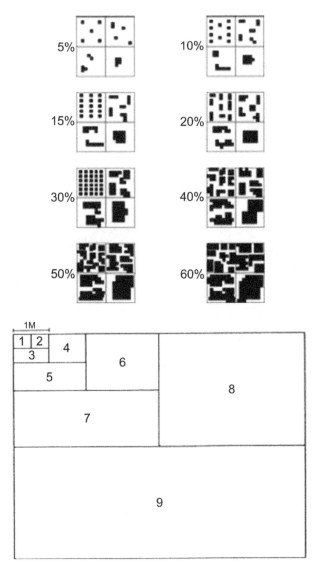

Figure 2.4. *Estimated abundance/dominance and minimum area according to Braun and Blanquet. The minimal areas of the species are estimated in a helical observation structure from an observation area of 1 m^2 of reference. The minimum area of a species is obtained when observed at least once*

In her PhD, Fanny Rhoné[1] mobilized this sampling solution at four nesting levels based on the reasoned and/or statistical method (Figure 2.5) to select "*at best*" the reference areas. The first level consists of targeting a bio-morpho-climato-agricultural geographic area considered to be homogeneous and representative: the slopes of a Pyrenean agropastoral valley for the first case (Ballongue, Ariège, FR); and the landscapes of the agrarian hills of Gers for the second. For each of these zones, n reference sectors are decided, according to a reasoned choice: accessibility; criteria for local differentiation; feasibility considering the material and human constraints of the observations and so on. For the landscape of the Gers, for example, six sites are retained, forming three representative couples of gradation of heterogeneity of the agricultural and vegetable texture and amplitudes of the relief in connection with the first hypothesis of the study (see above). An apiary, made up of about 10 beehives, is placed at the center of each site from which a geographical area with a radius of three kilometers is set as representative of the living area of the bees. Two sets of samples will therefore be mobilized. The first concerns observations at the level of the hives themselves, which include the observation period (March to November); frequency of observation (every 15 days); the type of measures envisaged (the frameworks of the hive for all the descriptors); and the analyses to be carried out (in particular, on the pollens). The second relates to vegetation; 50 points are sampled by pairs of sites in a non-aligned way based on compliance with land use quotas mapped from the visual interpretation of aerial photography. The method of minimum areas estimated by abundance/dominance is finally used for the surveys at the different strata encountered.

The geography sample does not only concern the geophysical and biological environment, it is mainly the population – in the sense of the natural persons – itself which interests the geographers in highlighting what makes sense in the society, which relates to socio-spatial practices. This is another way of understanding endogenous data through surveys and semi-structured interviews. The population is the focus of surveys of socio-spatial practices in order to determine what makes sense in the daily relationship between the individual, the group of individuals and geographical space. The socio-spatial practices of actors are addressed through surveys and/or semi-directive interviews. Surveys aim to visit the largest number of people on the basis of a simplified reading grid (closed questions), while the interviews target a small population whose purpose will be to analyze the presupposed in-depth and enlightened knowledge on the subject, targeted (open-ended questions whose content will have to be analyzed). Statistically, to a translation close to the matrix, the goal is the same: to make a typology of individuals based on the variables of the reduced number for the survey; to obtain this typology from the high number

---

1 Rhoné F., L'abeille à travers champs : quelles interactions entre Apis mellifera L et le paysage agricole (Gers 32) ? : le rôle des structures paysagères ligneuses dans l'apport de ressources trophiques et leurs répercussions sur les traits d'histoire de vie des colonies, PhD Thesis, edited by Laffly D., 2015.

of variables, deduced from the analysis of the content, for a limited number of individuals.

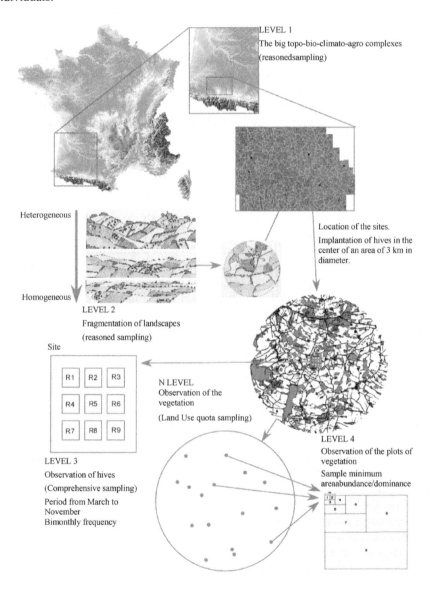

Figure 2.5. *Nesting Observation Scales and Sampling (modified from Rhoné 2015, ibid.). For a color version of this figure, see www.iste.co.uk/laffly/torus1.zip*

Defining a representative sample is therefore a rather delicate operation. Provided we have a census of the population where the survey is conducted, we can hope to have probabilistic representativeness or quotas based on the census variables (e.g. population structure by age, household income). Very general variables in view of the scientific questions that motivate the investigation, hence a rather vague representativity. Very often – especially for emerging countries – censuses do not exist or if they exist, the data are not made available to users – for many governments, data such as the map remains a sensitive area.

Statistically, the question of the sample amounts to defining its size and representativeness for a given margin of error. Statistical normality – in the sense of the large number theory and the so-called normal Laplace–Gauss law – theoretically calculates the smallest proportion of individuals to be selected for a sample [2.1]:

$$n = \frac{z^2 * p(1-p)}{e^2} \qquad\qquad [2.1]$$

where: n: sample size;

z: confidence level according to the normal centered-reduced law.

Confidence level	z-score
80 %	1.28
85 %	1.44
90 %	1.65
95 %	1.96
99 %	2.58

p: proportion for which the margin of error is calculated. By convention 0.5 because it is with this value that the margin of error is the largest, so we obtain a conservative result,

e: tolerance margin tolerated.

When p is unknown – i.e. almost always – with a default value of 0.5 the formula becomes [2.2]:

$$n = \frac{z^2}{4e^2} \qquad\qquad [2.2]$$

For example:

– to calculate a proportion with a confidence level of 95% and a margin of error of 7%, we obtain $n = (1.96)^2/4(0.07)^2 = 196$;

– to calculate a proportion with a confidence level of 95% and a margin of error of 5%, we obtain $n = (1.96)^2/4(0.05)^2 = 384.16$;

– to calculate a proportion with a confidence level of 99% and a margin of error of 2%, we get $n = (2.575)^2/4(0.02)^2 = 3218.75$.

It is desirable to take into account the size of the initial population to refine the sample, knowing that from 10,000 individuals, the number of people to be sampled becomes stable as described above. The formula becomes [2.3], and the margin of error is given by [2.4]:

$$n = \frac{\frac{z^2 * p(1-p)}{e^2}}{1 + \frac{z^2 * p(1-p)}{eN}} \qquad [2.3]$$

$$e = z\sqrt{\frac{p(1-p)}{n}} * \sqrt{\frac{N-n}{N-1}} \qquad [2.4]$$

where: N: population size.

As mentioned above, the sampling plan must also take into account the human, material and financial feasibility of the survey.

Anyway, one might think that with a sample of about 380 people, it would be possible to carry out a survey with a margin of error of 5% (to understand more or less 5% compared to the frequency of answers to a question) and a 95% confidence level (on the margin of error is the degree of certainty). It is actually much more difficult to know the margin of error and the degree of certainty because the socio-spatial behavior of individuals is not necessarily distributed according to a normal law and/or the population that constitutes the sample is strongly skewed: far too many occurrences of one category than another in relation to the target population (typically too many boys compared to girls, too many senior managers compared to workers, etc.); the variable or question asked is not or little known or conversely too simplistic. This explains the interest of testing a questionnaire before making it operational and to investigate as many individuals as possible and then to check the characteristics of the population afterwards. In all cases, an inquiry must meet four requirements, the first three of which are always quite similar:

– **Who** is it? Understand the general characterization of individuals (age, level of education, income, profession, etc.).

– **Where** is it? Understand the localization to make the link with the geographical space. This is rather delicate since it can cover several meanings that must all be targeted if possible: place of residence, workplace, place at the time of the investigation, etc.

– **When** is it? Understand the temporal dynamics of socio-spatial practices at different levels: date at the time of the survey, people's diary, etc.

– **What** is it? Understand the theme that motivates the survey that varies from one study to another.

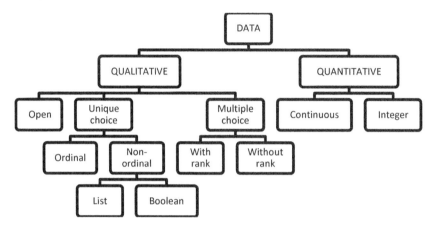

Figure 2.6. *Main data types*

While the semi-structured interviews are based on an open discussion – from which the content will have to be analyzed to code the information in Boolean terms – the surveys are generally based on so-called closed or categorical questions and thus qualitative variables, see Figure 2.6. It is strongly recommended to use ordinal, single choice, multiple choice, unclassified and last resort ranking variables. The number of combinations with multiple choice variables is quickly very troublesome, with three modalities (a, b and c, for example), there are seven possibilities of answer without classification (i.e. $1 + n!$ with n the number of modalities: a, b, c, ab/ba, ac/ca, cb/bc, abc/cba/bca/cab/acb/bac) and 15 with ranked (i.e. $n + ((n - 1)*n!)$: a, b, c, ab, ba, ac, ca, cb, bc, abc, cba, bca, cab, acb, bac). We go to 25 and 76 possible answer configurations for 4 modalities, to 121 and 485 for 5 modalities and so on or for several variables of this type, thousands of combinations for only a few hundred individuals. This makes no sense: while we seek to identify organizational structures that explain the behavior of groups of individuals, we add noise that isolates each individual in the group further.

A good example of the need for surveys is that of the RecycUrbs-Viet[2] on waste collection and recycling in the city of Hanoi: urban dynamics and metropolitan recomposition. T. H. Nguyen explains:

"The recyclable waste collection business in Hanoi occupies a large population in both the municipal and informal private sector. More than 10,000 street collectors and diggers roam the streets of the capital daily to buy or collect waste, which they then resell to intermediaries in several hundred 'bai' (recyclable waste depots) scattered throughout the Vietnamese capital. However, unlike other big cities in the South, Hanoi collectors are not poor people living in slums. Most collectors are seasonal migrants from the same coastal province of Nam Dinh. Among them, some are settled in the capital: they settled on their own as resellers of waste. Despite their non-recognition by the public sector, they collect and recycle more than 20% of the waste produced by this city in the midst of metropolitan renewal. This system of collection, sorting, resale and recycling of waste is unique because it relies on the flexibility of migrants' schedules, the informality of access to land and the migratory and artisanal networks of the actors. The second specificity of this system is its participation in the proto-industrial village transformation process. Indeed, it is integrated into the production chain of many clusters of craft villages of the Red River Delta that recycle waste metal, paper and plastic. This research project aims to understand the functioning of the network of informal collectors, its structure, its organizational rationality and its sustainability in a context of privatization of public spaces, growth and diversification of the volume of waste linked to economic growth."

Figure 2.7 shows the geographical location in the Hanoi district (Vietnam) of the 805 points surveyed for a study of the informal economy related to the collection, sorting and recycling of waste (grayscale density collection points per km²). Each site corresponds to a collection point where the waste is deposited daily by more than 10,000 individuals, who collect the waste by bicycle according to fixed itineraries; the person in charge of the structure is the person subjected to the questionnaire. In this example, almost all the collection points surveyed (815) are

---

2 See the 2017 RECYCURBS-VIET research project on the issue of collection and recycling of waste in Hanoi under the direction of Thai Huyen Nguyen, Hanoi Architectural University at: https://www.ird.fr/les-partenariats/renforcement-des-capacites/des-programmes-specifiques/jeunes-equipes-associees-a-l-ird-jeai/jeai-en-cours-de-soutien-par-departement-scientifique/departement-societes-et-mondialisation-soc/jeai-recycurbs-viet-vietnam-2017-2019.

visited for the survey, i.e. a margin of error of 0.36% for a 99% confidence level. Statistically, we could have investigated 260 collection points with a margin of error of 5% (and 95% confidence level) – a commonly accepted range – the fieldwork would have been greatly facilitated but the risk would have been to lose any possibility of understanding the spatial rules that prevail in the organization of this informal economy. Characteristics that are not highlighted by the analysis of the data from the survey (see below the factorial analysis of multiple correspondences) but by the cartographic representation of the data. That is, the "*order*", the spatial structuring, in the methodological chain that we intend to promote here.

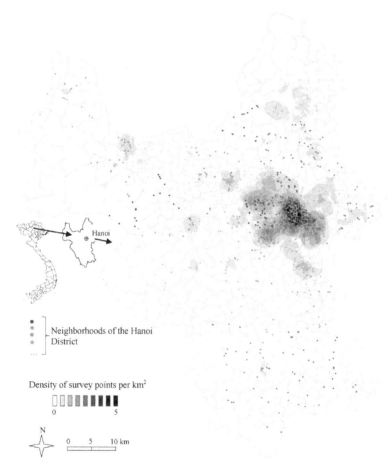

Figure 2.7. *Mapping associated with the field survey, the spatial dimension of information. The colors of the points correspond to different administrative units of the Hanoi District. For a color version of this figure, see www.iste.co.uk/laffly/torus1.zip*

For this study, each individual is a localized repository (see **"Where** is it?"). This location generates point cards as shown above or as shown in Figure 2.8. Each map is a representation of the modalities of a variable; it is, in fact, an additional graph of the data analysis which makes it possible to *"see"*, in the geographical space, if the modalities seem distributed randomly – in which case, there are no spatial structures – or not – in which case, there is a spatial structuring: center-periphery, spatial dichotomy, alignments, etc.

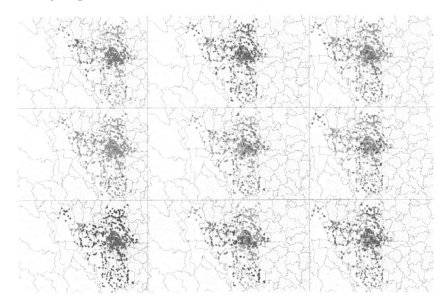

Figure 2.8. *Map collections to find what makes sense in the geographical area. For a color version of this figure, see www.iste.co.uk/laffly/torus1.zip*

2.1. References

Braun-Blanquet J. (1954). La végétation alpine nivale des Alpes françaises. *Travaux du comité scientifique du CAF*, 250.

## 3

Characterization of the Spatial Structure

We use the metrics of graph theory and landscape ecology to characterize the spatial fragmentation of a landscape. Ecologists integrate these dimensions to mainly study the habitats of one or more species. We are content here to draw up a list of quantitative indicators that are significant for the heterogeneity of geographical space. The indicators will be confronted later with the analysis of the data resulting from the investigations and observations *in situ*, to validate or not the role played by this dimension of the landscape.

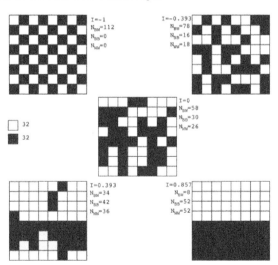

Figure 3.1. *Texture differences and space co-occurrence matrices (from Whingham P.A. and Dick G., "Evolutionary dynamics for the spatial Moran process", Genetic Programming and Evaluable Machines, vol. 9, issue 2, pp. 157–170, 2008)*

Chapter written by Dominique LAFFLY.

Figure 3.1 gives a simple example of what is the texture of an image. In all cases, the number of white and blue squares is the same – their frequency of appearance is identical – and does not distinguish local differences. It is necessary to resort to spatial statistics based on neighborhood relations, direct or indirect contiguity: it is the mathematics of spatial co-occurrences to which Haralick R.M., Shanmugan K. and Dinstein I. contributed decisively in a reference article published in 1973 in *IEEE Transactions on Systems, Man and Cybernetics*, entitled "Textural features for image classification". They described 14 texture indices for distinguishing and quantifying texture differences, the top 10 of which are presented in Figure 3.2.

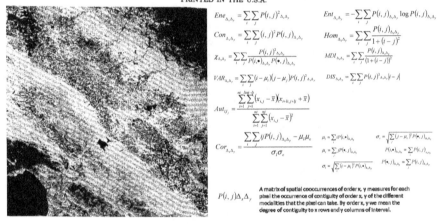

Textural Features for Image Classification

ROBERT M. HARALICK, K. SHANMUGAM, AND ITS'HAK DINSTEIN

Reprinted by permission from IEEE TRANSACTIONS ON SYSTEMS, MAN AND CYBERNETICS
Vol. SMC-3, No. 6, November 1973, pp. 610-621
Copyright 1973, by the Institute of Electrical and Electronics Engineers, Inc.
PRINTED IN THE U.S.A.

Figure 3.2. *The main texture indices calculated from space co-occurrence matrices*

– Energy (Ene), also called second angular momentum, measures the uniformity of the texture, maximum for a homogeneous zone.

– Entropy (Ent) measures the disorder of a picture, up to a random distribution of values.

– Contrast (Con) shows the difference between the highest and lowest values of a set of pixels. It translates a boundary effect when there is a large local variation

– Local homogeneity (Hom) measures the homogeneity of an image. It is highly negatively correlated with the contrast.

– Dissimilarity (DIS) also measures homogeneity.

– Correlation (Cor) measures the linear dependence of gray tones in the image. High correlation values involve a linear link between gray levels and pairs of pixels.

– Covariance (VAR) measures the spreading of the values of the normalized matrix around the diagonal.

– Chi2 (χ^2) compares the theoretical distribution of mathematical independence with the observed one. This measure is positively correlated with energy.

– Spatial autocorrelation (Aut), with qualitative data that do not express gradation of gray levels of a channel (e.g. land use classes) co-occurrence matrices are also representative of the texture by measuring the correlation between neighborhoods or spatial autocorrelation.

– Moment of the inverse difference (MDI) informs about the size of textural elements and their dimension.

For example, we used spatial co-occurrence matrices to map the potential biotopes of the woodland grouse – *Tetrao urogallus* – in the Jura Mountains (France, Figure 3.3). Without resorting to Haralick *et al.* (*op.cit.*), another solution for the characterization of spatial textures can be envisaged by defining reference zones – and the spatial co-occurrence matrices that characterize them – where it is known that gallinaceans are present (field observation). Thirty sites have been listed to define *in fine* five types of biotopes, according to the degree of openness and the plant composition in an area of 400 m^2 recommended by ornithologists. For each pixel, a sliding window of identical surface is applied, within which the matrix of spatial co-occurrences is calculated. Finally, to evaluate the level of similarity with the different reference zones, we calculate the Manhattan distance [3.1]. The results are expressed by isolines; we consider a maximum threshold of 0.55 as the lowest level of similarity. This value has been calibrated empirically from sites known to have an image texture that does not represent a potential biotope:

$$D_{Ct,Co} = \sum_{i=1}^{n} \sum_{j=1}^{n} |Ct_{i,j} - Co_{i,j}| \qquad [3.1]$$

where:

Ct: matrix of co-occurrences of a control zone;

Co: pixel-centric co-occurrence matrix;

n: number of classes in the image.

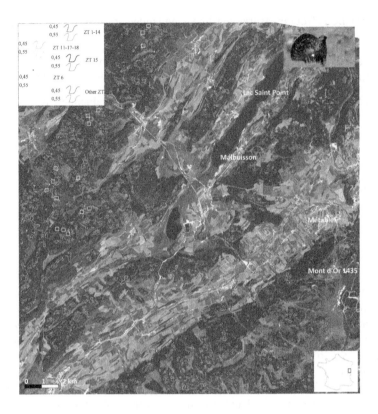

Figure 3.3. *Texture analysis applied to the biotope of* Tetrao urogallus *(Image Spot P). For a color version of this figure, see www.iste.co.uk/laffly/torus1.zip*

A similar use is proposed to identify small hamlet settlements in coffee and cocoa plantations in Ivory Coast, as part of health geography research on human African trypanosomiasis (HAT) – sleeping sickness.

The work of Laveissière and Hervouët showed that, for the same geographical area, the pathology does not have the same prevalence in populations of small hamlets – a few dozen individuals, lesser risk – as those living in camps – less than 10 people, higher risk. This distinction is explained by the different socio-spatial practices: dichotomy space socially open versus socially closed. In the first case, the inhabitants of the hamlets do not go to the plantations for the agricultural works. The rest of the time the social and family exchanges take place in the hamlet. In the second case, a camp where families reside, the inhabitants attend the plantations in addition to social visits to other camps. Apart from the fact that the same ethnic groups live in camps or hamlets, camp residents spend more time in infected areas of the potential tsetse fly *Glossina palpalis*. From this risk factor, we propose an environmental risk indicator developed from remote sensing (SPOT P[1] at 10 m) and texture analysis to identify encampments (Figure 3.4).

Analysis of multiscalar texture

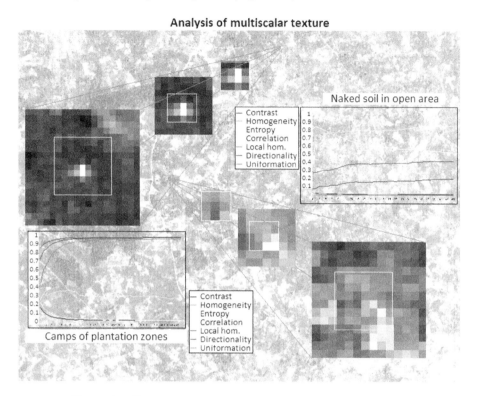

Figure 3.4. *Texture analysis to identify areas at risk of HAT. For a color version of this figure, see www.iste.co.uk/laffly/torus1.zip*

The principle is based on a moving window, for each pixel of the image, whose size is varied by systematically calculating the indices proposed by Haralick *et al.* so as to obtain a local signature of the texture and thus identify the camp areas in opposition to the hamlet areas which are the basis of the risk factors identified by Laveissière and Hervouët.

The analysis of the texture does not rely solely on the indices mentioned above that are calculated from raster data. It can also be applied to vector objects related to the theory of graphs: the point, line, the planar graph without isthmus – more

1 This analysis was performed in 2000 with Spot 4 imagery (launched March 23, 1998). Concerning panchromatic higher spatial resolution, it was the same definition (10 m).

commonly called "*polygon*". Depending on the nature of these objects, the spatial fragmentation indicators will aim to quantify the spatial distribution of point elements, the connections of linear elements and the contiguousness of surfaces. Figure 3.5 shows a simple illustration of the quantification by the Moran or Getis–Ord spatial autocorrelation index of the fragmentation of a set of polygons[2]. All these objects can be crossed to create mixed indicators, for example:

– proportion of one class in the total area (percentage of land, PLAND);

– density of patches by land use class (patch diversity, PD) – fragmentation;

– aggregation and degree of aggregation of the pixels of the same class (aggregation index, AI) – heterogeneity;

– average distance between two neighboring patches (Euclidian nearest neighbor, ENN) – connectivity;

– probability that two randomly selected individuals in a given environment are of the same species (Simpson diversity index, SDI) – diversity.

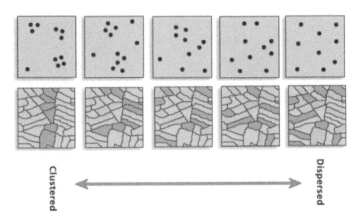

Figure 3.5. *Quantifying the heterogeneity of a landscape (source: ESRI). For a color version of this figure, see www.iste.co.uk/laffly/torus1.zip*

We will see later in the chapters on remote sensing and image processing that taking into account the texture is a key element for image segmentation and object recognition (semantic labeling). In the case of images, segmentation is initially based on the definition of a threshold, starting from an initial point, below which all the pixels will be grouped into homogeneous zones which will then have to be

---

2 FRAGSTATS is a free application that offers a very detailed collection of texture indices. It is available at: http://www.umass.edu/landeco/research/fragstats/fragstats.html.

labeled by a classification to identify, for example, land use. Depending on the value of the selected threshold, we can obtain very different results (Figure 3.5): either a myriad of zones, which are in fact pixels a little bigger than the original ones, or too few zones, which are in fact abusive groupings which have no geographical sense, a middle ground... But how to determine it (see Chapters 2 and 14)?

Figure 3.6. *Segmentation of a panchromatic image, but which threshold value to use? (modified from https://grass.osgeo.org/grass74/manuals/i.segment.html). For a color version of this figure, see www.iste.co.uk/laffly/torus1.zip*

## 4

Thematic Information Structures

When databases are available without prior knowledge of their contents, descriptive statistics – parametric and non-parametric depending on the nature of the data – are used to understand and organize the information. In addition to the stripping phase (i.e. univariate description), we are faced with matrices with n and m dimensions for which we look for a structure that underlies the organization of the data.

We use the whole battery of descriptive statistics:

– *Univariate*: variable by variable set the key parameters. With a qualitative variable, we identify each modality M_i by its number E_{M_i} that we then transform into frequency of appearance $F_{Mi} = \frac{E_{M_i}}{N}$, with N being the number of total individuals. With a quantitative variable, we calculate a set of parameters related to the normal law of Laplace-Gauss[1]: position parameters (minimum, maximum, arithmetic mean, quantile of order k); scope parameters (different amplitudes);

Chapter written by Dominique LAFFLY.

1 Basically, let's remember that it is the primal assumption of the so-called parametric statistic... *"In probability theory and in statistics, the normal law is one of the most appropriate probability laws for modeling natural phenomena coming from several random events. [...] It is also called the Gaussian law, the law of Gauss or the Laplace–Gauss law, after the names of Laplace (1749–1827) and Gauss (1777–1855), two mathematicians, astronomers and physicists who studied it. More formally, it is an absolutely continuous law of probability that depends on two parameters: its expectation, a real number noted µ, and its standard deviation. [...] The curve of this density is called the Gauss curve or bell curve, and has other names too. This is the best known representation of this law. The normal law of zero mean and standard deviation is called the normal law."* (fr.wikipedia.org/wiki/Loi_normale).

dispersion parameters (fluctuation of values, variance) and shape parameters (asymmetry and flattening).

– *Bivariate*: are the two variables dependent or not? If so, what is the intensity of the link and eventually its form? To answer these questions, with two qualitative variables, we use the Chi analysis (Tschuprow or Kappa coefficient), the variability analysis (ANOVA) with a qualitative variable and another quantitative (Fischer coefficient), and finally the regression with two quantitative variables (correlation coefficient).

– *Multivariate*: multiple regression type with quantitative variables when trying to explain one variable from several others – little or no use from survey data – or more global type factorial analysis whose purpose is to reduce initial dimensions while losing the least possible significance (principal component analysis – PCA, factorial correspondence analysis – FCA, multiple correspondence factor analysis – MFCA, canonical analysis – CA, procrustean factorial analysis – PFA, etc.). Clustering analysis is also a solution for multivariate analysis and can be applied to raw data or results data from factorial analysis: which strategy of aggregation and which distance? The commonly used ones are: Bayes, K-means, hierarchical ascending classification, support vector machine and random forests It is the nature of the data that will ultimately impose the choice of statistical elements, as summarized in Figure 4.1.

Beyond the statistical methods, we try to reduce the number of initial dimensions of the cloud of points formed by the data in order to see more clearly, simply. That is, how variables and individuals, in the statistical sense, organize each other. Let us keep in mind that surveys place us *de facto* in cases of inductive statistics. We cannot formulate an initial hypothesis by *a priori* lack of knowledge of the studied system itself, described almost exclusively by categorical data.

We therefore proceed to the exploration of data – an exploratory approach – to identify the hidden meaning of the information *a posteriori*, if there is one.

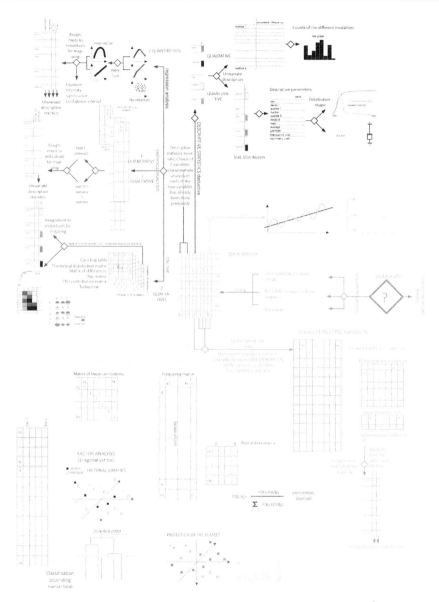

Figure 4.1. *Methodological chain of information processing*[2].
For a color version of this figure, see www.iste.co.uk/laffly/torus1.zip

2 The title of this essay can be translated as: "The Tô Lịch river in the landscape of Hanoi: Case study: The Ha Yên Quyêt (Cót) village & the Định Công Hạ village".

Jean-Paul Benzécri, the "father" of factorial correspondence analyses (FCA), whose work will be used a lot for this exploration says, after over 40 years devoted to this task:

> *"Then, by giving geometrical form to this analysis, one would end up looking for the principal axes of inertia of a cloud of massed points; classical problem, in dimension 3, but to treat here in one dimension, n, whatever. This requires, imperatively, diagonalizations of square matrices n*n, a computation that is infeasible without a machine, as soon as n exceeds 3 (or 4...). By 1963, diagonalizing a 7*7 matrix was a daunting task for a modestly equipped laboratory. Subsequently, the Ascending Hierarchical Classification asked for calculations even heavier than those of diagonalizations. But as the power of machines grew with the efficiency of algorithms, our career as statisticians grew. [we were put] at the service of constantly growing ambitions, techniques whose progress defied all dreams! Around 2000, on a microcomputer such as those offered to market customers, one could, in a few minutes, classify several thousand individuals. More precisely, it takes a few minutes for the classification and factor analysis algorithms. [...] But the data design, their formatting, the examination of the results take not only hours but months. [...] There are more, strictly speaking, calculation problems; but the very problem of Data Analysis remains; all the more so since calculation does not limit research, there is no excuse for stopping in the collection of data and meditation. Relative to 1960 [...], the relationship of difficulty, between intellectual projects and calculations is reversed."*[3]

Do Xuan Son, an architect, as part of his thesis of Geography, raises all these questions. In addition to his sensitivity as a trained architect, he turned to socio-spatial surveys of the populations of two urban villages (129 households surveyed) to measure their perception of urban facts and their sense of a sustainable city: Hạ Yên Quyết (Cót) examined 64 homes and Định Công Hạ examined 65 homes. The questionnaire was organized into several main themes:

– general information on age, professional status, studies and so on;

– the historical dimension of the villages (significance of the river);

– the cultural and economic activities of the home;

– landscape and esthetic perception;

3 Benzécri J.-P., "In memoriam... Pierre Bourdieu – L'@nalyse des données : histoire, bilan, projets, ..., perspective", *Revue MODULAD*, no. 35, 2006.

– urban morphology and green planning, the place of water in the local buildings;

– traffic and daily itinerary;

– habitat transformation;

– the sense of identity and attachment to a place.

The use of this qualitative database for the most part uses multivariate statistical methods of multiple correspondence analysis (MCA) which require recognized competencies in the field. After encoding, the matrix to be analyzed has 129 lines and 750 columns (all the modalities of all the questions). It is impossible to understand something as it is; the factorial methods consist of drastically reducing the number of dimensions of the matrix to retain only the organizational structures – called main axes – which should be interpreted thematically. Generally, three to four axes are sufficient to exhaust the total inertia of the initial cloud (to understand the amount of information) and to identify structures that explain how individuals organize their responses according to unsuspected structures.

Figure 4.2 presents the factorial space of the first three axes taken from the surveys of Don Xuan Son's thesis. The arrangement of the points representing the modalities and the individuals in the same factorial space – the principle of the distributional equivalence proper to MCA or double representativeness – makes it possible to interpret the thematic significance of the axes and thus the organizational structures of information. This is an extremely delicate task that only a specialist in the topic can consider:

– What are the reasons that at the end of an axis the "*modalities*" points and the "*individuals*" points are close (thus the modalities have a common meaning, the individuals have the same behavior, the individuals characterize the modalities) which oppose them to the reasons that explain the proximities on the side of the opposite end of the same axis?

– Similar "*modalities*" and/or "*individuals*" for one axis can be opposed for another axis.

– If there are thresholded quantitative variables (e.g. age) in n classes – in other words, conditions to be analyzed with the qualitative variables (e.g. age classes from 1 to n, i.e. from the "youngest" to the "oldest") – is there an order structure by an alignment along an underlying linear structure? If so, the axis that declines this alignment expresses a gradation of values (from the youngest to the oldest, for example).

Factorial space

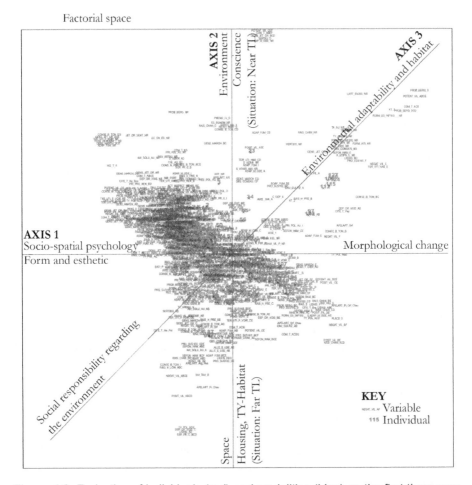

Figure 4.2. *Projection of individuals (red) and modalities (blue) on the first three axes of the MCA. Interpretation of the neighbors between the modalities, the individuals, the modalities and the individuals makes it possible to highlight the theme carried by each axis (according to Xuan S.D., ibid.). For a color version of this figure, see www.iste.co.uk/laffly/torus1.zip*

To complete the FCA, we use a classification whose principle is based on the definition of an aggregation rule and a metric between the points to be aggregated. The double representation of the data, as we have seen, allows an "easy" graphic reading of the factorial spaces where the visual proximity also reflects a thematic proximity. The distance between all the points can be calculated so as to order them from the nearest to the farthest ones. In other words, more like the most different. In statistics, such an aggregation strategy is called ascending hierarchical classification

(AHC) and several metrics can be considered (Euclidean, Euclidean squared, city-block, Ward, etc.). We prefer Ward's metric based on the notion of decomposition of variance which gives more open interpretation graphs. The points are grouped in a hierarchical or dendrogram tree, and a graph of aggregation distances is also associated with it. Depending on the distance chosen, the results of the final aggregation inevitably vary – they would vary even more if other aggregation rules were applied. Always keep in mind that a classification is a rather vague notion, some points are very "typed" while others are at the margin of several classes that can sometimes be aggregated to one or another of these classes.

Factorial analysis of correspondences and ascending hierarchical classification are intimately linked in our approach. The hierarchical tree can be truncated at different levels to then project into the factor space the cloud of points where the classes will be identified by colors (Figure 4.3). This nebula provides information on the intrinsic organization of the data and reinforces the thematic interpretation of the structures sought. In addition, when the individuals in the statistical population are geographical objects or attached to location-based locations, it is easy to map the factorial classes and to visualize in the geographical space whether the location influences – or not – the spatial distribution: if not, the geographical position is neutral; if yes, the geographical position is not neutral; how to explain it then?

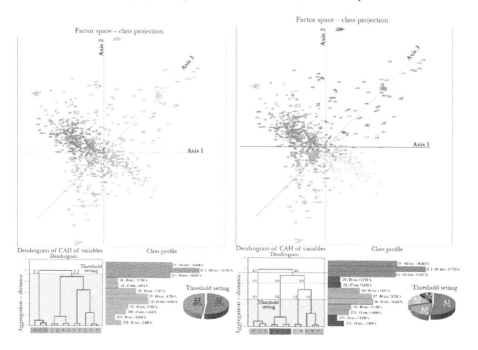

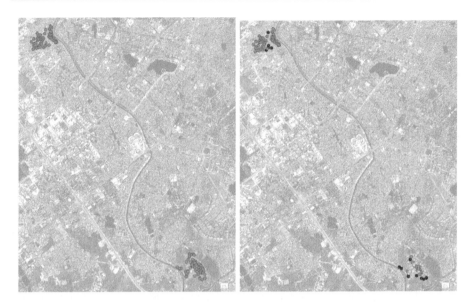

Figure 4.3. *Projection of classes in the factorial and geographical space (according to Xuan S.D. ibid.). The dendrogram can be truncated at different levels. For a color version of this figure, see www.iste.co.uk/laffly/torus1.zip*

In addition to the interest in the interpretation of the factor space and the typology itself, the classes obtained are as many subsets of the initial population. These new groups are defined by their own statistical parameters, occurrence profiles for categorical variables or descriptive statistics for continuous variables. These statistics are obtained directly from the data submitted to the AFC but can also be obtained for other variables. We will therefore have a solution – among others – to link endogenous and exogenous data.

In other words, a solution for developing a prediction from an apprenticeship.

From the Point to the Surface, How to Link Endogenous and Exogenous Data

In 1763, Richard Price posthumously published the works of his friend Thomas Bayes in a single article entitled *"An Essay towards a problem in the Doctrine of Chances"* which determines what was thereafter called the distribution *a posteriori* of the probability *p* of a binomial distribution or probability of the causes[1]. In probability theory, if we know the probabilities of events *A* and *B* and the probability of *B* knowing *A*, then it is possible to determine the probability of *A* knowing *B*. There is such a recent craze for the Bayes formula that some even consider it

---

Chapter written by Dominique LAFFLY.

1 It is interesting to note that Pierre-Simon Laplace – ignoring the work of Bayes – will demonstrate in 1774 the same theorem and promulgate the writing of the equation as we know it (Alberganti 2012): *"It is the dream, more or less conscious, of any scientist: to discover a universal law to understand and predict the natural phenomena of our universe. Few people succeed. And rare, too, are the equations that can claim a form of universality. In physics, for example, Einstein's theory of gravitation remains incompatible with quantum mechanics. [...] Strangely, the formula then dozes for more than two centuries. And more suddenly, around the year 2000, the number of scientific publications that mention it explodes. It goes from about 5000 mentions per year to more than 25,000 in 2010. It must be said that the fields of application of this formula, almost as simple as that of Newton, are extremely numerous. It allows us to better understand certain events in the evolution of species as well as certain mysteries of the universe. It can be used in the fields of weather and climatology, prediction of natural disasters, disease genetics, properties of matter, as well as cognitive science. For Stanislas Dehaene, professor of psychology at the Collège de France, we are in the middle of a Bayesian revolution in this field."*

a universal mathematical formula[2]: *By the way, Bayes the way!* This theorem corresponds to the following formula[3] [5.1]:

$$P(A|B) = \frac{P(B|A)\,P(A)}{P(B)}$$

[5.1]

where: P(A): *prior* probability of *A* (called marginal);

P(B): *prior* probability of *B*;

P(A|B): *a posterior* probability of *A* knowing *B* (or of *A* under condition *B* – conditional probability);

P(B|A): for a known *B*, likelihood function of *A*.

A more detailed form of the formula is also given as follows [5.2]:

$$P(A_i|B) = \frac{P(B|A_i)P(A_i)}{\sum_j P(B|A_j)P(A_j)}$$ for all A_i in the partition.

[5.2]

It is easy to schematize the Bayes formula as a superposition of two decision trees (Figure 5.1).

The conditional probabilities of Bayes assume an *a priori* knowledge of a distribution of probabilities of a partition (Figure 5.2). In our case, for each class resulting from the ascending hierarchical classification (AHC) carried out on the results of the multiple correspondence factor analysis (MFCA), the occurrences of the modalities of the variables of the classes will be considered here as this knowledge *a priori* of the studied system. For example, we assume a population partitioned into eight classes, for each of which we know the frequency of appearance of all the modalities of the variables. The Bayes formula makes it possible to calculate the probability of each modality for each of the classes. It is given by [5.3]:

---

2 See   http://www.franceculture.fr/emission-science-publique-une-formule-mathematique-universelle-existe-t-elle-2012-11-09.
3 Bayes blue neon theorem at Autonomy offices in Cambridge (https://fr.wikipedia.org/wiki/Théorème_de_Bayes).

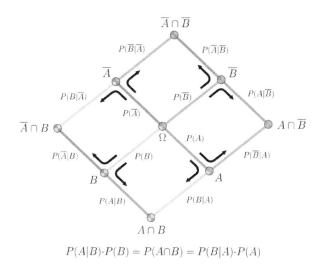

$$P(A|B) \cdot P(B) = P(A \cap B) = P(B|A) \cdot P(A)$$

Figure 5.1. *Bayes formula seen as the superposition of two decision trees (source: https://fr.wikipedia.org/wiki/Théorème_de_Bayes). For a color version of this figure, see www.iste.co.uk/laffly/torus1.zip*

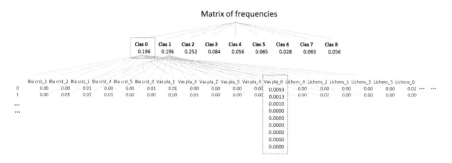

Figure 5.2. *Occurrence frequency matrices of classes and categories, i.e. the conditions of events a and b, as well as b knowing a. For a color version of this figure, see www.iste.co.uk/laffly/torus1.zip*

$$P(Vas\ pla\_0|Clas\ 0) = \frac{0.196*0.0093}{(0.196*0.0093)+(0.196*0.0013)+(0.196*0.001)} \approx 0.78 \quad [5.3]$$

$$P(Vas\ pla\_0|Clas\ 1) = \frac{0.196*0.0093}{(0.196*0.0093)+(0.196*0.0013)+(0.196*0.001)} \approx 0.78$$

$$P(Vas\ pla\_0|Clas\ 2) = \frac{0.252*0.0093}{(0.252*0.0093)+(0.252*0.0013)+(0.252*0.001)} \approx 0.80$$

The probability of observing the modality 0 (absence) of vascular plants – coded Vas_pla_0 – for classes 0 and 1 is 78%. Is 80% for class 2 and so on.

T. Brossard was one of the French geographers who indirectly introduced this method into landscape analysis from the late 1980s (Figure 5.3). We make this methodological basis our own by formalizing it more strictly, which offers an interesting solution for linking endogenous and exogenous data in a probabilistic way.

The frequencies of appearance of the modalities of the variables of a class (Figure 5.4) – resulting from the remote sensing or from an MCFA/AHC procedure – are considered as the marginal probability and this is the knowledge *a priori*. These frequencies combine the data that relate to the different levels of endogenous and exogenous observations (the examples given are indicative and do not correspond to the data systematically used):

– endogenous:

- vegetation surveys,

- local climatology,

- surveys of socio-spatial practices;

– exogenous:

- general topography (altitude, slope, orientation, shape of the relief, etc.),

- global climatology,

- land use (remote sensing),

- fragmentation and texture indices,

- dynamic synthetic indicators (diachronic vegetation indices),

- socio-economic attribute data by administrative unit.

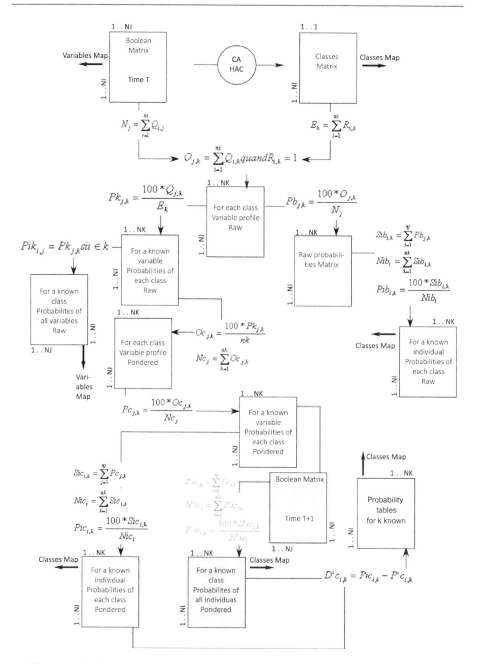

Figure 5.3. *Flow chart of the landscape data analysis (modified from Brossard, 1986). For a color version of this figure, see www.iste.co.uk/laffly/torus1.zip*

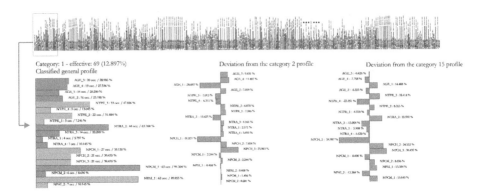

Figure 5.4. *Frequencies of appearance of the modalities of the variables for a class and deviations from the other classes. Example of biogeographic surveys at Spitsbergen. For a color version of this figure, see www.iste.co.uk/laffly/torus1.zip*

The Bayesian method is then mobilized in order to generalize in all points of space – via the exogenous data – the probability of occurrence of the elements initially observed in a specific way at the level of the field samples – the endogenous data. It should be checked first whether the relationships between the different levels of observations are statistically reliable. If so, then the method described here is excessively efficient and aesthetic.

Figure 5.5 shows the methodological progression that allows the prediction of plant composition in the small glacial age moraines at Spitsbergen by coupling *in situ* spot surveys of plant composition and aerial mapping of environmental variables given by satellite image radiometry, the description of terrain (altitude, slope, orientation, dominant form, etc.) and microclimatic conditions (temperature and wind).

For each precisely geolocated point (precision less than the size of the pixel – GNSS), we have a learning database where we compare the field readings and the "environmental" values of the pixels: all the elements are combined simultaneously in the MFCA; or the "environmental" variables are additional in the MFCA. In the end, for each class resulting from the MFCA, we know the profile of the field variables and the "environmental" variables. The final prediction consists of calculating the probability of each class for each pixel of the images and then deducing the probabilities of the modalities of the terrain variables: *Bayes, the way.*

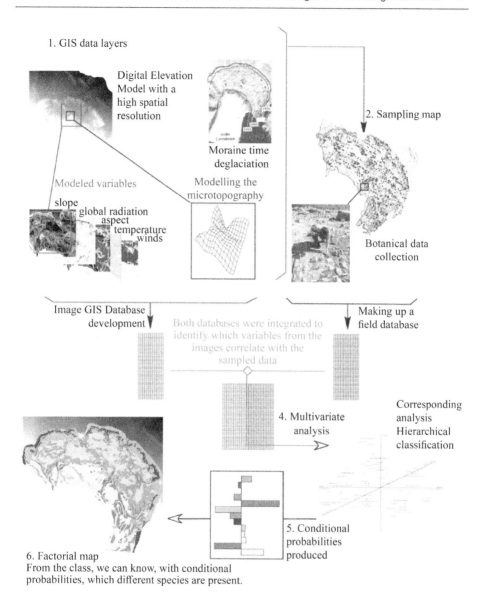

1. GIS data layers

Digital Elevation Model with a high spatial resolution

Moraine time deglaciation

Modeled variables

slope
global radiation
aspect
temperature
winds

Modelling the microtopography

2. Sampling map

Botanical data collection

Image GIS Database development

Both databases were integrated to identify which variables from the images correlate with the sampled data

Making up a field database

4. Multivariate analysis

Corresponding analysis
Hierarchical classification

5. Conditional probabilities produced

6. Factorial map
From the class, we can know, with conditional probabilities, which different species are present.

Figure 5.5. *From the point to the surface or how to link endogenous and exogenous data by the probabilities of Bayes causes (in Moreau et al., 2005, op. cit.). For a color version of this figure, see www.iste.co.uk/laffly/torus1.zip*

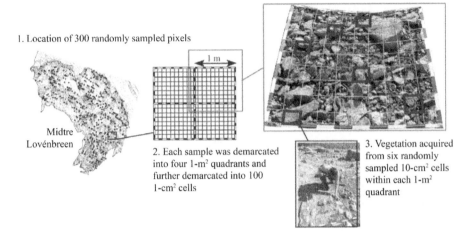

1. Location of 300 randomly sampled pixels

Midtre
Lovénbreen

1 m

2. Each sample was demarcated
into four 1-m² quadrants and
further demarcated into 100
1-cm² cells

3. Vegetation acquired
from six randomly
sampled 10-cm² cells
within each 1-m²
quadrant

Figure 5.6. *From the point to the surface or how to link endogenous and exogenous data by the probabilities of Bayes causes (in Moreau et al., 2005, op. cit.) For a color version of this figure, see www.iste.co.uk/laffly/torus1.zip*

Three levels of sampling:

– moraines of Little Ice Age (LIA);

– points localization;

– observation of vegetation.

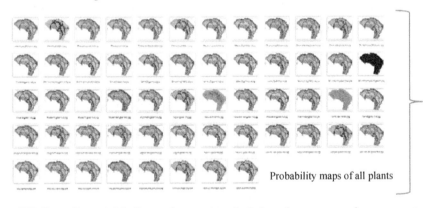

Probability maps of all plants

Figure 5.7. *From the point to the surface or how to link endogenous and exogenous data by the probabilities of Bayes causes (in Moreau et al., 2005, op. cit.)*

This example initially applied to biogeographic studies at Spitsbergen was later extended to the analysis of organic carbon in soil[4]. The methodological basis is the same. We associate *in situ* survey points with pixels in images to produce *in situ* data predictions from environmental data. We are now developing a similar approach based on social surveys and socio-economic data by administrative unit (Figure 5.8) as part of the research initiated by Thai Huyen Nguyen (RECYCURBS-VIET program, see above): 805 waste collection points were surveyed *in situ*; a classification on the results of an MFCA makes it possible to establish a standardized typology of the main structures that organize the data; the classes are summarized by administrative units for which socio-economic data are available (equivalent of a municipality); the Bayes model calculates the probability of a class based on socio-economic variables from which the probability of the modalities from the survey is known; the model can be applied to other agglomerations in a deductive approach.

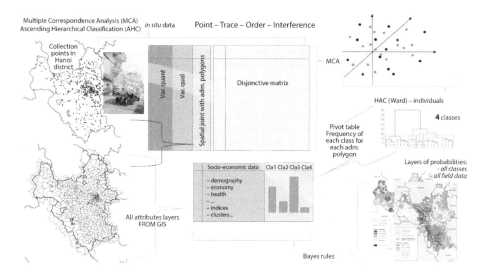

Figure 5.8. *From the prototype to an operational chain – point, trace, order and inference. For a color version of this figure, see www.iste.co.uk/laffly/torus1.zip*

The Bayesian solution is not the only one to remember; we recall the performance of the MCMC (Monte Carlo–Markovian Chain), which is based on

4 *Programme international SOCRATE* (Soil Organic Carbon in Arctic Environment) in collaboration with the KOPRI (Korea Polar Research Institute), University of Tromsø (Norway), l'EISTI and the University of Toulouse.

the Metropolis–Hastings algorithm. Villani[5] refers to them as *"random walk exploration"* and we could just as easily mention the other methods of machine learning: support vector machines, linear regressions, artificial neural networks, decision trees, k-means, logistic regressions, random forests, etc.

That is, ubiquitous methods in artificial intelligence brought up to date in the new era of Big Data.

5.1. References

Alberganti M. (2012). *Une formule mathématique universelle existe-t-elle ?* [Online]. Available at: https://www.franceculture.fr/emissions/science-publique/une-formule-mathematique-universelle-existe-t-elle.

Brossard T. (1991). "Pratiques des paysages en Baie du Roy et sa région". *Annales littéraires de l'université de Franche-Comté*, 428.

Moreau M., Laffly D., Joly D. and Brossard T. (2005). "Analysing the plant colonization of moraine since the end of Little Ice Age by means of remote sensed data and a Bayesian approach". *Remote Sensing of Environment*, 99(3), 244–253.

5 Villani C., *Théorème vivant*, Éditions Grasset at Fasquelle, Paris, 2013.

6

Big Data in Geography

NOTE.–Zettaoctet = a "byte" is equivalent to an "octet", for clarity, eight bits. A zettaoctet is 10^{21} octets, or 1,000,000,000,000,000,000,000 octets. A zettabyte is 10^{21} bytes (Wikipedia https:// en.wikipedia.org/wiki/Octet_(computing)):

Order of magnitude	International System (SI)			Binary prefixes		
	Unit	Notation	Value	Unit	Notation	Value
1	byte	B	1 byte	byte	B	1 byte
10^3	kilobyte	kB	10^3 bytes	kibibyte	KiB	2^{10} bytes
10^6	megabyte	MB	10^6 bytes	mebibyte	MiB	2^{20} bytes
10^9	gigabyte	GB	10^9 bytes	gibibyte	GiB	2^{30} bytes
10^{12}	terabyte	TB	10^{12} bytes	tebibyte	TiB	2^{40} bytes
10^{15}	petabyte	PB	10^{15} bytes	pebibyte	PiB	2^{50} bytes
10^{18}	exabyte	EB	10^{18} bytes	exbibyte	EiB	2^{60} bytes
10^{21}	zettabyte	ZB	10^{21} bytes	zebibyte	ZiB	2^{70} bytes
10^{24}	yottabyte	YB	10^{24} bytes	yobibyte	YiB	2^{80} bytes

Table 6.1. *Octets. For a color version of this figure, see www.iste.co.uk/laffly/torus1.zip*

Big Data is the new oil gold; the amounts of information now generated are astronomical: "the digital data created in the world would have gone from *1.2 zettaoctet* per year in 2010 to 1.8 zettabyte in 2011, then 2.8 zettabytes in 2012 and will rise to 40 zettabytes in 2020"[1]. A true universe with black holes that absorb most of the information without it even being processed – it is estimated that less

---

Chapter written by Dominique LAFFLY.
1 Wikipedia https://en.wikipedia.org/wiki/Zettabyte_Era.

than 3% of the data are actually marked and analyzed[2]. The numbers are beyond the comprehension of most of us[3]:

– "in 2011, 5 exabytes of data were generated every two days. This is now done in just 10 minutes;

– only 0.5% of these data are analyzed;

– there were only 130 exabytes of data in the digital universe in 2005. There should be more than 40,000 by 2020;

– in 2020, the data will represent the equivalent of more than 5,000 GBs per person;

– in 2012, 35% of this information would require protection, but this is the case only for 20% of it".

Big Data is a major issue now raised by the conferences of the parties (COP21, COP22 and COP23) and incorporates the UN Sustainable Development Goals that speak of data philanthropy.

"Global Big Data contains essential data 'to solve the climate equation', and in particular to improve the energy efficiency of cities and buildings, for smart grids, to verify the application of regulations to fight against deforestation, overfishing, land degradation, food waste or better managing waste, eco-consume or encourage investors to create smart cities… [but it does not go without asking moral and ethical questions]."[4]

In 2016, Taylor[5] asked the following: when Big Data is presented as a common or a public good, what good are we talking about? And to what audience do we really intend it? Futher, he mentioned Robert Kirkpatrick (Director of United Nations Global Pulse) for whom Big Data is like "a new kind of natural resource – or unnatural resource – infinitely renewable, increasingly ubiquitous – but one that has fallen into the hands of what's been an opaque and largely unregulated extractive industry that's just beginning to wake up to the recognition that it has a social opportunity – and perhaps a social responsibility – to make sure that this data reaches the people who need it most."

---

2 See https://www.emc.com/leadership/digital-universe/index.htm.
3 See https://www.blogdumoderateur.com/big-data-donnees-en-ligne.
4 Wikipedia https://en.wikipedia.org/wiki/Big_data.
5 Taylor L. "The ethics of big data as a public good: which public? Whose good?" Available at: http://rsta.royalsocietypublishing.org/content/374/2083/20160126?utm_source=TrendMD&utm_medium=cpc&utm_campaign=Philosophical_Transactions_A_TrendMD_0, 2016.

Technically, how to consider the exploitation of these data. Peter Norvig, Director of Research at Google, offers an S-curve to illustrate the link between the evolution of the amount of data and the quality of possible processing solutions (Figure 6.1). The switch between Small Data and Big Data is far behind us, and its dating depends on the disciplines and sectors of activity. Google's Big Data (24 petabytes a day) is not CERN's[6] or that of NASA[7] and even less than that of the geographer. Anyway, let us agree that from the moment the data accumulate faster than we have the time to analyze them, they require storage volumes that involve servers, and that the information is not systematically structured and we are indeed in a big data problem: we find the initial 3V's – volume, speed and variability.

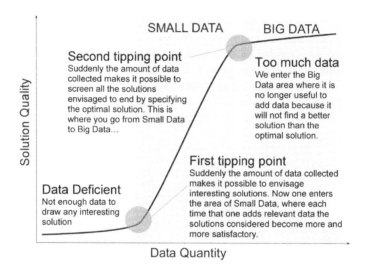

Figure 6.1. *S-curve of Peter Norvig (modified from Norvig P., "Computer Science, the Unreasonable Effectiveness of Data" and http://adnetis.com/traitement-donnees)*

6 And so, CERN's Large Hadron Collider uses around 150 million sensors that deliver data 40 million times per second. For 600 million collisions per second, after filtering, there are 100 collisions per second that are of interest, or 25 PBs of data to store each year, and 200 PBs after replication (https:// en.wikipedia.org/wiki/Large_Hadron_Collider).
7 Between 2017 and 2025, the volume of data in the EOSDIS (Earth Observing System Data and Information System) archive is expected to grow dramatically, accompanied by an order of magnitude increase in the rate of data ingest. To describe the enormous amount of data, 1 petabyte (PB) has been described as the data equivalent of roughly 20 million four-drawer file cabinets filled with text. EOSDIS is continually evolving its data systems to accommodate these expanding data and user requirements.

The geographer – and more broadly the geosciences in the broad sense of the term – is confronted with this triptych when he resorts to the systematic observation of a territory and a population from satellite images and information from social networks, for example. As far as we are concerned, it was in 2006 that the need to take the plunge became apparent in the context of research on the impact of global warming on the glacier balance of the Austre Lovénbreen at Spitsbergen (Svalbard, Norway – Figure 6.2). At this date, unlike today, the images at the spatial resolution adapted to our problem – optical remote sensing, of the order of 10 m and less – paid off and the costs were prohibitive when we considered a temporal follow-up. Nevertheless, we opted for the FORMOSAT 2 satellite[8] and a 3-year subscription of 12 images per year, i.e. two to three images per month between April and September, a permanent day in the Arctic and snowmelt and glacial melt. Complemented by meteorological, hydrological and geochemical field measurements, the images acquired every two weeks were to map the melting rhythms to feed a fusion-day model and to distinguish in the flows what came from the ice of the glacier, ground ice, snow and rain. In theory, because, in practice, even with a very high acquisition repeatability due to the high latitude, cloud cover prevents any systematic monitoring in polar optical remote sensing.

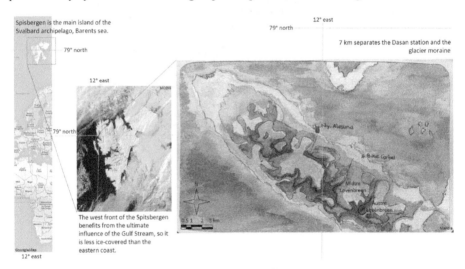

Figure 6.2. *King's Bay and Lovén glacier, a place of experimentation. For a color version of this figure, see www.iste.co.uk/laffly/torus1.zip*

---

8 See https://en.wikipedia.org/wiki/National_Space_Organization#FORMOSAT.

A few years later, in 2015, SPOT5's airborne de-orbitation allowed for a significant reduction in image acquisition cycles – from 26 days to 5 days – and provided free data for 150 sites, including ours, for a few months[9]. Even under these conditions, it was impossible to obtain regular monitoring, as seen in Figure 6.3: from April 9 to September 1, only three images (framed in red) were validated among the 50 proposed.

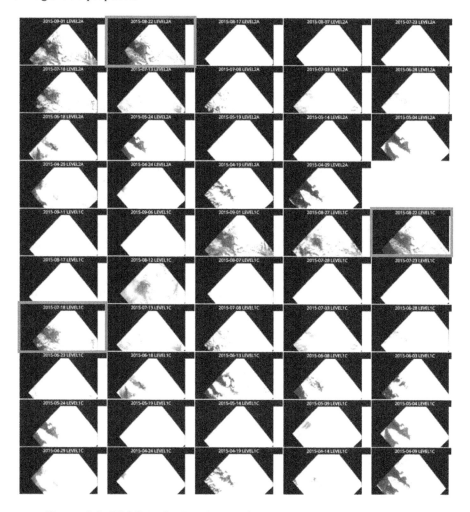

Figure 6.3. SPOT 5 take 5, only three images are available on one year. For a color version of this figure, see www.iste.co.uk/laffly/torus1.zip

---

9 See http://www.theia-land.fr/fr/produits/spot-5-take-5.

Hence the idea of proceeding differently, from within to acquire *in situ*, under the clouds, the data that will follow the melting[10]: six time lapse cameras programmed to acquire three images per day were installed around the glacier catchment area to cover almost the entire surface. In theory, for each acquisition cycle, the chain of treatments to be mobilized is simple: ortho-rectification; mosaicing; classification – snow(s), ice(s), other; equivalent height conversion.

In practice, it is much more complicated: the cameras are not calibrated, they can move slightly between shots[11], which prohibits the systematic use of a physical model[12] for orthorectification; some images are unusable[13]; for the same site, the dynamics of hues[14] may vary depending on lighting conditions; the quantity of images is quickly a brake to the systematic exploitation of the database – 6,570 images per year or 78,840 at the end of the year 2018. In addition, there were no systems at the time that were adapted to the constraints of the field: battery power and battery life (access difficulties preclude the use of heavy batteries); electronic management closer to consumption (the device must not remain lit between shots, see electric autonomy); storage on memory cards (the study area is located in a frequency protected area due to the radio-astronomical equipment of Ny-Ålesund); extreme weather conditions and so on. Hence the need to develop a dedicated system from photoscopes of the general public, in this case initially Leica D-Lux (collaboration with CNRS laboratory FEMTO in Besançon, France – Figure 6.4).

Ranisavljevic developed, in her thesis[15], cloud solutions to meet the volume constraints of the data and the treatments to be mobilized. These solutions are

---

10 For a program of ANR Hydro-Sensor flows: Griselin M., Marlin C., Laffly D. "Un glacier sous surveillance au Spitsberg". https://web.univ-pau.fr/RECHERCHE/SET/LAFFLY/docs_laffly/annee_polaire_internationale.pdf.
11 Under the action of an animal, when we assume the management of the system to recover the data and repair if necessary.
12 We will apply a geometric correction based on a dense network of Thiesen triangles. Either a model for each camera, all the images will have to be systematically brought into geometric conformity with the one that was used as a reference to develop the model (see previous note).
13 The camera may not have worked, the camera is in the fog, the lens is covered with drops of water or ice.
14 How to automatically distinguish different types of snow and ice when they can cover the entire range of gray?
15 Ranisavljevic É., Cloud computing appliquée au traitement multimodal d'images in-situ pour l'analyse des dynamiques environnementales, EISTI, Thesis, edited by Laffly D. and Le Nir Y., 2016.

considered as services (Software as a Service - SaaS) which are necessary to orchestrate dynamically to process databases (Figure 6.5).

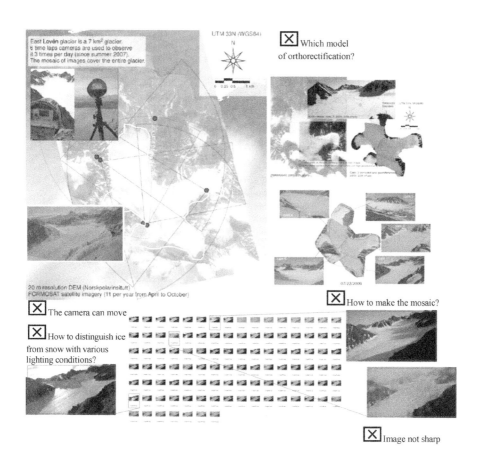

Figure 6.4. *Sequential tasks of a data framework. For a color version of this figure, see www.iste.co.uk/laffly/torus1.zip*

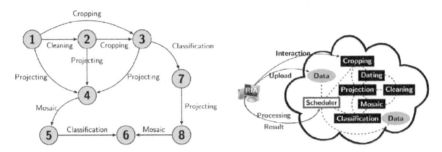

Sample workflow for image processing. The images are the vertices and the tasks are the edges.

Orchestration

Figure 6.5. *From the identification of services to their dynamic orchestration in the cloud. X as a Service – XaaS – new paradigm*

An excerpt from the remarks made in this thesis is sufficient to understand the need to learn to communicate between geosciences and computer science as TORUS promotes:

> *"Among the different methods of composition of services [...] we have made the choice to start from a composition in BPEL format, and to diversify it and make it more dynamic and adaptable to different scenarios by semantics. WS being developed in SOAP with a description WSDL for reasons of quantity of data to be transferred through the requests, the addition of the semantics to the various services was done through the annotations in SAWSDL. The ontological model used for the semantic annotations corresponds to the description of the different WSs defined for the process of the environmental analysis. It defines the families of processing types (classification services, mosaic services, etc.) as well as the different types of data used at the input and output of each of the services. Thus, by specific requests on this ontology, it is possible to define or diversify workflow according to the desired treatment."*

BPEL, WS, SOAP, WSDL, SAWSDL… what else?

Whether taken from space from a satellite, a plane or a drone or acquired *in situ*, remote sensing images are at the heart of massive data in environmental science. Data providers such as NASA or ESA have been developing cloud computing solutions for several years and offer a choice of archive and/or current images (a few hours after acquisition), most of which are free. We will discuss these aspects below in the chapter dedicated to remote sensing. Let us note here that since December 2016, Google offers a cloud computing platform that allows the online processing of environmental data: *Google Earth Exchange*[16]. This service is connected to the providers' systems mentioned above for the choice of data and offers either turnkey solutions – an already operational treatment – or a console mode where the user can develop their own code in Python. All from an ergonomic user interface integrated and directly usable from a browser without having to install any software or download any data on their workstation (Figure 6.6):

> *"Google Earth Engine is a computing platform that allows users to run geospatial analysis on Google's infrastructure. There are several ways to interact with the platform. The Code Editor is a Web-based IDE for writing and running scripts. The Explorer is a lightweight web app for exploring our data catalog and running simple analyses. The client libraries provide Python and JavaScript wrappers around our web API. Continue reading for an overview of each of these, or visit the Earth Engine's Developer Guide for an in-depth guide."*

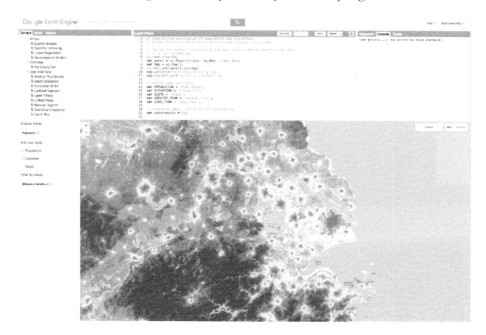

Figure 6.6. *Example of Google Earth Exchange environment. For a color version of this figure, see www.iste.co.uk/laffly/torus1.zip*

16 See https://earthengine.google.com.

Note that the free version is restricted, and does not allow an operational search.

Presented in December 2016 – halfway through TORUS – Google Earth Engine is typically what we hope to develop in TORUS. All in proportion, of course, but the proof is again there that we need to learn from each other, geosciences and computer science, because the real tools of tomorrow will be in the image of the one presented here by Google.

Conclusion to Part 1

Why Here But Not There?

We hope to have shown by our words that Geography is a science that offers a specific way of looking at the world, and whose underpinning can be summarized by the following question: *Why here and now but not there?* A primordial question (Figure C.1) – to which current issues around location-based information testify – common to many disciplines; more specifically, contemporary to many disciplines, and yet it is at the heart of Geography, heard beyond the French university, it is age-old. We like to quote the Jesuit Father Jean Francois who, in 1652, wrote in a book entitled *The Science of Geography*:

> "*Geography has had, until now, the job of distributing and enumerating the parts that compose the globe. Until now, this has been an art of memory rather than due to a discourse of reason. But the understanding, on the contrary, needs a master who teaches him to see and understand.*"

Then, there is the incredible speech that actualizes A. Frémont in 1984:

> "*But geographers, and particularly French geographers, were they made for remote sensing space…? Without falling into an excessive pessimism or a too sharp critical mind, it seems that the negative answer is imperative. […] It* [Geography] *now collects the disadvantages when its 'specialists' are considered technically under-qualified. […] Faced with the current stakes, the geographers of the 1980s do not seem to me any more to have the choice of hesitations, on pain of accompanying their discipline in the decline of archaisms. With computer science for data processing, automatic mapping and infographic, remote sensing space is undoubtedly one of the*

Conclusion written by Dominique LAFFLY.

instruments of technological change in the discipline. […] Refusing these perspectives and the consequences they imply is most likely to be definitively resolved to provincial dimensions for the school or the French schools."

We make ours the conclusion of A. Frémont: *"Faced with the current stakes, the geographers of the years [2010] no longer seem to me to have the choice of hesitations, on pain of accompanying their discipline in the decline of archaisms."*

Figure C.1. *The feeling of landscape (modified from Schuiten F. and Peeters B., The Invisible Border, Casterman Editions, 2002). For a color version of this figure, see www.iste.co.uk/laffly/torus1.zip*

We have seen that these issues are those of massive data, artificial intelligence and cloud computing. Integrating these methods and mastering these techniques will contribute positively to the evolution of the questioning inherent in Geography. First and foremost, it is now unthinkable to not evolve in a multidisciplinary context that is ideally transdisciplinary. Mutual recognition and a common language are now the true keystones of science.

TORUS has been a program that has met all these expectations of contemporary science. And since we are all geographers, now I invite G. Bertrand[1] to conclude:

"You have to use geography to cross other disciplines as long as you draw a path. As Antonio Machado says, 'the way is done by walking'. We must consider that when we talk about landscape, the environment,

---

1 See http://cafe-geo.net/wp-content/uploads/CR-Paysage-22.10.03-.pdf.

development or territory, we always talk about the same subject. It is a set that can't be used with a single methodology. It is a paradigm that takes into consideration all the elements and hybridizes the opposites (example: nature/society, individual/collective, ordinary/extra-ordinary)."

The way we do it is by walking… what else do we do here by opening cloud computing and artificial intelligence to Geography, to delve deep into massive data? (Figure C.2).

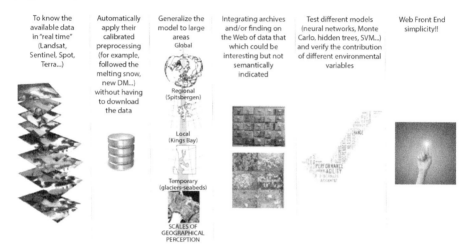

Figure C.2. *The ideal of geoscience in the age of Big Data and cloud computing. For a color version of this figure, see www.iste.co.uk/laffly/torus1.zip*

How to not conclude about cloud computing, Big Data, satellite imagery, social network with the "Anatomy of a Killing"[2] (Figure C.3). *"From a simple amateur video, the BBC managed to identify the place, the date and the perpetrators of a massacre that occurred in Cameroon in July. A scientific survey that relies on Big Data, and allows journalists a new exploitation of images."* (*Le Monde*, October 6, 2018). Illustration of datajournalism, *"In this context, would the image become a database like any other?"* This is what Karen Bastien, co-founder of WeDoData, an agency specializing in data visualization, argues: *"A digital image is a set of pixels in which we can now detect a modification, a 're-work', that, on the colorimetric, luminosity or other side, it has metadata that describe it and are attached to it, and that can also be exploited. And if, until recently, the images had to be analyzed at length by a human eye, now the technologies that analyze them massively have become accessible and make it possible to identify stronger correlations because*

2 See https://www.youtube.com/watch?v=4G9S-eoLgX4.

they no longer rely on one but on hundreds, thousands or even tens of thousands of images. Crossed with other databases, the video reviewed by the BBC has revealed many secrets." (ibid.)

Figure C.3. *Datajournalism or how journalists have identified the murderers with the help of Big Data and artifical intelligence on the cloud – Where, When and Who? Unfortunatly we know Why (from the BBC, see footnote 2 of this chapter). For a color version of this figure, see www.iste.co.uk/laffly/torus1.zip*

PART 2

Basic Mathematical, Statistical and Computational Tools

An Introduction to Machine Learning

7.1. Predictive modeling: introduction

In many applications of machine learning, the goal is to learn a classification/prediction model from the data that can be used to predict the classes/values of new (future or test) cases/instances. Formally, apply a prediction function, f, to a feature representation, $\mathbf{x}$, of the data to get a desired output y:

$$y = f(x). \tag{7.1}$$

Two major approaches are often used to estimate the prediction function f:

1) **Supervised learning**, in which the training data are labeled. Here, the goal is to take a vector x of input features and to assign it to one of C alternative classes labeled by a vector y, a C-dimensional binary vector in which all elements are zero except the one corresponding to the class. The two most common types of supervised learning are **classification** (where the outputs are discrete labels, for example, land cover classification) and **regression** (where the outputs are real-valued, for example, time-series prediction/forecasting).

2) And **unsupervised learning**, in which we are given a collection of unlabeled data, which we wish to discover patterns within. **Clustering** is one of such approaches.

7.2. Bayesian modeling

In this chapter, we will mainly focus on **Bayesian** methods. Bayesian probability theory is distinguished by defining probabilities as *degrees of certainty*, which

Chapter written by Hichem SAHLI.

provides a system for reasoning with uncertainty. In the following, we will introduce basic probability theory, the Bayes rule, along with the notions of parameters estimation, these being the basic notions for statistical machine learning.

7.2.1. *Basic probability theory*

This section gives an overview of probability theory.

The basic rules of probability theory are as follows [BER 03]:

– the probability $P(\mathbf{A})$ of a statement $\mathbf{A}$ is a real number $\in [0, 1]$. $P(\mathbf{A}) = 1$ indicates absolute certainty that $\mathbf{A}$ is true, $P(\mathbf{A}) = 0$ indicates absolute certainty that $\mathbf{A}$ is false and values between 0 and 1 correspond to varying degrees of certainty;

– the **joint probability** $P(\mathbf{A}, \mathbf{B})$ of two statements $\mathbf{A}$ and $\mathbf{B}$ is the probability that both statements are true (clearly, $P(\mathbf{A}, \mathbf{B}) = P(\mathbf{B}, \mathbf{A})$);

– the **conditional probability** $P(\mathbf{A}|\mathbf{B})$ of $\mathbf{A}$ given $\mathbf{B}$ is the probability that we would assign $\mathbf{A}$ as true, **if** we knew $\mathbf{B}$ to be true. The conditional probability is defined as $P(\mathbf{A}|\mathbf{B}) = P(\mathbf{A}, \mathbf{B})/P(\mathbf{B})$;

– **the product rule**: the probability that $\mathbf{A}$ and $\mathbf{B}$ are both true is given by the probability that $\mathbf{B}$ is true, multiplied by the probability we would assign to $\mathbf{A}$ if we knew $\mathbf{B}$ to be true:

$$P(\mathbf{A}, \mathbf{B}) = P(\mathbf{A}|\mathbf{B})P(\mathbf{B}) \qquad [7.2]$$

Similarly, $P(\mathbf{A}, \mathbf{B}) = P(\mathbf{B}|\mathbf{A})P(\mathbf{A})$. This rule follows directly from the definition of conditional probability;

– **the sum rule**: the probability of a statement being true and the probability that it is false must sum to 1:

$$P(\mathbf{A}) + P(\bar{\mathbf{A}}) = 1 \qquad [7.3]$$

As a result, given a set of mutually exclusive statements $\mathbf{A}_i$, we have

$$\sum_i P(\mathbf{A}_i) = 1 \qquad [7.4]$$

– **marginalization**:

$$P(\mathbf{B}) = \sum_i P(\mathbf{A}_i, \mathbf{B}) \qquad [7.5]$$

where $\mathbf{A}_i$ are mutually exclusive statements, of which exactly one must be true. In the simplest case where the statement $\mathbf{A}$ may be true or false we can derive:

$$P(\mathbf{B}) = P(\mathbf{A}, \mathbf{B}) + P(\bar{\mathbf{A}}, \mathbf{B}) \qquad [7.6]$$

– **independence**: two statements are independent if and only if $P(\mathbf{A}, \mathbf{B}) = P(\mathbf{A})P(\mathbf{B})$. If $\mathbf{A}$ and $\mathbf{B}$ are independent, then it follows that $P(\mathbf{A}|\mathbf{B}) = P(\mathbf{A})$.

7.2.2. *Bayes rule*

In statistical machine learning, our goal is to determine the model f from observed data x. Indeed, the model is described by some unknown variables, and we observe some data; our goal is to determine the model from the data. This can be made possible using the **Bayes rule**:

$$\underbrace{p(model|data)}_{posterior} = \frac{\overbrace{P(data|model)}^{likelihood}\overbrace{p(model)}^{prior}}{\underbrace{p(data)}_{evidence}} \tag{7.7}$$

The different terms of the above equation are defined as follows:

– the **likelihood** distribution describes the likelihood of data given by the model. It reflects our assumptions about how the data are generated;

– the **prior distribution** describes our assumptions about the model before observing the data;

– the **posterior distribution** describes our knowledge of the model, incorporating both the data and the prior;

– the **evidence** is useful in model selection and will be discussed later. Here, its only role is to normalize the posterior PDF.

7.2.3. *Parameter estimation*

Parameter estimation is used in many machine learning problems. We are interested in finding a single estimate of the value of an unknown parameter from observed data. In this section, we give a general description of the approaches that are mainly used, namely maximum A posterior (MAP) and maximum likelihood (ML).

MAP is defined as: select the parameter value θ that maximizes the posterior, i.e.:

$$\hat{\theta} = arg \max_{\theta} p(\theta|\mathcal{D}) \tag{7.8}$$

$$= arg \max_{\theta} P(\mathcal{D}|\theta)p(\theta) \tag{7.9}$$

Generally, it is more convenient to minimize the negative log of the objective function (ln is a monotonic decreasing function) and pose MAP estimation as:

$$\hat{\theta}_{MAP} = arg \max_{\theta} P(\mathcal{D}|\theta)p(\theta) \qquad [7.10]$$

$$= arg \min_{\theta} - \ln(P(\mathcal{D}|\theta)p(\theta)) \qquad [7.11]$$

$$= arg \min_{\theta} - \ln P(\mathcal{D}|\theta) - \ln p(\theta)) \qquad [7.12]$$

The objective breaks into a part corresponding to the likelihood and a part corresponding to the prior. Often, we assume a *uniform prior*, in this case, the $p(\theta)$ term can be ignored from MAP learning, and we are left with only maximizing the likelihood, which defines the *maximum likelihood* (ML) estimator:

$$\hat{\theta}_{ML} = arg \max_{\theta} P(\mathcal{D}|\theta) \qquad [7.13]$$

7.2.4. *Learning Gaussians*

Let us consider the problem of learning a Gaussian distribution from N training samples $\mathbf{x}_{1:N}$. We first start by defining a Gaussian probability distribution function (PDF) over a scalar value x, given by:

$$p(x|\mu, \sigma^2) = \frac{1}{\sqrt{2\pi\sigma^2}} exp(-\frac{1}{2\sigma^2}(x - \mu)^2) \qquad [7.14]$$

with μ the mean and σ^2 the variance. The mean specifies the center of the distribution, and the variance tells us how spread-out the PDF is.

The PDF for D-dimensional vector $\mathbf{x}$, the elements of which are jointly distributed with a Gaussian density function, is given by:

$$p(\mathbf{x}|\mu, \Sigma) = \mathbf{G}(\mathbf{x}; \mu, \Sigma) \equiv \frac{1}{\sqrt{(2\pi)^{\mathbf{D}}|\Sigma|}} \exp(-(\mathbf{x} - \mu)^{\mathbf{T}}\Sigma^{-1}(\mathbf{x} - \mu)/\mathbf{2}) \qquad [7.15]$$

where μ is the mean vector, Σ is a $D \times D$ covariance matrix and $|\Sigma|$ denotes the determinant of the matrix Σ. The covariance matrix Σ must be symmetric and positive definite ($|\Sigma| > 0$).

An important special case is when the Gaussian is isotropic (rotationally invariant). In this case, the covariance matrix can be written as $\Sigma = \sigma^2\mathbf{I}$, where $\mathbf{I}$ is the identity matrix. This is called a spherical or isotropic covariance matrix. In this case, the PDF reduces to:

$$p(\mathbf{x}|\mu, \sigma^2) = \frac{1}{\sqrt{(2\pi)^D \sigma^{2D}}} \exp(-\frac{1}{2\sigma^2}||\mathbf{x} - \mu||^2) \qquad [7.16]$$

Coming back to our problem of learning a Gaussian distribution from N training samples $\mathbf{x}_{1:N}$, maximum likelihood learning of the parameters μ and Σ entails maximizing the likelihood:

$$p(\mathbf{x}_{1:N}|\mu, \Sigma) \qquad [7.17]$$

We assume here that the data points are drawn independently and come from a Gaussian. Hence, the joint likelihood over the entire set of data is the product of the likelihoods for each individual datum:

$$p(\mathbf{x}_{1:N}|\mu, \Sigma) = \prod_{i=1}^{N} p(\mathbf{x}_{1:N}|\mu, \Sigma) \qquad [7.18]$$

$$= \prod_{i=1}^{N} \frac{1}{\sqrt{(2\pi)^D |\Sigma|}} exp(-\frac{1}{2}(\mathbf{x_i} - \mu)^{\mathbf{T}}\Sigma^{-1}(\mathbf{x_i} - \mu)) \qquad [7.19]$$

where D is the dimensionality of $\mathbf{x_i}$. From section 7.2.3, it is more convenient to minimize the negative log likelihood:

$$L(\mu, \Sigma) \equiv -\ln p(\mathbf{x}_{1:N}|\mu, \Sigma) \qquad [7.20]$$

$$= -\sum_i \ln p(\mathbf{x_i}|\mu, \Sigma) \qquad [7.21]$$

$$= \sum_i \frac{(\mathbf{x_i} - \mu)^{\mathbf{T}}\Sigma^{-1}(\mathbf{x_i} - \mu)}{2} + \frac{N}{2}\ln|\Sigma| + \frac{NM}{2}ln(2\pi) \qquad [7.22]$$

Solving for μ and Σ by setting $\partial L/\partial \mu = \mathbf{0}$ and $\partial L/\partial \Sigma = 0$ (subject to the constraint that Σ is symmetric) and gives the maximum likelihood estimates:

$$\hat{\mu} = \frac{1}{N}\sum_i \mathbf{x_i} \qquad [7.23]$$

$$\hat{\Sigma} = \frac{1}{N}\sum_i (\mathbf{x_i} - \hat{\mu})(\mathbf{x_i} - \hat{\mu})^{\mathbf{T}} \qquad [7.24]$$

In summary, we estimate the Gaussian's mean as the sample mean of the data and the Gaussian's covariance as the sample covariance of the data.

7.3. **Generative versus discriminative models**

As introduced in section 7.1, in many applications of machine learning, we are given a training dataset X comprising N input vectors $X = \{x_1, \cdots, x_N\}$ together with a set of corresponding labels $Y = \{y_1, \cdots, y_N\}$, in which we assume that the input vectors, and their labels, are drawn independently from the same distribution. Our goal is to predict the class $\hat{y}$ for a new input vector $\hat{x}$, so we require the conditional distribution:

$$p(\hat{y}|\hat{x}, X, Y) \qquad [7.25]$$

To determine this distribution, we introduce a parametric model governed by a set of parameters θ. *Discriminative methods* define the conditional distribution $p(y|x, \theta)$, where θ are the parameters of the model. The likelihood function is then given by:

$$L(\theta) = p(Y|X, \theta) = \prod_{n=1}^{N} p(y_n|x_n, \theta) \qquad [7.26]$$

The likelihood function can be combined with a prior $p(\theta)$, to give a joint distribution

$$p(\theta, Y|X) = p(\theta)L(\theta) \qquad [7.27]$$

from which we can obtain the posterior distribution by normalizing:

$$p(\theta|X, Y) = \frac{p(\theta)L(\theta)}{p(Y|X)} \qquad [7.28]$$

where

$$p(Y|X) = \int p(\theta)L(\theta)d\theta \qquad [7.29]$$

Predictions for new inputs are then made by marginalizing the predictive distribution with respect to θ weighted by the posterior distribution:

$$p(\hat{y}|\hat{x}, X, Y) = \int p(\hat{y}|\hat{x}, \theta)p(\theta|X, Y)d\theta \qquad [7.30]$$

In practice, this marginalization is rarely tractable. Having enough data, an estimate for θ can be made by maximizing the posterior distribution to give θ_{MAP}, and the predictive distribution can then be estimated using:

$$p(\hat{y}|\hat{x}, X, Y) \simeq p(\hat{y}|\hat{x}, \theta_{MAP}) \qquad [7.31]$$

Discriminative methods give good predictive performance and have been widely used in many applications when labeled data are available. However, in many cases, it is impossible to provide enough labeled training examples, so there is increasing use of *semi-supervised* learning in which the labeled training examples are augmented with a much larger quantity of unlabeled examples. In such cases, *generative models*, which define a joint distribution $p(x, y|\theta)$ over both input vectors and class labels, have been proposed [JEB 06].

In summary:

1) **generative models**, such as the Naïve Bayes classifier, describe the complete probability of the data $p(x, y)$;

2) **discriminative models**, such as logistic regression (LR), artificial neural networks (ANNs) and k-nearest neighbor (KNN), describe the conditional probability of the output given the input: $p(y|x)$.

Generative models allow us to put more prior knowledge into how we build the model, but classification may often involve difficult optimization of $p(y|x)$. Discriminative methods are typically more efficient and generic, but are harder to specialize to particular problems.

7.4. Classification

In classification, we are trying to learn a mapping f from a set of features x to a set of labels y. For example, we might want to determine whether a remote sensing image contains a road. Such a detection task is a *binary classification* problem. In *multi-class classification* problems, we are interested in determining which of the multiple categories the input belongs to. For example, given a satellite image, we might wish to recognize all land cover classes.

The input x might be a vector of real numbers or a discrete feature vector. In the case of binary classification problems, the output y might be an element of the set $\{-1, 1\}$, while for a multi-class problem with C categories, the output might be an integer in $\{1, ..., C\}$.

The general goal of classification is to learn a *decision boundary*, with the purpose to identity the regions of the input space that correspond to each class. For binary classification, the decision boundary is the surface in the feature space that divides the test inputs into two classes: points x for which $f(x) < 0$ are in the first class, while points for which $f(x) > 0$ are in the other. The points on the decision boundary, $f(x) = 0$, are those inputs for which the two classes are equally probable.

In this section, we introduce several basic methods for classification, focusing mainly on binary classification problems to ease understanding. These methods can be easily extended to multi-class.

7.4.1. *Naïve Bayes*

Let us consider that we have two mutually exclusive classes C_1 and C_2. Each class has a distribution for its data: $p(\boldsymbol{x}|C_1)$ and $p(\boldsymbol{x}|C_2)$. The prior probability of a sample from class C_1 is $P(C_1)$ and $P(C_2) = 1 - P(C_1)$. Given labeled training data $(\boldsymbol{x}_i, y_i)$, we can estimate the distribution for each class by maximum likelihood and estimate $P(C_1)$ by computing the ratio of the number of samples from class C_1 to the total number of samples.

Once we have trained the parameters of this *generative* model, we perform classification by comparing the posterior class probabilities:

$$P(C_1|\boldsymbol{x}) > P(C_2|\boldsymbol{x})? \qquad [7.32]$$

or by defining a decision function f as a posterior ratio:

$$f = \frac{p(\boldsymbol{x}|C_1)P(C_1)}{p(\boldsymbol{x}|C_2)P(C_2)} \qquad [7.33]$$

If $f(\boldsymbol{x}) > 1$, then we classify $\boldsymbol{x}$ as belonging to class C_1, and C_2 otherwise.

The quantities $P(C_i|\boldsymbol{x})$ are computed using the Bayes rule (equation [7.7]) as:

$$P(C_i|\boldsymbol{x}) = \frac{p(\boldsymbol{x}|C_i)P(C_i)}{p(\boldsymbol{x})} \qquad [7.34]$$

As a concrete example, let us consider a model in which the inputs associated with each class are modeled with a Gaussian distribution:

$$p(\boldsymbol{x}|C_i) = G(\boldsymbol{x}; \boldsymbol{\mu}_i, \Sigma_i) \qquad [7.35]$$

Also, let us assume that the prior class probabilities are equal:

$$P(C_i) = \frac{1}{2} \qquad [7.36]$$

The values of $\boldsymbol{\mu}_i$ and Σ_i can be estimated by maximum likelihood, as explained in section 7.2.3, on the individual classes in the training data.

With such a model, we can demonstrate that the log of the posterior ratio equation [7.33] is given by:

$$f(\boldsymbol{x}) = -\frac{1}{2}(\boldsymbol{x} - \boldsymbol{\mu}_1)^T \Sigma_1^{-1}(\boldsymbol{x} - \boldsymbol{\mu}_1) - \frac{1}{2}ln|\Sigma_1|$$
$$+ \frac{1}{2}(\boldsymbol{x} - \boldsymbol{\mu}_2)^T \Sigma_2^{-1}(\boldsymbol{x} - \boldsymbol{\mu}_2) + \frac{1}{2}ln|\Sigma_2| \qquad [7.37]$$

The sign of f determines the class of $\boldsymbol{x}$.

The issue of the above-described approach concerns the large number of parameters required to learn the likelihood model. In the case of Gaussian class conditional models, with D-dimensional input vectors, we need to estimate the class mean and class covariance matrix for each class. The mean will be a D-dimensional vector, and the covariance is a $D \times D$ matrix.

Naïve Bayes aims to simplify the estimation problem by assuming that the different input features $\boldsymbol{x} \in \mathbb{R}^D$ are conditionally independent:

$$p(\boldsymbol{x}|C) = \prod_{i=1}^{D} p(x_i|C). \qquad [7.38]$$

This assumption allows us to estimate D 1-dimensional densities rather than estimating one D-dimensional density. In the above Gaussian case, the Naïve Bayes model effectively replaces the general $D \times D$ covariance matrix by a diagonal matrix.

7.4.2. *Support vector machines*

Suppose we are given N training vectors $\{(\boldsymbol{x}_i, y_i)\}$, where $\boldsymbol{x} \in \mathbb{R}^D$, $y \in \{-1, 1\}$, and we want to learn a classifier

$$f(\boldsymbol{x}) = \boldsymbol{w}^T \phi(\boldsymbol{x}) + b \qquad [7.39]$$

so that the classifier's output for a new $\boldsymbol{x}$ is $sign(f(\mathbf{x}))$.

Suppose that our training data are linearly separable in the feature space $\phi(\mathbf{x})$, as illustrated in Figure 7.1, the two classes of training exemplars are a sufficiently well-separated hyperplane in the feature space.

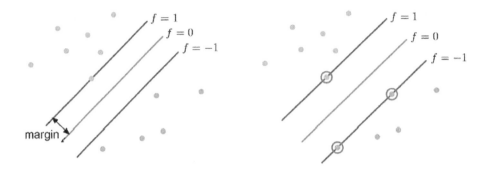

Figure 7.1. *Left: the margin for a decision boundary is the distance to the nearest data point. Right: in SVMs, we find the boundary with maximum margin. Figure adapted from [BIS 06]. For a color version of this figure, see www.iste.co.uk/laffly/torus1.zip*

The idea is to place the boundary such that it maximizes the **margin**, i.e. the distance from the hyperplane to the closest data point in either class. As such, we want to optimize the following objective function:

$$\max_{\boldsymbol{w},b} \min_i dist(\boldsymbol{x}_i, \boldsymbol{w}, b) \qquad [7.40]$$

$$\text{such that, for all } i,\, y_i(\boldsymbol{w}^T \phi(\boldsymbol{x}_i) + b) \geq 0 \qquad [7.41]$$

where $dist(\boldsymbol{x}, \boldsymbol{w}, b)$ is the Euclidean distance from the feature point $\phi(\boldsymbol{x})$ to the hyperplane defined by $\boldsymbol{w}$ and b. This objective function allows us to maximize the distance from the decision boundary $\boldsymbol{w}^T \phi(\boldsymbol{x}) + b = 0$ to the nearest point $\boldsymbol{x}_i$ and the constraint forces us to find a decision boundary that classifies all training data correctly.

The distance from a point $\phi(\boldsymbol{x}_i)$ to a hyperplane $\boldsymbol{w}^T \phi(\boldsymbol{x}) + b = 0$ is given by $\frac{|\boldsymbol{w}^T \phi(\boldsymbol{x}_i)+b|}{||\boldsymbol{w}||}$. Substituting this expression for $dist(\boldsymbol{x}, \boldsymbol{w}, b)$ into the above objective function, we get:

$$\max_{\boldsymbol{w},b} \min_i \frac{y_i(\boldsymbol{w}^T \phi(\boldsymbol{x}_i) + b)}{||\boldsymbol{w}||} \qquad [7.42]$$

$$\text{such that, for all } i,\, y_i(\boldsymbol{w}^T \phi(\boldsymbol{x}_i) + b) \geq 0 \qquad [7.43]$$

Because of the normalization by $||\boldsymbol{w}||$ in equation [7.42], the scale of $\boldsymbol{w}$ is arbitrary; thus, we can rewrite the objective function and the constraint as:

$$\max_{\boldsymbol{w},b} \frac{1}{||\boldsymbol{w}||} \qquad [7.44]$$

such that, for all i, $y_i(\boldsymbol{w}^T \phi(\boldsymbol{x}_i) + b) \geq 0$ [7.45]

Finally, considering that maximizing $1/||\boldsymbol{w}||$ is the same as minimizing $||\boldsymbol{w}||^2/2$, we get:

$$\min_{w,b} \frac{1}{2}||\boldsymbol{w}||^2$$ [7.46]

such that, for all i, $y_i(\boldsymbol{w}^T \phi(\boldsymbol{x}_i) + b) \geq 0$ [7.47]

7.5. Evaluation metrics for classification evaluation

When dealing with a classification problem, one should define an evaluation metric used at two different stages. During training, the evaluation metric can be used to optimize the parameters of the classifier. During the testing stage, the evaluation metric is used to measure the effectiveness of the produced classifier results when tested in unseen data. In this section, we give an overview of the mostly used evaluation measures.

7.5.1. Confusion matrix-based measures

For binary classification problems, the evaluation of the best (optimal) solution during training can be defined based on a confusion matrix, as shown in Table 7.1. The rows of the table represent the predicted class, while the columns represent the actual class. In the table, tp and tn denote the number of positive and negative instances that are correctly classified respectively. Meanwhile, fp and fn denote the number of misclassified negative and positive instances respectively.

From Table 7.1, several commonly used metrics have been defined to evaluate the performance of classifiers as listed in Table 7.2. For multi-class problems, the last four metrics are often used.

	Actual positive class	Actual negative class
Predicted positive class	True positive (tp)	False negative (fn)
Predicted negative class	False positive (fp)	True negative (tn)

Table 7.1. *Confusion matrix for binary classification*

The *accuracy* is the most used evaluation metric for binary or multi-class classification problems. The complement metric of accuracy is *error rate*, which evaluates the produced solution by its percentage of incorrect predictions.

Metrics	Formula	Evaluation focus
Accuracy (acc)	$\frac{tp+tn}{tp+fp+tn+fn}$	In general, the accuracy metric measures the ratio of correct predictions to the total number of instances evaluated.
Error Rate (err)	$\frac{fp+fn}{tp+fp+tn+fn}$	Misclassification error measures the ratio of incorrect predictions to the total number of instances evaluated.
Sensitivity (sn)	$\frac{tp}{tp+fn}$	This metric is used to measure the fraction of positive patterns that are correctly classified.
Specificity (sp)	$\frac{tn}{tn+fp}$	This metric is used to measure the fraction of negative patterns that are correctly classified.
Precision (p)	$\frac{tp}{tp+fp}$	Precision is used to measure the positive patterns that are correctly predicted from the total predicted patterns in a positive class.
Recall (r)	$\frac{tp}{tp+tn}$	Recall is used to measure the fraction of positive patterns that are correctly classified.
F-Measure (FM)	$\frac{2*p*r}{p+r}$	This metric represents the harmonic mean between recall and precision values.
Geometric-mean (GM)	$\sqrt{tp*tn}$	This metric is used to maximize the tp rate and the tn rate, and simultaneously keeping both rates relatively balanced.
Averaged Accuracy	$\frac{\sum_{i=1}^{l}\frac{tp_i+tn_i}{tp_i+fn_i+fp_i+}}{l}$	The average effectiveness of all classes.
Averaged Error rate	$\frac{\sum_{i=1}^{l}\frac{fp_i+fn_i}{tp_i+fn_i+fp_i+}}{l}$	The average error rate of all classes.
Averaged Precision	$\frac{\sum_{i=1}^{l}\frac{tp_i}{tp_i+fp_i}}{l}$	The average of per-class precision.
Averaged Recall	$\frac{\sum_{i=1}^{l}\frac{tp_i}{tp_i+fn_i}}{l}$	The average of per-class recall.
Averaged F-measure	$\frac{2*p_M*r_M}{p_M+r_M}$	The average of per-class F-measure.

Note: tp_i - true positive for C_i; fp_i - false positive for C_i; fn_i - false negative for C_i; tn_i s- true negative for C_i; and M macro-averaging.

Table 7.2. *Metrics for classification evaluations (adapted from [HOS 15])*

7.5.2. *Area under the ROC curve (AUC)*

The AUC value reflects the overall ranking performance of a classifier. For a two-class problem, the AUC value can be calculated as:

$$AUC = \frac{S_p - n_p(n_n + 1)/2}{n_p n_n} \qquad [7.48]$$

where S_p is the sum of all positive examples ranked, while n_p and n_n denote the number of positive and negative examples respectively.

Although the performance of AUC is excellent for evaluation and discrimination processes, its computational cost is high, especially for discriminating a volume of generated solutions of multi-class problems. To compute the AUC for multi-class problems of C classes, the time complexity is $O(|C|nlogn)$.

7.6. Cross-validation and over-fitting

Cross-validation [BOU 03] is a statistical method of evaluating and comparing learning algorithms by dividing data into two sets: one used to train a model and the other used to validate the model. In typical cross-validation, the training and validation sets must cross over in successive rounds such that each data point has a chance of being validated against. It works as follows: in each iteration, one or more learning algorithms use $k - 1$ folds of data to learn a model, and subsequently, the learned model is used on the validation set for prediction. The performance of the model on each fold is evaluated using one of the metrics of section 7.5. When completed, k samples of the performance metric will be available. Averaging is then used to obtain an aggregate measure from these samples.

The basic form of cross-validation is k-fold cross-validation. Other forms of cross-validation are special cases of k-fold cross-validation or involve repeated rounds of k-fold cross-validation. In k-fold cross-validation, the data are first partitioned into k equally sized samples or folds. Subsequently, k iterations of training and validation are performed such that within each iteration, a different fold of the data is held out for validation while the remaining $k - 1$ folds are used for learning. In machine learning, 10-fold cross-validation ($k = 10$) is the most common.

To obtain reliable performance estimation, a large number of estimates are always preferred. A commonly used method to increase the number of estimates is to run k-fold cross-validation multiple times. The data are reshuffled and re-stratified before each round.

The leave-one-out cross-validation (LOOCV) is a special case of k-fold cross-validation, where k equals the number of instances in the data. In other words, in each iteration, nearly all the data except for a single observation are used for training and the model is evaluated on that single observation.

When evaluating a classifier, one has to find a way to simultaneously balance (over)fitting and generalization by adjusting the inferred systems (i.e. the positive and negative systems) obtained from the classification algorithm. The balance of the two systems will target at minimizing the total misclassification costs of the final system. Let us denote C_{FP}, C_{FN} and C_{UC} as penalty costs for the false-positive, false-negative and unclassifiable cases respectively. Let $RATE_FP$, $RATE_FN$ and $RATE_UC$ be the false-positive, false-negative and unclassifiable rates respectively. Then, the problem is to achieve a balance between (over)fitting and generalization that would minimize the total misclassification cost (TC). The problem is defined in the following expression:

$$TC = \min(C_{FP}.RATE_FP + C_{FN}.RATE_FN + C_{UC}.RATE_UC) \quad [7.49]$$

This methodology creates classification systems that would be optimal in the sense that their total misclassification cost would be minimized.

7.7. References

[BER 03] BERTSEKAS D., TSITSIKLIS J., *Introduction to Probability*, Athena Scientific, 2003.

[BIS 06] BISHOP C., *Pattern Recognition and Machine Learning*, Springer, 2006.

[BOU 03] BOUCKAERT R.R., "Choosing between two learning algorithms based on calibrated tests", *Proceedings of the 20th International Conference on Machine Learning*, pp. 51–58, 2003.

[HOS 15] HOSSIN M., SULAIMAN M.N., "A review on evaluation metrics for data classification evaluations", *International Journal of Data Mining and Knowledge Management Process*, vol. 5, pp. 01–11, 2015.

[JEB 06] JEBARA T., MEILA M., "Machine learning: Discriminative and generative", *The Mathematical Intelligencer*, vol. 28, no. 1, pp. 67–69, Springer, 2006.

## 8

Multivariate Data Analysis

Multivariate analysis is a set of methods used for analyzing a dataset that contains more than one variable. They are used to extract hidden information from a database table in order to make intelligent decisions.

In this chapter, we introduce descriptive methods. The aim is to study the link between variables, proximity between data points or find patterns in the dataset.

8.1. Introduction

With the growth of computational power, multivariate methodology plays an important role in data analysis, especially to study the link between variables or to discover patterns in the data. Among the multitude of data, obtaining a clear summary of the dataset to understand what is going on and making clever decisions are a challenge. Multivariate data analysis is a powerful tool to process information in a meaningful fashion.

There are many ways to perform multivariate analysis. Which one you choose depends on your goal of course, but it also depends on the type of variables involved in the study:

– quantitative variables are numerical and represent a measurable quantity (continuous or discrete). They are resumed with location parameters (mean, median, quantiles) and dispersion parameters (variance, median absolute deviation, etc.) (Figure 8.1 left);

– categorical variables (also called factors) take on values that are names or labels (Figure 8.1 right).

Chapter written by Astrid JOURDAN and Dominique LAFFLY.

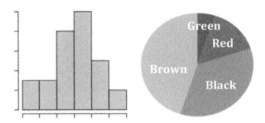

Figure 8.1. *Different types of graphs for quantitative and qualitative variables. For a color version of this figure, see www.iste.co.uk/laffly/torus1.zip*

They are resumed in a contingency table that displays the frequency of each label.

In this chapter, we describe three descriptive methods. The principal component analysis (PCA) and correspondence analysis (CA) allow us to represent a dataset on meaningful two-dimensional graphics. The PCA method is for quantitative variables, and the CA method is for categorical variables. The third method is a way to discover patterns in the dataset, called clustering. All these methods require a dataset.

A dataset is a matrix with p columns for the variables and n rows for the data points (individuals) of the observed statistical unit

$$X = \begin{pmatrix} x_{11} & x_{1j} & x_{1p} \\ x_{21} & x_{2j} & x_{2p} \\ & \vdots & \\ x_{i1} & \cdots & x_{ij} & \cdots & x_{ip} \\ & \vdots & \\ x_{n1} & x_{nj} & x_{np} \end{pmatrix}$$

The variables are denoted by X_j, j = 1, ..., p and the data points by x_i, I = 1..., n.

REMARK.– The task of obtaining a dataset is very long and boring (data extraction, data cleaning, missing data, etc.). We used to say that this step takes up 80% of the task's time, but it is necessary.

8.2. Principal component analysis

We suppose that all the variables X_1, ..., X_p are quantitative. Each row of the dataset can be considered as a point $x_i = (x_{i1}, ..., x_{ip}) \in IR^p$, described in a p-coordinate system defined by the variables.

To illustrate this chapter, we consider the dataset in Table 8.1. The statistical unit is a country described by nine quantitative variables (population, density, Net.migration, etc.) and a categorical variable, the region (ASIA, NORTHERN AFRICA, etc.). The dataset represents the 100 most populated countries in the world.

	Population	Density	Net.migration	...	Region
Afghanistan	31056997	48	23.06		ASIA (EX. NEAR EAST)
Algeria	32930091	13.8	-0.39		NORTHERN AFRICA
Angola	12127071	9.7	0		SUB-SAHARAN AFRICA
Argentina	39921833	14.4	0.61		LATIN AMER. & CARIB.
Australia	20264082	2.6	3.98		OCEANIA
Austria	8192880	97.7	2		WESTERN EUROPE
...					
mean	63086863	181.43	0.06		
standard dev.	172025557	640.83	3.15		

Table 8.1. *The 100 most populated countries in the world (https://www.kaggle.com/)*

Figure 8.2. *Source: J.P. Fenelon*

Since the countries are points in a 9-coordinate system, it is impossible to obtain a good picture of the dataset. The main idea of PCA is to project the points onto a 2D or 3D graphic with a minimum loss of information. The initial p-coordinate system $(X_1,...,X_p)$ is transformed into an orthogonal p-coordinate system $(U_1,...,U_p)$, such that the first components contain a maximum of the dataset information.

8.2.1. *How to measure the information*

The information of a dataset is the inertia of the points:

$$ I = \frac{1}{n}\sum_{i=1}^{n} \| x_i - g \|^2 , $$

where $g = (\bar{x}_1,...,\bar{x}_p)$ is the barycenter and $\|\cdot\|$ is the usual L_2-norm in IR ^{p}.

If we denote $\bar{x}_j$ and s_j the mean and the standard deviation of X_j, $j = 1, ..., p$, and V the variance–covariance matrix of the variables, we note that $I = tr(V)$ [1]. With the example in Table 8.1, the barycenter is g = (63086863,181.43, 0.06, ...) and the inertia is I = $172025557^2 + 640.83^2 + 3.15^2 + ... = 2.96 \cdot 10^{16}$.

Notation

Let us denote x = $(x_1, ..., x_n)$ and y = $(y_1, ..., y_n)$ two vectors in IR ^{n}. We have:

$$ \bar{x} = \frac{1}{n}\sum_{i=1}^{n} x_i \text{ (mean)}, \qquad s_x^2 = \frac{1}{n}\sum_{i=1}^{n}(x_i - \bar{x})^2 \text{ (variance)}, $$

$$ c_{xy} = \frac{1}{n}\sum_{i=1}^{n}(x_i - \bar{x})(y_i - \bar{y}) \text{ (covariance)}, \qquad r_{xy} = \frac{c_{xy}}{s_x s_y} \text{ (coefficient of correlation)} $$

$$ d^2(x,y) = \sum_{i=1}^{n}(x_i - y_i)^2 \text{ (distance between x and y)}, \qquad \|x\|^2 = \sum_{i=1}^{n} x_i^2 \text{ (norm}^2 \text{ of x)} $$

Since the variables do not have the same scale, some of them can be negligible in the computation of the inertia. In the following example, we can see that the

---

1 $I = \frac{1}{n}\sum_{i=1}^{n}\|x_i - g\|^2 = \frac{1}{n}\sum_{i=1}^{n}\sum_{j=1}^{p}(x_{ij} - g_j)^2 = \sum_{j=1}^{p}\frac{1}{n}\sum_{i=1}^{n}(x_{ij} - g_j)^2 = \sum_{j=1}^{p} s_j^2.$

variables density and net migration have no impact on the distance between Afghanistan and Algeria.

$$d^2(\text{Afghanistan, Algeria}) = (31056997 - 32930091)^2$$
$$+(48 - 13,8)^2 + (23,06 - (-0,39))^2 + \ldots$$

$$\cong (31056997 - 32930091)^2.$$

To avoid this problem, the variables are scaled with mean and variance values equal to 0 and 1 respectively

$$x_{ij} \leftarrow \frac{x_{ij} - \overline{x}_j}{s_j}, \; i \in \{1, \ldots, n\}, \; j \in \{1, \ldots, p\}.$$

	Population	Density	Net.migration	...	Region
Afghanistan	-0,19	-0,21	7,34		ASIA (EX. NEAR EAST)
Algeria	-0,18	-0,26	-0,14		NORTHERN AFRICA
Angola	-0,30	-0,27	-0,02		SUB-SAHARAN AFRICA
Argentina	-0,14	-0,26	0,18		LATIN AMER. & CARIB.
Australia	-0,25	-0,28	1,25		OCEANIA
Austria	-0,32	-0,13	0,62		WESTERN EUROPE
...					
mean	0	0	0		
standard dev.	1	1	1		

Table 8.2. *The scaled dataset*

With scaled variables, the barycenter is the center of the coordinate system, $g = (0,0,0,\ldots)$ and the inertia is d, the number of variables, $I = \text{trace}(V) = 1^2 + 1^2 + 1^2 + \ldots = p$.

With the scaled dataset (Table 8.2), we have the variance–covariance matrix given in Table 8.3.

	Population	Density	Net.migration	Infant.mortality	GDP	Literacy	Phones	Birthrate	Deathrate
Population	1	0.00	0.00	-0.06	-0.01	0.01	0.05	-0.12	-0.12
Density	0.00	1	0.15	-0.15	0.25	0.08	0.21	-0.17	-0.12
Net.migration	0.00	0.15	1	0.09	0.32	-0.08	0.27	-0.02	0.25
Infant.mortality	-0.06	-0.15	0.09	1	-0.64	-0.76	-0.69	0.86	0.68
GDP	-0.01	0.25	0.32	-0.64	1	0.56	0.94	-0.68	-0.22
Literacy	0.01	0.07	-0.08	-0.76	0.56	1	0.62	-0.81	-0.40
Phones	0.05	0.21	0.27	-0.69	0.94	0.62	1	-0.74	-0.25
Birthrate	-0.12	-0.17	-0.02	0.86	-0.68	-0.81	-0.74	1	0.49
Deathrate	-0.12	-0.12	0.25	0.68	-0.22	-0.40	-0.25	0.49	1

Table 8.3. *Variance–covariance matrix V of the scaled dataset*

8.2.2. *Scalar product and orthogonal variables*

In order to obtain an orthogonal coordinate system, we need a scalar product between variables. Since the variables can be viewed as vectors in IR ^{n}, we use the usual scalar product

$$< X_j, X_k > = \frac{1}{n} \sum_{i=1}^{n} x_{ij} x_{ik} \text{ ,}$$

The associated norm is

$$\| X_j \|^2 = \frac{1}{n} \sum_{i=1}^{n} x_{ij}^2 \text{ .}$$

We note that for scaled variables,

$$\| X_j \|^2 = \text{var}(X_j) = 1 \quad \text{and} \quad < X_j, X_k > = \text{cov}(X_j, X_k) = corr(X_j, X_k),$$

then

$$\cos(X_j, \hat{X}_k) = \frac{< X_j, X_k >}{\| X_j \| \| X_k \|} = corr(X_j, X_k) \cdot$$

Two variables are orthogonal if they are uncorrelated. Since their norm is 1, they can be represented in the unit n-ball, and the cosine of the angle between two variables is their correlation.

8.2.3. *Construction of the principal axes*

The problem is building a new coordinate system $(U_1,...,U_p)$, where U_j is a linear combination of $(X_1,...,X_p)$ and

– the first principal axis (U_1) catches a maximum variance (inertia);

– the second principal axis (U_2) catches the maximum of the remaining variance and is orthogonal to the first axis;

– each succeeding component is built in the same way until the last axis (U_p).

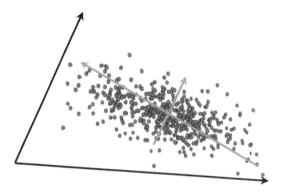

Figure 8.3. *Illustration of the principal axes. For a color version of this figure, see www.iste.co.uk/laffly/torus1.zip*

We can demonstrate that the solutions of this problem are the eigenvectors associated with the eigenvalues λ_1, ..., λ_p of the covariance matrix V such that $\lambda_1 > \lambda_p$. Moreover, we have:

– inertia of the data projected on U_j is λ_j;

– inertia of the data projected on Vect$\{U_1,...,U_j\}$ is $\lambda_1+ ... +\lambda_j$;

– total inertia is $I = \lambda_1 + ... + \lambda_p$.

Hence, the percentage of variance explained by the jth axis is λ_j/I. With the scaled dataset, we have the eigenvalues given in Table 8.4. We note that the sum of the eigenvalues equals 9.

	Eigenvalue	Percentage of variance	Cumulative percentage of variance
λ_1	4.24	47.08	47.08
λ_2	1.52	16.92	64.00
λ_3	1.01	11.27	75.27
λ_4	0.94	10.42	85.70
λ_5	0.57	6.32	92.01
λ_6	0.40	4.48	96.50
λ_7	0.17	1.89	98.38
λ_8	0.09	1.07	99.41
λ_9	0.05	0.59	100.00
Tot	9.00	100.00	

Table 8.4. *Eigenvalues of matrix V in Table 8.3*

We keep in the study only k << p axes and k is selected such that:

– the cumulative variance explained by the k axes is greater than 70–80%;

– adding the (k + 1)th axis does not significantly increase the cumulative variance ("elbow rule").

In Figure 8.4 and Table 8.4, we can see that the first axis explained 47% of the information, the second axis 17%, and so on. With the first two axes, we lose 36% of the information. With the third axis, we reduce the loss to 25%. However, if we include the third axis, we also need to keep the fourth axis since it explains nearly the same percentage of variance as the third axis.

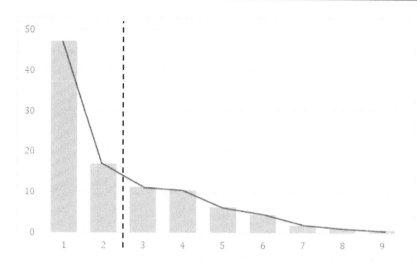

Figure 8.4. *Percentage of variance explained by the principal axes.
For a color version of this figure, see www.iste.co.uk/laffly/torus1.zip*

The components of the principal axis are given by the eigenvectors in Table 8.5. The *principal components* are the components of the data points projected on the principal axis. They are given by

$$C_j = X\,U_j, j = 1,\dots,p$$

U_1	U_2	U_3	U_4	U_5	U_6	U_7	U_8	U_9
−0.041	0.14	0.9063	−0.351	0.161	0.018	−0.0606	0.065	−0.0289
−0.123	−0.25	0.3172	0.859	0.269	−0.091	−0.0114	0.026	0.0285
−0.041	−0.68	0.1516	−0.137	−0.549	−0.436	0.0078	0.051	0.0164
0.446	−0.20	0.0400	−0.032	0.138	0.029	−0.3996	−0.759	−0.0336
−0.406	−0.33	−0.0523	−0.078	0.039	0.483	−0.2214	0.021	−0.6580
−0.402	0.14	−0.1699	−0.116	0.293	−0.573	−0.5977	0.068	0.0052
−0.425	−0.28	−0.0301	−0.142	0.100	0.389	−0.0751	−0.131	0.7330
0.450	−0.08	0.0019	0.075	−0.118	0.270	−0.5868	0.573	0.1606
0.270	−0.45	−0.1445	−0.271	0.685	−0.117	0.2832	0.255	−0.0291

Table 8.5. *Eigenvectors of matrix V in Table 8.3*

With the example, if we keep only two principal axes, we can plot the dataset points on a 2D graphic (C_2 vs. C_1) with a minimum loss of information (Figure 8.5).

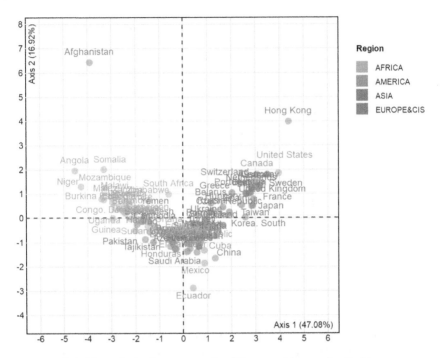

Figure 8.5. *The principal components of the countries on the first two axes.*
For a color version of this figure, see www.iste.co.uk/laffly/torus1.zip

The problem now is to interpret the axes. We can see that the first component of the United States is very high and the second component of Afghanistan is low – but what does that mean?

8.2.4. *Analysis of the principal axes*

The principal axes are linear combinations of the variables. In order to understand the previous graphic, we need to know which variables contribute to the construction of U_1 (axis 1) and U_2 (axis 2) and which variables are correlated with U_1 and U_2.

The variables are represented in the unit ball which can be projected on U_1 and U_2 to obtain the second graphic (Figure 8.6). The correlation between X_j and U_k is the cosine of the angle between them. Here, we can see that U_1 is strongly correlated with Infant.mortality, GDP, Literacy, Phones, Birthrate and to a less extent with Deathrate. These results are also available in the correlation table (Table 8.6). This means that on the right side of Figure 8.4, we found countries with high Birthrate,

Deathrate and Infant.mortality rates. On the left side, we have countries with a high level for Literacy, GDP and Phones.

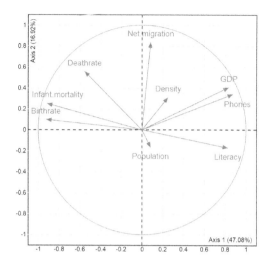

Figure 8.6. *Variable map on U_1 and U_2*

	U_1	U_2	U_3	U_4	...
Population	0.08	−0.2	0.913	0.34	
Density	0.25	0.3	0.319	−0.83	
Net.migration	0.09	0.8	0.153	0.13	
Infant.mortality	−0.92	0.3	0.040	0.03	
GDP	0.84	0.4	−0.053	0.08	
Literacy	0.83	−0.2	−0.171	0.11	
Phones	0.88	0.3	−0.030	0.14	
Birthrate	−0.93	0.1	0.002	−0.07	
Deathrate	−0.55	0.6	−0.146	0.26	

Table 8.6. *Correlation between $X_1, ..., X_9$ and $U_1, ..., U_9$*

We note that the projections of the variables are no longer unit vectors (arrows smaller than the unit circle), especially Population and Density. This is due to the angle of projection (Figure 8.7). If a variable is orthogonal to the subspace vect$\{U_1, U_2\}$, we lose all the information given by this variable. Only the well-projected variables (near the circle) are taken into account for the interpretation of the new axes.

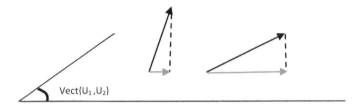

Figure 8.7. *Vector projections of the subspace generated by U_1 and U_2. For a color version of this figure, see www.iste.co.uk/laffly/torus1.zip*

8.2.5. *Analysis of the data points*

Before analyzing a data point, we must find on which axes it is well-projected. For that, the square cosine of the projection angle must be close to 1 (Figure 8.7).

The United States has a good projection on U_1 (Table 8.7), and then we can say that this country has a high level for Literacy, GDP and (or) Phones. Afghanistan is well-represented on U_2, and so we can conclude that this country has a high Net.migration rate. Contrarity, South Africa is not well-projected on U_1, nor on U_2, so we can say nothing about this country. If a data point is close to the origin in the data point map, we cannot know if this is because it is close to the barycenter in IR ^{P}, or if it is because it is orthogonal to the subspace generated by U_1 and U_2. In this case, the information regarding this point is lost with the projection.

	Cos²						Contribution (%)					
	U_1	U_2	U_3	U_4	U_5	...	U_1	U_2	U_3	U_4	U_5	...
Afghanistan	0.20	**0.55**	0.02	0.02	0.13		3.61	**27.30**	1.18	1.64	17.60	
Angola	**0.71**	0.13	0.00	0.01	0.09		4.86	2.51	0.08	0.31	4.48	
Ecuador	0.02	**0.82**	0.04	0.04	0.04		0.04	5.56	0.43	0.45	0.68	
South Africa	0.05	0.14	0.05	0.11	**0.50**		0.08	0.62	0.34	0.79	6.05	
United States	**0.60**	0.13	0.03	0.09	0.00		3.77	2.26	0.89	2.62	0.00	
...						...						...

Table 8.7. *Square cosine of the angle of projection and the contribution (%) of the countries to the construction of the principal axes*

Outliers

Since PCA is based on variance decomposition, the result is sensitive to outliers.

The mean contribution of a data point to the axis construction is 1/n. If the contribution is much higher, the point may be an outlier. This means that the result depends strongly on this point. If we remove it from the dataset, and if we compute the PCA again, the result will be completely different.

In this case, we can add this point as a supplementary data point. This means that it does not contribute to the computation of the principal axes but it is projected on the data point graphic.

In our example, the mean contribution is 1% (100 countries). In Table 8.7, we note that the contribution of Afghanistan to the construction of U_2 is much higher (27.30%). However, Afghanistan is not an outlier since, when we remove it from the dataset, the result does not change. In fact, it has a high contribution but for an axis which explains 26.92% of the variance only. Figure 8.8 gives the graphical result of PCA on the first two axes for a dataset with a new country. We note that the interpretation of axes U_1 and U_2 is completely different only because of this new point. The new country is an outlier and must be removed from the study.

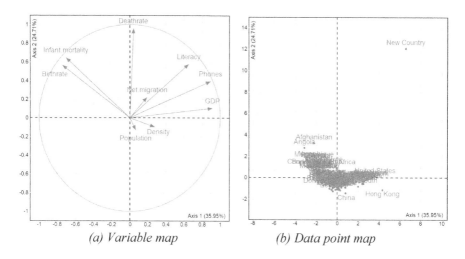

(a) Variable map   (b) Data point map

Figure 8.8. Result of PCA with a new country

	Population	Density	Net. migration	Infant. mortality	GDP	Literacy	Phones	Birthrate	Deathrate
New country	63086863	181.428	0.0559	130	40000	500	2000	50	70

Table 8.8. Component of the new country

8.3. Multiple correspondence analysis

The previous method is defined for quantitative variables. In the case of categorical variables (also called factors), the notion of distance is meaningless, even if the levels are coded with integers. The multiple correspondence analysis (MCA) deals with categorical variables. The aim is similar: provide a meaningful picture of the dataset.

This chapter is illustrated with the previous dataset. The quantitative variables are transformed into categorical variables with 5 equidistributed levels (L1 for the smallest values and L5 for the highest values). The countries are grouped into four regions: Africa, Europe&CIS, Asia (Asia, Oceania, Near East) and America (South, Central and North America) (Table 8.9).

The objectives of MCA are to:

– Study the proximity of two data points. Can we say that France is *closer* to the US than it is to Somalia?

– Study the proximity of two levels. Is it possible to establish a link between GDP and the region?

– Determine which levels characterize a data point. Is the US defined by its GDP or by its infant mortality?

We are dealing with factors that lead to the following questions: How do we compute the distance between rows? How do we quantify the information? How do we measure the link between variables?

The main problem is that distance, average, variance and correlation are meaningless with factors.

Country	Inf.mortality	GDP	Region
France	L1	L5	EUROPE&CIS
Belgium	L1	L5	EUROPE&CIS
Samolia	L5	L1	AFRICA
US	L1	L5	AMERICA
...			

Table 8.9. *Extract of the dataset*

8.3.1. *Indicator matrix*

In order to compute distance between rows, we have to transform the dataset into a table with numeric entries. We use a binary coding for each factor. The ith component of this vector is 1 if the ith data point takes the level, and 0 otherwise.

	Inf.mortality $m_1 = 5$			GDP $m_2 = 5$			Region $m_3 = 4$					
	L1	...	L5	L1	...	L5	EUROPE&CIS	AFRICA	...		...	sum
France	1	0	0	0	0	1	1	0	0			p
Belgium	1	0	0	0	0	1	1	0	0			
Samolia	0	0	1	1	0	0	0	1	0			p
US	1	0	0	0	0	1	1	0	1			p
...												
sum	n_{11}	...	n_{15}	n_{21}	...	n_{25}	n_{31}	n_{32}	...			np
	$n_{11} + ... + n_{15} = n$			$n_{21} + ... + n_{25} = n$			$n_{31} + ... + n_{34} = n$					

Table 8.10. *Indicator table*

Let m_j denote the number of levels of factor X_j, and $m = m_1 + ... + m_p$. The indicator table is an $n \cdot m$ matrix, $K = (k_{ij})_{i \in \{1,...,n\}, j \in \{1,...,m\}}$, where the sum of the m columns is p (the number of factors) and the rank is m-p-1 (since we have only one level per factor per variable).

In our example, the nine transformed variables have 5 levels each and the REGION has 4 levels. The size of the indicator matrix is $100 \cdot 49$ and its rank is $49 - 10 - 1 = 38$.

For each factor, the sum of the level occurrences is n. Then, the sum of the entries of K is np. We define the frequency table as:

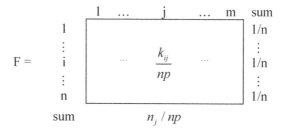

where $f_{ij} = \dfrac{k_{ij}}{np}$ if data point i takes level j and 0 if not.

MCA processes as PCA but with two clouds of points, one for the data points (rows) and one for the levels (columns).

– The weight of each row (data point) is $\dfrac{1}{np}$. We note $r = \left(\cdots, \dfrac{1}{n}, \cdots\right)' \in \text{IR}^{\,n}$ the weight vector of data points.

– The weight of each column (level) is $\dfrac{n_j}{np}$. The weight increases when the level is frequent. We note $c = \left(\cdots, \dfrac{n_j}{np}, \cdots\right)' \in \text{IR}^{\,m}$ the weight vector of levels.

8.3.2. *Cloud of data points*

The cloud of data points is defined by the matrix of row profiles, which is the level frequencies per data point:

$$
R = \quad
\begin{array}{c|ccccc|c}
 & 1 & \cdots & j & \cdots & m & \text{sum} \\
\hline
1 & & & & & & 1 \\
\vdots & & & & & & \vdots \\
i & \cdots & & \dfrac{k_{ij}}{p} & & \cdots & 1 \\
\vdots & & & & & & \vdots \\
n & & & & & & 1 \\
\end{array}
$$

The distance between two data points i and i' is the χ^2 distance between the corresponding two row profiles

$$
d^2(i, i') = \sum_{j=1}^{m} \frac{np}{n_j}\left(\frac{k_{ij}}{p} - \frac{k_{i'j}}{p}\right)^2 = \frac{n}{p}\sum_{j=1}^{m}\frac{1}{n_j}(k_{ij} - k_{i'j})^2 .
$$

This distance is defined such that:

– if two data points share the same level j, $k_{ij} - k_{i'j} = 0$, and if they share all the levels, the distance is 0;

– if two data points have in common a rare level (small n_j), they are closed even if they take different levels for the other factors.

The barycenter of this cloud is c, and the distance between data point I and the barycenter is

$$d^2(i,c) = \frac{n}{p} \sum_{j=1}^{m} \frac{k_{ij}}{n_j} - 1.$$

We can demonstrate that the inertia of the cloud of data points is

$$I = \frac{1}{n} \sum_{i=1}^{n} d^2(i,c) = \frac{m}{p} - 1.$$

In order to illustrate the data point proximity, we use the small data extract given in Table 8.11. The US is "closer" to France than to Somalia since the US shares two levels with France (Inf.mortality and GDP) but none with Somalia.

A first result of MCA is a graphical representation of this proximity. It is obtained by applying the PCA method to the dataset defined by the row profiles. Figure 8.9 gives the projection on the two first components.

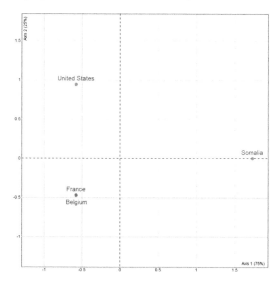

Figure 8.9. *Projection of the data point cloud on axis 1 and axis 2. If two data points are well-projected (cos²~1) and if they are close on the map, we can say that they share many levels*

8.3.3. *Cloud of levels*

The cloud of levels is defined by the matrix of column profiles, which is the level frequencies per level,

$$
C = \quad
\begin{array}{c}
1 \\ \vdots \\ i \\ \vdots \\ n \\ \text{sum}
\end{array}
\begin{array}{ccccc}
1 & \cdots & j & \cdots & m \\
\hline
 & & & & \\
 & \cdots & \dfrac{k_{ij}}{n_j} & \cdots & \\
 & & & & \\
\hline
1 & \cdots & 1 & \cdots & 1
\end{array}
$$

The distance between two levels j and j' is the χ^2 distance between the corresponding two column profiles

$$
d^2(j,j') = \sum_{i=1}^{n} n\left(\frac{k_{ij}}{n_j} - \frac{k_{ij'}}{n_{j'}}\right)^2 .
$$

This distance is defined such that:

– two levels are closed which have many common data points which take these levels;

– rare levels are far from the other;

– two levels of the same factor are necessarily far from each other.

The barycenter of this cloud is r, and the distance between level j and the barycenter is

$$
d^2(j,r) = \frac{n}{n_j} - 1 .
$$

We can demonstrate that the inertia of the cloud of levels is

$$
I = \frac{1}{m}\sum_{j=1}^{m} d^2(j,r) = \frac{m}{p} - 1 .
$$

The two clouds have the same inertia.

It follows that a rare level is far from the barycenter and contributes a lot to the inertia. It is recommended not to use MCA with rare levels.

$\Rightarrow$ We put together rare levels of the same factor.

Moreover, the contribution of a factor increases with the number of its levels. It is better to have factors with a small number of levels.

$\Rightarrow$ We transform the factors in order to obtain factors with nearly the same number of levels.

A second result of MCA is a graphical representation of the level proximity. It is obtained by applying the PCA method to the dataset defined by the column profiles. Figure 8.10 gives the projection on the two first components. Level 1 of Inf. mortality and level 5 of GDP are closed since they are taken by three data points (France, US and Belgium). Levels 5 and 1 of GDP (or Inf.mortality) are at opposite sides of axis 1. And AMERICA, AFRICA and EUROPE&CIS are spread throughout the principal plane.

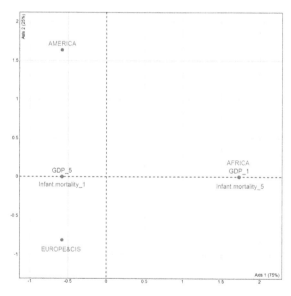

Figure 8.10. *Projection of the level cloud on axis 1 and axis 2. For a color version of this figure, see www.iste.co.uk/laffly/torus1.zip*

8.3.4. MCA or PCA?

The nature of the data determines the choice of method – PCA for quantitative variables and MCA for factors. But to show that both are from the same family of methods, we will compare the results of the PCA with those of the MCA on the quantitative variables divided into classes.

The analysis of the principal plane (Figure 8.11) shows the same organizational structures. For example, Birthrate and Inf.mortality significantly explain axis 1 for PCA and MCA. On axis 2, we observe the same thing with Net.migration, while Density is not structuring on this plane for both methods.

In this particular case of classes generated by a quantitative variable, it is interesting to observe that there is a gradation (or order structure) drawn by the levels of the variable with the MCA method. Figure 8.11 illustrates this case; the different Birthrate levels are linked by a curve that draws a gradation of the values on axis 1. Without this gradation, axis 1 reflects an opposition between the extreme values (classes) of the variable. The MCA offers the opportunity for a more detailed analysis.

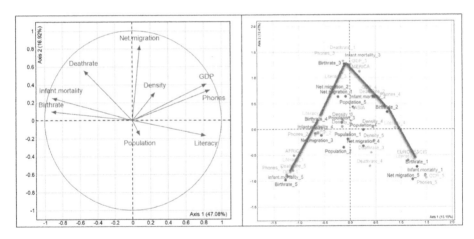

Figure 8.11. *Variable results on the X_1X_2 plane for PCA (left) and MCA (right). For a color version of this figure, see www.iste.co.uk/laffly/torus1.zip*

Another advantage of MCA is the possibility to simultaneously represent the two clouds in the same graphic. In this representation, a data point is in the middle of its levels and a level is in the middle of the data points which take this level. In Figure 8.12, we can see that the US is in the middle of its levels, for example.

MCA factor map

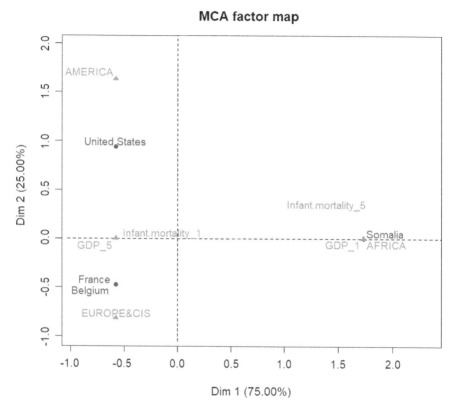

Figure 8.12. *Biplot with data points and levels obtained with the dataset presented in Table 8.9. For a color version of this figure, see www.iste.co.uk/laffly/torus1.zip*

Contrarily, using MCA instead of PCA with quantitative variables divided into classes may lead to a confused result. In addition, it considerably increases the dimension of the problem (since each level of each variable is transformed into an indicator variable) and the information (inertia) is scattered on many axes (see Figure 8.13).

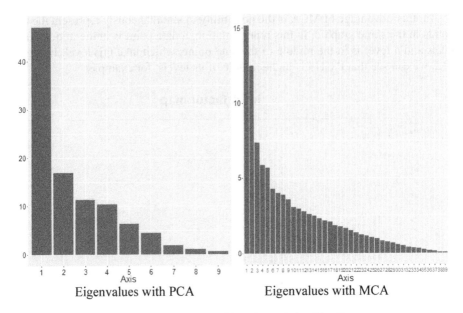

Figure 8.13. *Percentage of inertia explained by the axes*

8.4. Clustering

The aim of clustering is to distinguish homogeneous groups of data points (called clusters) within a large volume of data. The tasks of clustering are:

– grouping data points with similar characteristics within the same cluster;

– building the most dissimilar clusters as possible.

An exhaustive research of the best partition is impossible since the number of partitions of n objects is

$$\frac{1}{e}\sum_{k\geq 1}\frac{k^n}{k!}.$$

For example, the number of partitions in a dataset of 30 data points is 10^{23}. An algorithm is necessary to build, not the best, but nearly the best partition. Sections 8.4.4 and 8.4.5 present two commonly used algorithms. The first one, called k-means, puts similar data points in the same cluster. This algorithm requires a distance between data points. The second one, called agglomerative hierarchical clustering (AHC), merges similar clusters together and requires a dissimilarity criterion between clusters.

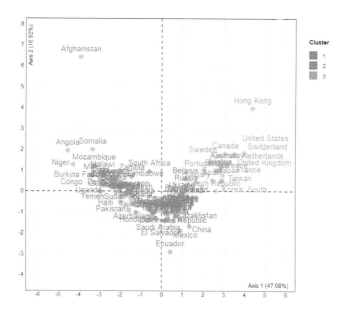

Figure 8.14. *Three clusters for the countries. For a color version of this figure, see www.iste.co.uk/laffly/torus1.zip*

8.4.1. *Distance between data points*

The choice of an appropriate distance will influence the shape of the clusters, as some elements may be close to one another according to one distance and farther away according to another.

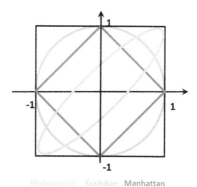

Figure 8.15. *Illustration of the three distances. For a color version of this figure, see www.iste.co.uk/laffly/torus1.zip*

The Euclidian distance leads to spherical clouds of data points:

$$d_2(x_i,x_j) = \left(\sum_{k=1}^{p} (x_{ik} - x_{jk})^2 \right)^{1/2}$$

The Manhattan distance is less impacted by outliers:

$$d_1(x_i,x_j) = \sum_{k=1}^{p} \left| x_{ik} - x_{jk} \right|$$

The Mahalanobis distance takes into account clouds of points with an ovoid shape:

$$d(x_i,x_j) = \left((x_i - x_j)^T \Sigma^{-1} (x_i - x_j) \right)^{1/2}$$

where Σ is the variance–covariance matrix.

REMARK.– A data point is a point that varies within a d-dimensional hypercube defined by the minimal and maximal values of each variable. Without loss of generality, we can suppose that the variation domain is the unit hypercube. A point provides information about a neighborhood around it, according to the Euclidian distance, for example. The surface of the largest circle recovers 78.5% of the unit hypercube surface in 2D, 31% in 3D and only 0.2% in 10D. This means that, when the dimension is high, data points are far from each other.

8.4.2. *Dissimilarity criteria between clusters*

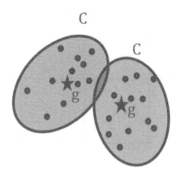

Figure 8.16. *For a color version of this figure, see www.iste.co.uk/laffly/torus1.zip*

We need a dissimilarity criterion to build clusters which are "far" from each other.

We consider two clusters C_1 and C_2, with n_1 and n_2 points respectively. We note g_1 and g_2 as their barycenters.

The minimal distance detects ovoid or even sinuous shapes. But it is sensitive to the effect of chain structure (two distant points are considered as belonging to the same cluster because they are connected by a series of points close to each other):

$$d_{\min}(C_1, C_2) = \min_{x \in C_1, y \in C_2} d(x, y).$$

The maximal distance is sensible to outliers:

$$d_{\min}(C_1, C_2) = \max_{x \in C_1, y \in C_2} d(x, y).$$

The average distance is less sensible but produces clusters with the same variance:

$$d_{\min}(C_1, C_2) = \operatorname{mean}_{x \in C_1, y \in C_2} d(x, y).$$

The ward distance is the most used. It tends to produce spherical clusters of the same size:

$$d_{Ward}(C_1, C_2) = \frac{n_1 \times n_2}{n_1 + n_2} d^2(g_1, g_2).$$

8.4.3. *Variance (inertia) decomposition*

The total inertia of the data

$$I_{tot} = \frac{1}{n} \sum_{i=1}^{n} d^2(x_i, g)$$

where d is the Euclidian distance and g is the barycenter can be decomposed in two parts (see Figure 8.17): $I_{tot} = I_{between} + I_{within}$.

– $I_{between}$ is the inertia between the clusters. Each cluster, C_k, is summarized by its barycenter, g_k, and weighted by its size, n_k:

$$I_{between} = \frac{1}{n}\sum_{k=1}^{r} n_k d^2(g_k, g)$$

where r is the number of clusters.

– I_{within} is the inertia within clusters, which is the average of the variances within the clusters, s_k^2, weighted by the size of the cluster:

$$I_{within} = \frac{1}{n}\sum_{k=1}^{r} n_k s_k^2 .$$

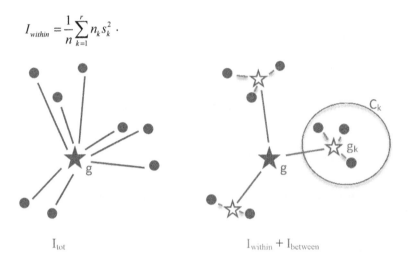

I_{tot} $I_{within} + I_{between}$

Figure 8.17. *Variance decomposition. For a color version of this figure, see www.iste.co.uk/laffly/torus1.zip*

We search a partition that:

– maximizes the inertia between clusters in order to obtain dissimilar clusters;

– minimizes the inertia within the clusters in order to have homogeneous data points in each cluster.

The quality of the partition is measured with the percentage of total inertia explained by the clusters:

$$R^2 = \frac{I_{between}}{I_{tot}} .$$

The aim is to obtain a partition with R^2 close to 1 and a minimum number of clusters. In fact, the coefficient R^2 increases with the number of clusters (we can easily see that: $r = n \Rightarrow R^2 = 1$). This criterion can be used to:

– select the best partition among partitions with the same number of clusters;

– choose the number of clusters with the elbow rule (as in the PCA method) in the graph of R^2 versus the number of clusters (Figure 8.18).

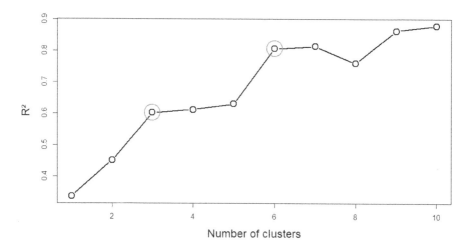

Figure 8.18. *Elbow rule for selecting the number of clusters. For a color version of this figure, see www.iste.co.uk/laffly/torus1.zip*

8.4.4. *k-means method*

k-means is a *partitional* clustering algorithm. It determines k clusters at once, where k is specified by the user. Each cluster is defined by its barycenter, also called its centroid.

Algorithm (Figure 8.19)

Step 1. Randomly choose k centroids among the data points.

Step 2. Compute the distances between all the data points and the k centroids.

Step 3. Assign each data point to the closest centroid.

Step 4. Re-compute the centroids with the current points in the clusters.

Repeat steps 3 and 4 until the convergence criterion is met.

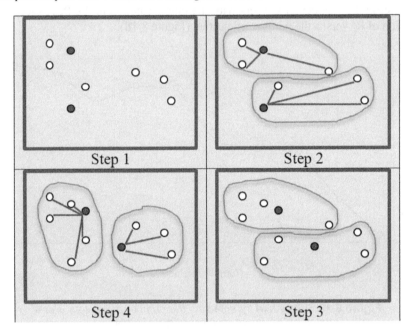

Figure 8.19. *Steps of the k-means algorithm*

The convergence criteria are:

– no or minimum change in clusters (no re-assignment of points or no change of centroids);

– minimum decrease of R^2.

The number of clusters is chosen according to the elbow rule. The algorithm is repeated with k = 2, 3, 4, and so on.

The algorithm may finish at a local optimum. And the result depends on the random initialization of the centroids. It is recommended to restart the algorithm several times and keep the best partition (higher R^2). The algorithm is sensitive to outliers since outliers attract the centroids. It is better to remove them from the dataset (Figure 8.20).

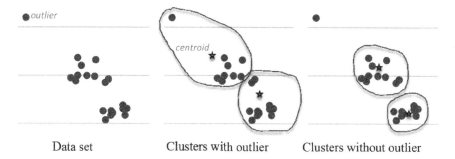

Data set   Clusters with outlier   Clusters without outlier

Figure 8.20. *Influence of outliers on the clusters*

k-means is the most popular clustering algorithm due to its simplicity and its efficiency (the time complexity is $O(n)$ for one iteration and $O(nrk)$ for r restarts and k number of clusters tested).

If we have mixed variables (categorical and numerical), then we use the sum

$$d(x_i,x_j) = \frac{1}{p}\sum_{k=1}^{p} \delta_k(x_i,x_j)$$

where Δ_k is the contribution of variables X_k and is defined such that: $0 \le \Delta_k \le 1$ and $\Delta_k(a,b) = 0 \Rightarrow a = b$. For categorical variable, the contribution is:

$$\delta_k(x_i,x_j) = \begin{cases} 1 & \text{if } x_{ik} = x_{jk} \\ 0 & \text{elseif} \end{cases},$$

and for quantitative variables:

$$\delta_k(x_i,x_j) = \left(\frac{x_{ik} - x_{jk}}{s_k}\right)^2 \frac{1}{\max_m (x_{mk}/s_k) - \min_m (x_{mk}/s_k)}.$$

8.4.5. *Agglomerative hierarchical clustering*

The AHC merges similar clusters.

Algorithm

Step 1. Initialization of n singleton clusters with the n data points.

Step 2. Compute the measure of dissimilarity.

Step 3. Merge the two nearest clusters (c clusters → c-1 clusters).

Repeat steps 2 and 3 until only one cluster remains.

The results of hierarchical clustering are usually presented in a dendrogram (Figure 8.21). The dendrogram represents the clusters obtained during the algorithm. The y-axis represents a measure of dissimilarity between clusters (based on R^2). The number of clusters (and the clusters) is chosen by cutting the dendrogram at the last gap of the dissimilarity measure.

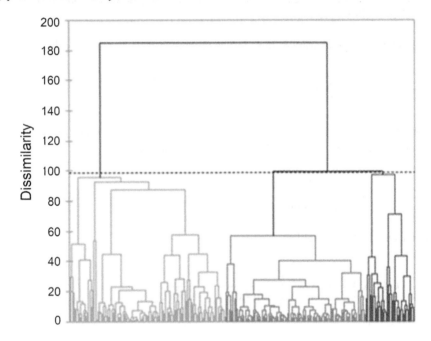

Figure 8.21. *Dendrogram. For a color version of this figure, see www.iste.co.uk/laffly/torus1.zip*

The hierarchical agglomerative clustering algorithm has a time complexity of $O(n^3)$ (some improved algorithms decrease the time complexity to $O(n^2)$) and requires $O(n^2)$ memory. It makes the algorithm unusable for high datasets.

REMARK.– A "top-down" version of hierarchical clustering exists. All data points start in a single cluster, and splits are performed recursively.

A clustering algorithm will always give a result, even if there are no clusters in the dataset. With a bit of practice, you can easily guess if they are clusters or not in the dataset (Figure 8.22).

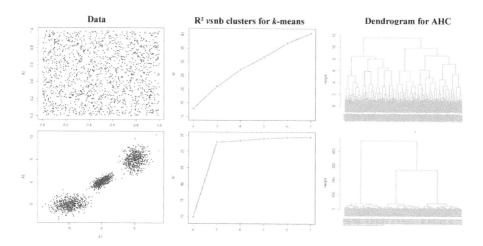

Figure 8.22. *Graphics to determine the number of clusters for two different kinds of data*

8.5. References

[EVE 11] EVERITT B., HOTHORN T., *An Introduction to Applied Multivariate Analysis with R.* Springer, 2011.

[HUS 11] HUSSON F., LÊ S., PAGÈS J., *Exploratory Multivariate Analysis by Example Using R.* Computer Science and Data Analysis Series. CRC Press, Taylor & Francis Group, 2011.

[JAM 13] JAMES G., WITTEN D., HASTIE T. *et al.*, *An Introduction to Statistical Learning with Applications in R.* Springer Texts in Statistics, 2013.

[KAU 90] KAUFMAN L., ROUSSEW P.J., *Finding Groups in Data: An Introduction to Cluster Analysis*. John Wiley & Sons, 1990.

[REN 02] RENCHER A.C. *Methods of Multivariate Analysis*. Wiley, 2002.

[ROK 05] ROKACH L., MAIMON O., "Clustering methods", *Data Mining and Knowledge Discovery Handbook*. Springer US, pp. 321–352, 2005.

9

Sensitivity Analysis

9.1. Generalities

Many scientific phenomena are simulated by expensive computer codes. A code is a black box with input variables $X_1, ..., X_d$, which represent some governing parameters of the physical phenomena. Given a set of values for the input variables, the code computes an output Y, which is the target variable. The aim of *Sensitivity Analysis* (*SA*) is to study the impact of the input variables on computer response. More precisely, the objectives are to:

– detect which variables govern the physical phenomena and which ones are negligible;

– better understand the link between the input and the output variables (monotonous, variable interactions, etc.).

Saltelli, in [SAL 02], defines SA as: "the study of how the uncertainty in the output of a model can be apportioned to different sources of uncertainty in the model input. The SA is hence considered as a prerequisite for model building in any setting, be it diagnostic or prognostic, and in any field where models are used." Uncertainty means the variability of data, a variable.

The underlying idea of this definition is the study of the effect of an input variable offset on the model output (or response). SA allows us to identify which variable has a huge influence on the response and, in turn, which variable has the least influence. It also allows us to explore the model in order to deduce its properties (linearity,

---

Chapter written by Astrid JOURDAN and Peio LOUBIÈRE.

nonlinearity, correlation, etc.). Usually, it is used in simulation and/or modeling, with many application domains, such as climatology, population dynamics, biology, and macro-economy.

In the context of environmental modeling, SA has been used for identifying input factors influence [MAN 18], models calibration in hydrology (soil and water assessment tool, SWAT) [ARN 12]) or air pollution [OST 10], both model calibration and identification of non-sensitive input factors, using one-at-a-time [HOL 05], Morris or Sobol' methods [SAR 16]. Those methods will be described in this chapter.

We suppose that the input variables vary between minimal and maximal values. The variation domain is then a hypercube. A naive way to study the impact of the input variables on the computer response is to discretize each variable into q levels and run the code for the q levels of the variables by moving only one variable at a time (One-at-time (OAT)). It amounts to discretize the hypercube into a grid with q^d cells (Figure 9.5).

When the dimension d (number of input variables) increases, the number of cells becomes so large that it is impossible to run the computer code so many times. If we suppose that the computer response has a monotonous behavior, we only have to test the minimal and maximal values for each variable (Figure 9.4). Even in this case, the number of runs is prohibitive (e.g. $d = 20$ variables implies $2^{20} = 1.048, 576$ runs). Moreover, this naive method does not allow us to catch variable interactions since only one variable varies at a time. This is a consequence of the curse of dimensionality.

The curse of dimensionality is a concept introduced by Bellman [BEL 57], illustrated by the following example. We consider a problem with $d = 2$ variables varying between $[-1, 1]$. We suppose that the middle point of the square $[-1, 1]^2$ gives information around it, according to the bigger circle of the variation domain. Then, the inscribed circle covers 78.5% of the variation domain (see Figure 9.1 [KEO 10, pp. 257–258]).

If we generalize this problem to $d > 2$ variables, the coverage ratio decreases drastically (as illustrated in Figure 9.1). For example, with $d = 10$ variables, the hypersphere covers only 0.2% of the hypercube $[-1, 1]^d$. So, even with a lot of points (data), it is very difficult to efficiently cover the entire variation domain.

The more the dimension increases, the more the space between points is significant. The curse of dimensionality leads to two good practices:

– *dimension reduction*: it is necessary to remove negligible or irrelevant variables before a data analysis. This is one objective of SA;

– *experimental design*: in the hope of obtaining a good coverage of the variation domain, it is recommended to use an experimental design (space-filling design) to determine the values of the points to be evaluated[1].

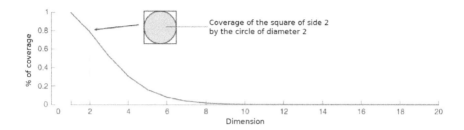

Figure 9.1. *Evolution of the ratio of the hypercube coverage by the hypersphere*

Figure 9.2 [IOO 15] illustrates the mapping of different SA methods. It presents advised methods, according to several criteria as the model uncertainty (linear, nonlinear behavior of the response function), and the number of evaluations that must be done to proceed the analysis (proportionally to the number d of the model variables).

In this chapter, we present three methods: linear and rank regression, Morris method and Sobol indices. Each method is illustrated by a simple example using the Sensitivity R package.

9.2. Methods based on linear regression

9.2.1. *Presentation*

For a d-dimensional model, consider n points $X^i = (X_1^i, ..., X_d^i)$ and their n evaluations by the model Y, according to equation [9.1]:

$$Y = \beta_0 \sum_{i=1}^{d} \beta_i X_i. \tag{9.1}$$

Among all regression-based methods, two main methods that can be applied in a linear or monotonous context are presented thereafter. The sensitivity indices can be computed using linear regression techniques. These indices provide information on

---

1 https://spacefillingdesigns.nl/.

the influence of each input variable on the model output evaluation. They also provide information on each variable weight that can help sort them to discriminate the most valuable ones.

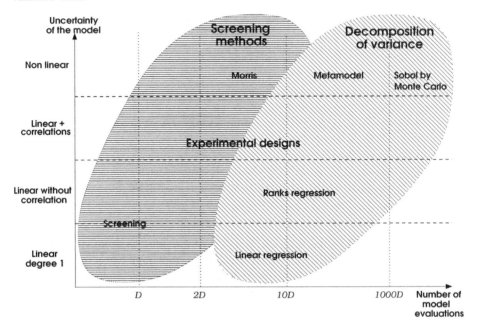

Figure 9.2. *Map of sensitivity analysis methods [IOO 15]*

Suppose now that X_i are independent, then:

$$Var(Y) = \sum_{i=1}^{d} \beta_i^2 Var(X_i). \tag{9.2}$$

The first method is to evaluate the linear correlation coefficients (also known as Pearson coefficients) $\rho(.,.)$ between an input variable X_j and the output Y. The standardized regression coefficient SRC_i, given by equation [9.3], is the percentage of the output variance explained by X_i.

$$SRC_i = \frac{\beta_i^2 Var(X_i)}{Var(Y)}. \tag{9.3}$$

It is easy to prove that $Cov(X_i, Y) = \beta_i Var(X_i)$ and then:

$$SRC_i = \rho^2_{(X_i,Y)} = \frac{Cov(X_i, Y)}{\sqrt{Var(X_i)Var(Y)}}. \qquad [9.4]$$

This method is simple and only needs a few evaluations ($n \geq d+1$), but it is based on a strong assumption that is the linear link between Y and X_i, equation [9.1].

In the case of a monotonous model (i.e. either increasing or decreasing on its definition domain), the linear correlation coefficient does not transliterate precisely the relation between the variables. In this case, a method of computation of rank-based correlation coefficients, the Spearman coefficient, can be applied. The idea is to transform a monotonous relation between variables in a linear relation between these variable ranks.

The coefficient, denoted $\rho^s(.,.)$, is based on each input variable rank and on the output variable. The vector $R_X = (R_{X_1}, \ldots, R_{X_d})$ is defined as the vector of input variables ranks and the vector R_Y, one of the output ranks.

For example, if $X_1 = (5.1, 0.9, 12.5, 2.6)$, then $R_{X_1} = (3, 1, 4, 2)$.

Equation [9.5] gives the coefficients computation formula:

$$\rho^s_i = \rho^s(X_i, Y) = \rho(R_{X_i}, R_Y). \qquad [9.5]$$

These two linear regression methods are not exhaustive; other methods exist as the standard regression coefficients or partial regression coefficients, but these methods are more expensive in terms of computation. Such methods are detailed in [FAI 13].

9.2.2. R practice

In order to illustrate linear correlation coefficients with R, we consider the following test function:

$$f(X) = X_1 + X_2 + X_3,$$

where $X_1 \in [0.5, 1.5], X_2 \in [1.5, 4.5]$ and $X_3 \in [4.5, 13.5]$. Due to its variation range, X_3 has a bigger impact on the response than X_1 or X_2.

```
library("sensitivity")

# Definition of f
Test=function(X)
{return(X[,1]+X[,2]+X[,3])}

# Definition of the experimental design
n <- 5
X <- data.frame(X1 = runif(n, 0.5, 1.5),
X2 = runif(n, 1.5, 4.5),
X3 = runif(n, 4.5, 13.5))

# Computation of the outputs at the design points
y=Test(X)

# Computation of the SRC coefficients.
# A bootstrap estimation is used
# in order to obtain a confidence interval for the coefficients.
SRCoef <- src(X, y, nboot = 100)
print(SRCoef)

# Graphic of the SRC coefficients
barplot(SRCoef$SRC$original,names.arg = c("X1","X2","X3"))
```

Code 9.1. *R practice: linear regression[2]*

```
    Call:
src(X = X, y = y, nboot = 100)
Standardized Regression Coefficients (SRC):
 original     bias        std. error    min. c.i.    max. c.i.
X1  0.1067023  0.0004085751  0.007111664  0.09066879   0.1197709
X2  0.3315320  0.0016566063  0.019614124  0.28690837   0.3676839
X3  0.9895911  0.0000581783  0.037008313  0.91650937   1.0611127
```

The coefficients are given by the attribute SRCoriginal. The two last columns give the minimal and maximal values of the confidence interval. We can see that the SRC coefficient of X_3 is much higher than the others.

---

2 For color versions of the codes in this chapter, see www.iste.co.uk/laffly/torus1.zip.

```
# Computation the rank_based SRC coefficients
SRRCoef <- src(X, y, nboot = 100,rank=TRUE)
```

Code 9.2. *R pratice for SRC coefficients*

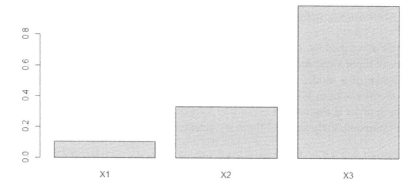

Figure 9.3. *Effects of each variable*

The previous methods treat the case of linear effect. They are very cheap in terms of function evaluations since only two levels need to be tested for each variable. Only the minimal and maximal values are necessary to catch linear or monotonic effects. However, with these methods, if the effect of a variable is nonlinear, this variable can be considered as negligible (Figure 9.4).

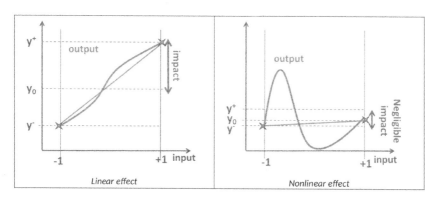

Figure 9.4. *Effect according to variability. For a color version of this figure, see www.iste.co.uk/laffly/torus1.zip*

Other methods deal with nonlinear effects, but they require much more runs in order to have a good exploration of the variation domain (not only the edges). We present two of these methods in the next sections.

9.3. Morris' method

9.3.1. *Elementary effects method (Morris' method)*

Morris developed the elementary effects method [MOR 91] which can detect the influence of input variables on the model response. Morris' method allows us to detect the influence of a model variables in the case of linear or nonlinear behaviors, as well as the interactions between these variables. As with the naive OAT method, the variation domain is discretized according to a regular grid. Not all the points of the grid are evaluated. Only some of them are selected according to a set of r trajectories.

Considering a point X^j, a trajectory offsets a single variable X_i^j according to a certain value (Δ_i), with the other variables fixed. The offset is repeated for each variable (see Figure 9.5). This means that a trajectory contains $(d + 1)$ points.

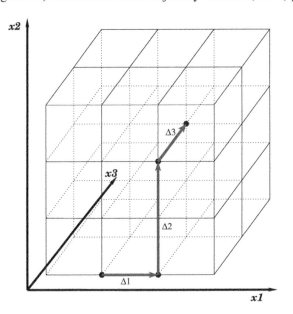

Figure 9.5. *Morris' OAT method: point trajectory. For a color version of this figure, see www.iste.co.uk/laffly/torus1.zip*

Usually the value is proportional to:

$$\delta = \frac{q}{2(q-1)},$$

where q is the number of discretization levels of the variation domain. Then, the method computes the elementary effect $EE_i(X^j)$ of this offset on the model response, according to equation [9.6]:

$$EE_i(X^j) = \frac{f(X_1^j, \ldots, X_i^j + \Delta_i, \ldots, X_d^j) - f(X^j)}{\Delta_i}. \qquad [9.6]$$

The elementary effect described by equation [9.6] provides a local evaluation of the sensitivity of the jth point's i^{th} variable. The global analysis is given by a set of r trajectories randomly chosen in the variation domain.

Each variable sensitivity is then computed by the mean of elementary effects, according to equation [9.7]:

$$\mu_i = \frac{1}{r} \sum_{j=1}^{r} EE_i(X^j). \qquad [9.7]$$

For a correct analysis of the results, a low value of μ_i indicates that the ith variable has a low effect on the model; on the contrary, a high value indicates a high effect on the model.

However, this information is not sufficient. Even if it is a good indicator, considering only the mean value, important information could be missed on the nonlinear behavior of one or many variables. For a complete study, there is also the computation of the elementary effects standard deviation, according to equation [9.8]:

$$\sigma_i = \sqrt{\frac{1}{r} \sum_{j=1}^{r} (EE_i(X^j) - \mu_i)^2}. \qquad [9.8]$$

The standard deviation σ_i study provides more information on variable effects. Considering the values of the couple mean/standard deviation (μ, σ), four cases of behavior can be made out to qualify the variable effect (see Figure 9.6):

– two low values for both mean and standard deviation imply that the variable *does not has (or has a low) effect* on the model;

– a low standard deviation value and a high mean value indicate that the variable has a *high linear effect* on the model;

– a low mean value and a high standard deviation value indicate that the variable has a *high nonlinear effect* on the model;

– two high values for both the mean and standard deviation describe a variable that *has a high nonlinear effect* on the model and/or *interactions* with other variables.

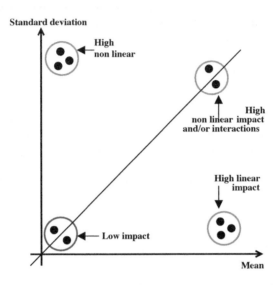

Figure 9.6. *Variable effect according to the couple (mean, standard deviation). For a color version of this figure, see www.iste.co.uk/laffly/torus1.zip*

In [CAM 07], Campolongo *et al.* suggest to use the elementary effect absolute mean indicator, μ^*, to evaluate a variable effect. Indeed, they consider the fact that μ^* provides a good approximation of the total sensitivity index defined by Saltelli *et al.* in [SAL 02] and described by equation [9.9].

$$\mu_i^* = \frac{1}{r} \sum_{j=1}^{r} |EE_i(X^j)|. \tag{9.9}$$

The complete process of Morris' method is detailed in Algorithm 1.

The main advantage of Morris' method is that much less computation effort is needed. It allows us to detect linear as well as nonlinear effect and interactions between variables. However, this method is constrained by its experimental design. Indeed, it does not compute the elementary effects on a set of random points. It demands an initial set of points, then performs multiple unidimensional offsets on each of these points, building discretized trajectories. Moreover, it can guess if a variable has influence (or not) on the model, but it cannot precisely quantify this influence.

Algorithm 1: Morris'method algorithm.

1: Randomly initialize r points and their evaluations
2: **for** $i \leftarrow 1$ *to* d **do**
3:      **for** $j \leftarrow 1$ *to* r **do**
4:          $\Delta \leftarrow random()$
5:          $X^{j\prime} \leftarrow (X_1^j, \dots, X_i^j + \Delta, \dots, X_d^j)$
6:          $EE_i(X^j) \leftarrow \frac{f(X^{j\prime}) - f(X^j)}{\Delta}$
7:          $X^j \leftarrow X^{j\prime}$
8:      **end**
9:      Compute μ_i^* and σ_i, according to [9.9] and [9.8]
10: **end**

To go further, it can be noted that other methods are inspired by the trajectories built to define elementary effects, such as the spiral staircase method [JAN 99].

9.3.2. *R practice*

The first step is the construction of the experimental design, i.e. the trajectories for the offset of the input variables. Hereafter, we consider two input variables (factors=2) discretized into five levels (levels=5) and three trajectories (r=3). For each offset, the variable shifts three levels (grid.jump=3). See code 9.3.

```
library("sensitivity")
M=morris(model = NULL, factors = 2, r = 3,
design=list(type = "oat", levels = 5, grid.jump = 3))
attributes(M)
```

Code 9.3. *R practice for Morris' method*

```
$names
[1] "model" "factors" "r" "design" "binf" "bsup" "scale"
[8] "X" "call"
$class
[1] "morris"
```

The experimental design is called X in the list generated by the `Morris` function.

```
Design=M$X
```

```
         x1    x2
[1,] 1.00 0.25
[2,] 1.00 1.00
[3,] 0.25 1.00
[4,] 0.75 0.00
[5,] 0.75 0.75
[6,] 0.00 0.75
[7,] 0.25 1.00
[8,] 0.25 0.25
[9,] 1.00 0.25
```

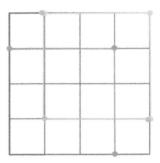

Figure 9.7. *Graphical overview of the design. For a color version of this figure, see www.iste.co.uk/laffly/torus1.zip*

The size of the experimental design is $n = r*(d+1)$. We note that the experimental design is built with entries in $[0, 1]$. A linear transformation is necessary to obtain the good variation range for each variable. We test the Morris' method with the following simple function:

$$f(x) = sin(x_1) + 2x_2 + x_3 + 0x_4,$$

where $x_i \in [0, 1]$. Variable X_4 has no impact on the response, X_1 has a nonlinear impact and X_2 has a bigger linear impact than X_3. This function is evaluated on the design points and the elementary effects are computed with the function `tell`. See code 9.4.

```
# Definition of f
Test=function(X)
{return(sin(X[,1])+2*X[,2]+X[,3]+0*X[,4])}
# Construction of the experimental design
M=morris(model = NULL, factors = 4, r = 3,
design=list(type = "oat", levels = 10, grid.jump = 3))
Design=M$X
Y=Test(Design)
Result=tell(M,Y)
print(M)
plot(M)
```

Code 9.4. *Toy example for Morris' method*

```
Call:
morris(model = NULL, factors = 4, r = 3, design = list(type =
"oat", levels = 10, grid.jump = 3))
Model runs: 15
        mu   mu.star   sigma
X1  0.8371365  0.8371365  1.453476e-01
X2  2.0000000  2.0000000  5.661049e-16
X3  1.0000000  1.0000000  7.850462e-17
X4  0.0000000  0.0000000  0.000000e+00
```

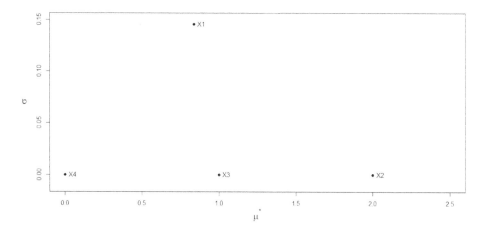

Figure 9.8. *Graphical overview of each variable effect*

9.4. Methods based on variance analysis

Morris' method gives a ranking of the input variables, but it does not assume that the variables have a real impact on the computer response. It may provide a ranking between negligible variables.

The methods based on variance analysis allow one to quantify the impact of the input variables. As for the methods based on linear regression (see section 9.2), a sensitivity index is defined as a ratio of the output variance, but without the assumption of linear behavior for the computer response. However, they assume that the input variables are uncorrelated and that the output distribution can be characterized by its variance (see Figure 9.9).

Hereafter, we present two sensitivity indices: the main index (also called first-order index) and the total index. These indices' estimation requests a very large number of sampled points and evaluations.

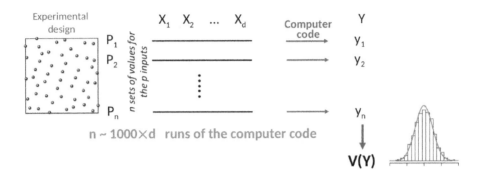

Figure 9.9. *Sobol' method. For a color version of this figure, see www.iste.co.uk/laffly/torus1.zip*

9.4.1. *Sobol' indices*

Sobol' indices method [SAL 02] is the most attractive method considering the fact that it is able to precisely quantify the effect of each variable on the variance of the output Y. The response variance is based on the mathematical decomposition of Var(Y). Each term represents the variability of the response due to a variable or due to an interaction of several variables.

For example, in the case of two independent random variables uniformly distributed on $[0, 1]$, where f_0 is a constant and f_1, f_2 and f_{12} are independent

$$
\begin{aligned}
Y = f(X_1, X_2) &= E(Y) &&\longleftarrow f_0 \\
&+ E(Y|X_1) - E(Y) &&\longleftarrow f_1 \\
&+ E(Y|X_2) - E(Y) &&\longleftarrow f_2 \\
&+ E(Y|X_1, X_2) - E(Y|X_1) - E(Y|X_2) + E(Y) &&\longleftarrow f_{12}
\end{aligned}
$$

random variables. Then,

$$
Var(Y) = Var(f_1) + Var(f_2) + Var(f_{12}). \tag{9.10}
$$

Then, dividing by $Var(Y)$, we obtain:

$$
1 = \frac{Var(f_1)}{Var(Y)} + \frac{Var(f_2)}{Var(Y)} + \frac{Var(f_{12})}{Var(Y)} = S_1 + S_2 + S_{12},
$$

where S_i is the percentage of the output variance explained by X_i and S_{12} is the percentage explained by the interactions between X_1 and X_2.

Efron *et al.* [EFR 81] generalized the decomposition to d independent random variables:

where $f_0 = E(Y), f_i(X_i) = E(Y|X_i) - E(Y)$ and so on.

The first-order index of the ith variable,

$$S_i = \frac{Var(f_i(X_i))}{Var(Y)} = \frac{Var\,[\mathbb{E}(Y|X_i)]}{Var(Y)} \qquad [9.11]$$

$$Y = f(X_1, \ldots, X_d) = f_0$$
$$+ \sum_{1 \le i \le d} f_i(X_i)$$
$$+ \sum_{1 \le i < j \le d} f_{ij}(X_j)$$
$$+ \ldots$$
$$+ f_{1..d}(X_1, \ldots, X_d),$$

is the main effect of X_i, i.e. the percentage of the output variance explained by X_i.

In the same way, we can define $2^{nd}, 3^{rd}, \ldots$ and higher-order indices. However, the number of indices increases rapidly (2^{d-1}). So, it is preferable to use the total sensitivity index defined by:

$$S_{T_i} = \frac{\mathbb{E}\,[Var(Y|X_j, \, j \ne i)]}{Var(Y)}. \qquad [9.12]$$

This index is the sum of all indices involving X_i. It measures the contribution of X_i on the response variance and its interactions with the other variables. For example, with two variables, $S_{T_1} = S_1 + S_{12}$. It is no more a percentage of the response variance. If the total index of X_i is higher than its first-order index, it means that X_i has a non-negligible interaction with other variables.

To illustrate these indices with an example, let us consider the Ishigami function in dimension $d = 3$:

$$f(X) = \sin(X_1) + 7\sin^2(X_2) + 0,1\,\sin(X_1)\sin^4(X_3),$$

where all X_i are uniformly distributed on $[-\pi, \pi]$.

The computation of all Sobol' indices leads to the conclusion that 31.4% of the response variance are imputable to the first variable X_1; 44.2% are due to the second variable X_2 and 24.4% are explained by an interaction between X_1 and X_3.

Considering the previous example, the Ishigami function, the total index of variable S_{T_1} is 55.8%, of S_{T_2} is 44.2% and of S_{T_3} is 24.4%. Note that the sum of the total effects is greater than 100%. The total indices of X_1 and X_3 are higher than their first-order indices, which translate their interaction.

Figure 9.10. *Sobol' indices for the Ishigami function. For a color version of this figure, see www.iste.co.uk/laffly/torus1.zip*

9.4.2. *Estimation of the Sobol' indices*

The Sobol' index computation requires the estimation of integrals,

$$u \subset [1, .., d], D_u = \int_{[0,1]^d} f_u^2(x) dx$$

A Monte-Carlo method is used to estimate these integrals[3]. Two samplings of size N recombined in order to obtain an experimental computer design of size $N(d + 2)$ (Figure 9.11). The computer code is evaluated at the design points, and the output is used to estimate the indices. A Monte Carlo estimation of the Sobol' indices is expensive in terms of computational time.

Other methods allow us to reduce the number of evaluations of the computer response.

For example, *Fourier Amplitude Sensitivity Test* (*FAST*) method uses a sampling composed of trajectories across the variation domain according to different frequencies [CUK 78].

Another way to reduce the cost is to replace the computer code by a surrogate model, usually a Gaussian process model [FAI 13, SAN 03, FAN 06].

---

3 https://en.wikipedia.org/wiki/Variance-based_sensitivity_analysis.

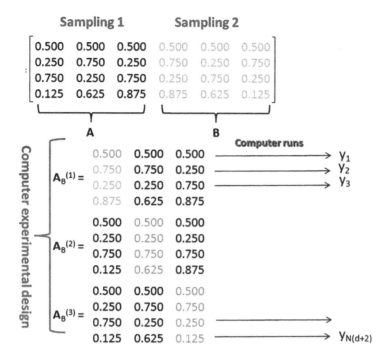

Figure 9.11. *Sobol' indices experimental design example. For a color version of this figure, see www.iste.co.uk/laffly/torus1.zip*

9.4.3. R practice

The first step is the construction of the experimental design, which is a combination of two samplings. Hereafter, we consider an example with $d = 4$ input variables and two samples of size $N = 2$ each. See code 9.5.

```
$names
[1]  "model"  "factors"  "r"  "design"  "binf"  "bsup"  "scale"
[8]  "X"  "call"
$class
[1]  "morris"
```

The experimental design is called X in the list generated by sobol2002 function. The size of the design $n = N * (d + 2) = 2 * (4 + 2) = 12$ (see Figure 9.12).

```
library("sensitivity")
sampling1=matrix(0,nrow=2,ncol=4)
sampling1[1,1]=1
sampling1[2,2]=1
sampling2=matrix(0,nrow=2,ncol=4)
sampling2[1,3]=1
sampling2[2,4]=1
S=sobol2002(model=NULL,X1=sampling1,X2=sampling2)
attributes(S)
Design=as.data.frame(S$X)
```

Code 9.5. *R practice: Sobol' method*

```
Design=as.data.frame(S$X)
```

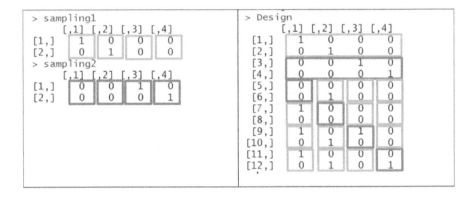

Figure 9.12. *Experimental design illustration. For a color version of this figure, see www.iste.co.uk/laffly/torus1.zip*

First, we test the Sobol' method with a simple example:

$$f(x) = x_1 + x_2 + 0x_3 + 0x_4,$$

where $x_i \in [0,1]$. This function is evaluated on the design points and the Sobol' indices are computed with the function tell. See code 9.6.

```
# Definition of f
Test=function(X)
{return(X[,1]+X[,2])}
sampling1=data.frame(matrix(runif(20000),nrow=5000,ncol=4))
sampling2=data.frame(matrix(runif(20000),nrow=5000,ncol=4))
S=sobol2002(model=NULL,X1=sampling1,X2=sampling2)
Design=S$X
y=Test(Design)
tell(S,y)
print(S)
```

Code 9.6. *Toy example for Sobol' method*

```
Call:
sobol2002(model = NULL, X1 = sampling1, X2 = sampling2)
Model runs: 30000
```

First order indices:

```
     original
X1   0.524127168
X2   0.497259838
X3   0.001208165
X4   0.001208165
```

Total indices:

```
     original
X1    0.458505594
X2    0.516237304
X3   -0.001203595
X4   -0.001203595
```

We note that X_3 and X_4 are negligible. Since the main effect of X_1 and X_2 are nearly equal to their total effect, we can conclude that there is no interaction between them. We also note some incoherence due to the Monte Carlo estimation of the indices. The sum of the first-order indices is greater than 1, and the total indices of X_3 and X_4 are negative. Moreover, the main effect of X_1 is greater than its total index.

Now we can use the Sobol' method to estimate the sensitivity indices of the famous Ishigami function (see code 9.7).

```
sampling1=data.frame(matrix(runif(15000),nrow=5000,ncol=3))
sampling2=data.frame(matrix(runif(15000),nrow=5000,ncol=3))
S=sobol2002(model=NULL,X1=sampling1,X2=sampling2)
Design= 2*pi*S$X-pi
# In order to have values in [-pi, pi]
y=ishigami.fun(Design)
tell(S,y)
print(S)
```

Code 9.7. *Ishigami function for Sobol' method*

```
Call:
sobol2002(model = NULL, X1 = sampling1, X2 = sampling2)
Model runs: 25000
```

First-order indices:

```
    original
X1  0.29379897
X2  0.44224361
X3  0.01465167
```

Total indices:

```
  original
X1  0.5570840
X2  0.4383746
X3  0.2229927
```

The estimated indices are not very far from the true values.

9.5. Conclusion

In this chapter, we have presented the context and objectives of the use of sensitivity analysis methods, as well as the methods mainly used. We have presented methods in the case of use with linear/nonlinear models, in the case of sorting, prioritizing variables or precisely evaluating their influence for reduction of problem dimension.

To go further, the interested reader should learn deeper on sampling techniques for building experimental designs, such as Monte Carlo sampling, mathematical sequences (Halton, Sobol'), and Latin hypercube design (LHD). Moreover, as introduced in the previous section, the use of metamodels can be an alternative to the expensive estimation of Sobol' indices; many methods allow us to approximate such surfaces (Gaussian process, SVM, neural networks, etc.) [SAN 03, FAN 06, BIS 95].

9.6. References

[ARN 12] ARNOLD J.G., MORIASI D.N., GASSMAN P.W. *et al.*, "SWAT: Model use, calibration, and validation", *Transactions of the ASABE*, vol. 55, no. 4, pp. 1491–1508, American Society of Agricultural and Biological Engineers, 2012.

[BEL 57] BELLMAN R.E., *Dynamic Programming*, Princeton University Press, Rand Corporation, 1957.

[BIS 95] BISHOP C.M., *Neural Networks for Pattern Recognition*, Oxford University Press, 1995.

[CAM 07] CAMPOLONGO F., CARIBONI J., SALTELLI A., "An effective screening design for sensitivity analysis of large models", *Environmental Modelling & Software*, vol. 22, no. 10, pp. 1509–1518, 2007.

[CUK 78] CUKIER R., LEVINE H., SHULER K., "Nonlinear sensitivity analysis of multiparameter model systems", *Journal of Computational Physics*, vol. 26, no. 1, pp. 1–42, Elsevier, 1978.

[EFR 81] EFRON B., STEIN C., "The jackknife estimate of variance", *The Annals of Statistics*, vol. 9, no. 3, pp. 586–596, JSTOR, 1981.

[FAI 13] FAIVRE R., IOOSS B., MAHÉVAS S. *et al.*, *Analyse de sensibilité et exploration de modèles*, Editions Quae, 2013.

[FAN 06] FANG K., LI R., SUDJIANTO A., *Design and Modeling for Computer Experiments*, Chapman & Hall/CRC, Computer Science and Data Analysis, 2006.

[HOL 05] HOLVOET K., VAN GRIENSVEN A., SEUNTJENS P. *et al.*, "Sensitivity analysis for hydrology and pesticide supply towards the river in SWAT", *Physics and Chemistry of the Earth, Parts A/B/C*, vol. 30, nos 8–10, pp. 518–526, Elsevier, 2005.

[IOO 15] IOOSS B., LEMAÎTRE P., "A review on global sensitivity analysis methods", DELLINO G., MELONI C. (eds), *Uncertainty Management in Simulation-Optimization of Complex Systems: Algorithms and Applications*, pp. 101–122, Springer, Boston, 2015.

[JAN 99] JANSEN M.J., "Analysis of variance designs for model output", *Computer Physics Communications*, vol. 117, no. 1, pp. 35–43, Elsevier, 1999.

[KEO 10] KEOGH E., MUEEN A., *Curse of Dimensionality*, Springer, Boston, 2010.

[MAN 18] MANNINA G., COSENZA A., NEUMANN M. *et al.*, "Global sensitivity analysis in wastewater treatment modelling", *Advances in Wastewater Treatment*, p. 363, 2018.

[MOR 91] MORRIS M.D., "Factorial sampling plans for preliminary computational experiments", *Technometrics*, vol. 33, no. 2, pp. 161–174, American Society for Quality Control and American Statistical Association, April 1991.

[OST 10] OSTROMSKY T., DIMOV I., GEORGIEVA R. *et al.*, "Sensitivity analysis of a large-scale air pollution model: Numerical aspects and a highly parallel implementation", *Large-Scale Scientific Computing*, Springer Berlin Heidelberg, pp. 197–205, 2010.

[SAL 02] SALTELLI A., "Sensitivity analysis for importance assessment", *Risk Analysis*, vol. 22, no. 3, pp. 579–590, Blackwell Publishing, Inc., 2002.

[SAN 03] SANTNER T.J., WILLIAMS B.J., NOTZ W., *The Design and Analysis of Computer Experiments*, Springer, 2003.

[SAR 16] SARRAZIN F., PIANOSI F., WAGENER T., "Global sensitivity analysis of environmental models: Convergence and validation", *Environmental Modelling & Software*, vol. 79, pp. 135–152, Elsevier, 2016.

Using R for Multivariate Analysis

10.1. Introduction

R is a programming language oriented toward data analysis, data mining and statistics. It allows us to quickly and flexibly organize and process large volumes of data, and to represent this data using a wide variety of available graphs.

Originally developed in the early 1990s by Ross Ihaka and Robert Gentleman, this language is now maintained and updated by a team of developers within the R Project. This structure ensures frequent updates. Among its interesting features, we note:

– this language is based on the notion of vector, which simplifies mathematical calculations and considerably reduces the use of iterative structures (loops for, while, etc.). In addition, there is no typing or declaration of variables required. This makes it possible to write very short programs (usually only a few lines of code) and considerably reduce computer development time;

– it allows us to easily create customizable graphs to better visualize data and results;

– it is free under the GPL license, which means that the sources are available and can be modified. A very active community of users is constantly developing new functionalities (libraries called 'packages') for the project. It runs on a variety of UNIX platforms, plus, Windows, Mac OS or Linux.

Chapter written by Astrid JOURDAN.

RStudio is an integrated development environment (IDE) specifically created to work with R. Its popularity has grown dramatically since 2014. It allows us to view the script files, the R code line, help files, graphics, etc., in a user-friendly interface. The RStudio interface (Figure 10.1) consists of four windows:

– edit window (top left): in this window appear the files containing the R scripts. At the top of this window, icons are used to save the file, execute a selected piece of code or the entire code contained in the file. Saving the file with the extension .R allows syntax highlighted to be adapted to the R language;

– command window (bottom left): this window contains a console in which R code lines are entered for execution;

– workspace/history window (top right): this window contains the objects in memory, which can be viewed by clicking on their names, as well as the history of the commands executed;

– window for files / graphics / packages / help (bottom right): the explorer allows us to move through the directory tree and the graphic window contains the graphics drawn by R (it is possible to export them). The package window shows the installed and currently-loaded packages, and the help window contains the documentation on functions and packages.

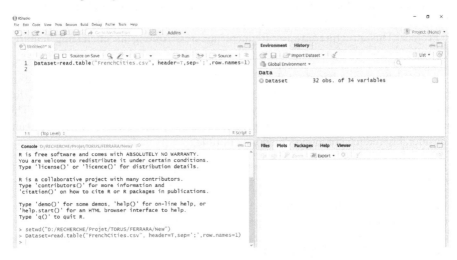

Figure 10.1. *RStudio Interface. For a color version of this figure, see www.iste.co.uk/laffly/torus1.zip*

Select a work directory (where you put your data):

Session → Set Working Directory → Choose Directory …

Open a new R script:

File → New File → R Script

REMARK.– Reading this chapter requires the prerequisites of the Chapter 8 Multivariate Analysis chapter.

10.1.1. *The dataset*

The toy dataset used to illustrate the principal component analysis is about French towns (Figure 10.2).

The statistical unit is a town. Thirty-two cities have been observed for 34 variables:

CLIMAT: Kind of climate (Continental=1/Mediterranean=2/Oceanic=3/semi-oceanic=4);

NO2: Nitrogen dioxide;

DENSITY: People per km^2;

RAINFALL: Average annual rainfall (mm);

"MONTH"+r: Average monthly rainfall (12 variables);

DAY_RAINFALL: Average annual number of rainy days;

"MONTH"=dr: Average monthly number of rainy days (12 variables);

TEMP: Average annual temperature (degree Celsius);

TEMP_RANGE: Temperature variation;

SUNSHINE: Average of sunny days (hours per day);

LATITUDE: Latitude;

LONGITUDE: Longitude.

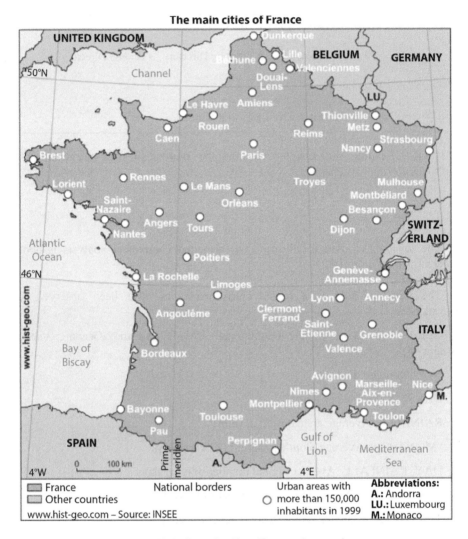

Figure 10.2. *French cities. For a color version of this figure, see www.iste.co.uk/laffly/torus1.zip*

The dataset is called "FrenchCities.csv". In order to import the dataset in R, we use the instruction `read.table`. Write the following instruction in the R script, select the line and click the button ⟶ Run to run it.

```
Dataset=read.table("FrenchCities.csv",
header=T,sep=';',row.names=1)
```

`header=T` indicates that the first line is the column names.

`row.names=1` indicates that the first column is the row names.

`sep=';'` indicates that the field separator character is a semi-colon.

The result of `read.table` is a *dataframe* visible in the Global Environment window (Figure 10.2). The blue arrow on the left gives the list of variables. You can also use the instruction `attributes(Dataset)`. The square on the right displays the dataset in a new window.

10.1.1.1. *How to select a variable?*

```
# Display the names of the variables
names(Dataset)

# with the attribute $var
Dataset$NO2

# with the column number
Dataset[,2]

# with the column name
Dataset[,"NO2"]
```

10.1.1.2. *How to select data points?*

```
# Display the names of the data points
row.names(Dataset)

# Select Rows 10, 11 and 12
Dataset[10:12,]

# Remove the rows 1, 4 and 7
Dataset[-c(1,4,7),]

# Create a subset of Dataset according to the logical
expression
subset(Dataset,NO2>50)

# Select a data point by its name
subset(Dataset,row.names(Dataset)=="Paris")
```

The function `write.table` prints the dataframe x into a file

```
write.table(x,file='name.file',sep=';',row.names=T,col.n
ames=T,....)
```

10.1.2. *The variables*

The type of categorical variables is *factor*, and the type of quantitative variables is *num* or *int*. Function `str` gives the variable types.

```
str(Dataset)
```

The type of variable CLIMAT is integer. We have to transform it into factor with labels:

– CONT=1;

– MED=2;

– OCEAN=3;

– SEMI_OCEAN=4.

`as.xx(var)` transforms var into type `xx`. `is.xx(var)` returns TRUE if var is type `xx`. `levels(var)` gives the labels of a categorical variable.

```
# Transform variable CLIMAT into factor
Dataset$CLIMAT=as.factor(Dataset$CLIMAT)
is.factor(Dataset$CLIMAT)

# Rename its labels
levels(Dataset$CLIMAT) # print the current labels
levels(Dataset$CLIMAT)=c("CONT","MED","OCEAN","SEMI_OCEAN")
levels(Dataset$CLIMAT) # print the new labels
```

summary provides numerical indicators (mean, median, etc.) if the variable is quantitative and the label frequencies for categorical variables.

```
summary(Dataset)
```

10.1.2.1. *Quantitative variable*

Numerical summarization:

```
mean(Dataset$NO2) # Mean value
sd(Dataset$NO2) # Standard deviation
median(Dataset$NO2) # middle value when the values are sorted
quantile(Dataset$NO2)# Split the ordered values into 4 equal
parts
                         # and gives the points between the
quarters
cor(Dataset[,1:5]) # correlation matrix of the five first
variables
```

Graphical summarization:

```
# Quantile boxplot
boxplot(Dataset$TEMP,main='Boxplot of
TEMP',ylab='TEMP',col='grey')
# Histogram
hist(Dataset$TEMP,main='Histogram of
TEMP',xlab='TEMP',col='blue')
# Scatterplot
plot(Dataset$LATITUDE,Dataset$TEMP,main='TEMP vs LATITUDE',
      xlab='LATITUDE',ylab='TEMP',col="red",lwd=2) # lwd=line
width
text(Dataset$LATITUDE,Dataset$TEMP,row.names(Dataset))
# Add the names of the points
# Scatterplot matrix for the five first quantitative variables
pairs(Dataset[,2:6])
```

Error is not a French city but an outlier. We remove it from the dataset.

```
Dataset0=Dataset # Dataset0 is the dataset with error
Dataset=subset(Dataset,TEMP>0) # Dataset is the data without
                               # Error (since TEMP=0 for
Error)
boxplot(Dataset$TEMP,main='Boxplot of TEMP',ylab='TEMP',col=
'grey')
hist(Dataset$TEMP,main='Histogram of TEMP',xlab='TEMP',col=
'blue')
plot(Dataset$LATITUDE,Dataset$TEMP,main='TEMP vs
LATITUDE',xlab=
'LATITUDE',ylab='TEMP',col='grey',lwd=2)
text(Dataset$LATITUDE,Dataset$TEMP,row.names(Dataset))
# add the names of the points
```

10.1.2.2. *Categorical variables*

– contingency table for one categorical variable and graphics

```
tab=table(Dataset$CLIMAT)
tab
pie(tab)
barplot(tab)
barplot(as.matrix(tab),legend=TRUE)
prop.table(tab)
addmargins(tab)
```

– contingency table for two categorical variables.

Since there is only one categorical variable in the dataset, we have to create a new one. We consider a Boolean variable, SHINY, which takes TRUE value if the average of sunny days is greater than 2000 hours per day. And we cross it with CLIMATE variable.

```
SHINY=Dataset[,32]>2000
SHINY=as.factor(SHINY)
tab=table(SHINY,Dataset$CLIMAT)
tab
barplot(tab)
```

10.2. Principal component analysis

FactoMineR is a package dedicated to multivariate analysis. We need to install it. Click on Packages tab and then on Install tab (Figure 10.3).

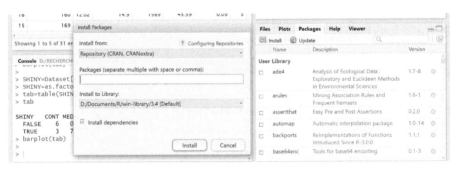

Figure 10.3. *Package installation. For a color version of this figure, see www.iste.co.uk/laffly/torus1.zip*

When the package is installed, we need to load it in the R session. Just check it in the list of installed packages or write the following instruction.

library(FactoMineR)

Every time you use R Studio for multivariate analysis, you have to load it in your new R session (but not to install it again).

The function *PCA* creates a dataframe with the results of the principal analysis components.

PCA(Dataset, scale.unit=TRUE, ...)

For more details about PCA type help(PCA).

Do not forget to scale the variables as explained in Multivariate analysis section!

```
res=PCA(Dataset[,-1],scale.unit=TRUE)
attributes(res)
```

PCA gives three main results, one about the eigenvalues, one about the variables and one about the data points.

10.2.1. *Eigenvalues*

res$eig gives a matrix containing all the eigenvalues of the covariance matrix, the percentage of variance and the cumulative percentage of variance

Here, the three first components contain more than 87% of the information. We can reduce the space to dimension 3.

```
# display the eigenvalues
res$eig
# barplot of the percentages of variance explained by the
principal axes
barplot(res$eig[,2])
```

10.2.1.1. *Variables*

res$var gives a list of matrices containing all the results for the active variables. The results are given for the five first principal axes (but are calculated for all axes). More axes can be displayed by using the argument ncp in the PCA function.

– *resvarcoord* gives the variable coordinates in the new coordinate system. The coordinates are used to draw the correlation circle (Figure 10.4).

```
# plot the correlation circle for axes 1 and 2
plot.PCA(res,choix="var",axes=c(1,2))
```

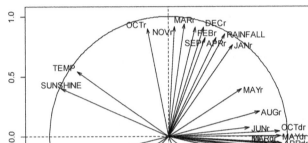

Figure 10.4. *Variable map for the principal plan Axes 1 and 2*

– *resvarcos2* gives the square cosines of the angle of variable projections on the axes. A variable is well projected on an axis if the square cosine is close to 1. An arrow near the circle indicates a good projection while a small arrow indicates that the information provided by the variable is lost when projecting on the axes.

	Dim.1	Dim.2	Dim.3	Dim.4
NO2	0.18	0.07	0.07	**0.53**
SUNSHINE	**0.81**	0.16	1.3e-03	0.15

Table 10.1. *Square cosines for variables NO2 and SUNSHINE projected on Axes 1, 2, 3 and 4*

In Figure 10.4, we can see that SUNSHINE is well projected on the principal plan contrary to NO2. Table 10.1 gives more information. The square cosine of SUNSHINE with Axis 1 is 0.81. Much of the information contained in SUNSHINE is taped by Axis 1. The square cosines of NO2 with the two first principal axes are very small. If we want a good representation of NO2, we have to draw the correlation circle with Axes 4. But Axis 4 is not interesting since it catches only 4% of the inertia.

```
# plot the correlation circle for axes 1 and 4
plot.PCA(res,choix="var",axes=c(1,4))
```

– resvarcontrib gives the percentage contribution of a variable to the construction of an axis. The mean contribution is 3% (since we have 33 variables). The variables which have a contribution more than 3% for the construction of Axis 1 are related to the number of wet days (annual and monthly) since Axis 2 is mainly built with rainfall variables.

```
sort(res$var$contrib[,"Dim.1"],decreasing = TRUE)
sort(res$var$contrib[,"Dim.2"],decreasing = TRUE)
```

– *Interpretation.* In Chapter 8, Multivariate Analysis, it is explained that the cosine of the angle between two variables is the correlation.

- if they are co-linear in the same direction, they are positively correlated. For example, SUNSHINE and TEMP are positively correlated. This means that a city with a lot of shinny days has also a high temperature average;

- if they are co-linear in the opposite direction, they are negatively correlated. For example, SUNSHINE and DAYS-RAINFALL are negatively correlated. This means that when the number of shinny days is big, the number of rainy days is small (obviously!);

- if they are orthogonal, they are uncorrelated. For example, TEMP and RAINFALL are uncorrelated. This means that a city with high precipitation can have high or low temperatures.

Caution, the interpretation is valid only if the variables are well projected on the map.

10.2.2. *Data points (Individuals)*

res$ind gives a list of matrices containing all the results for the active individuals (coordinates, square cosine, contributions). *plot.PCA* with argument *choix='ind'* plot the principal components.

– *resindcos2*. In order to interpret an individual, we need to know where it is well projected, so we display the square cosines of the data points (Table 10.2).

```
plot.PCA(res,choix="ind",axes=c(1,2))
res$ind$cos2
```

	Dim.1	Dim.2	Dim.3	Dim.4
Ajaccio	**0.690**	0.0328	0.09878	0.03045
Angers	0.111	0.1375	0.39507	0.13872
Angoulme	0.474	0.0779	0.04759	0.21581
Besancon	0.471	0.1364	0.31754	0.01016
Biarritz	0.294	**0.6658**	0.01307	0.00046

Table 10.2. *Square cosines for some cities projected on Axes 1, 2, 3 and 4*

Individuals factor map (PCA)

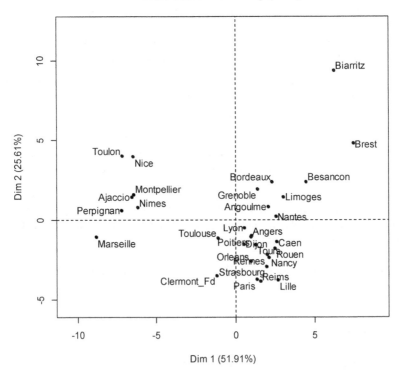

Figure 10.5. *Individual map for the principal plan Axes 1 and 2*

Ajaccio is well projected on Axis 1. We use the correlation circle to interpret this city. Ajaccio can be called a sunny city, with high temperatures and few days of rain. Biarritz (near Bayonne on France map Figure 10.2) is well projected on Axis 2. We can say that Biarritz is a city with high rainfall. Data points in the middle of the map are either near the barycenter, or orthogonal to the principal plan and then bad projected. Then, we can say nothing about them:

– *resindcontrib*. The mean contribution is 3.2% (since we have 31 cities). A high contribution can indicate outliers.

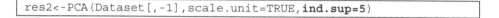

```
sort(res$ind$contrib[,"Dim.1"],decreasing = TRUE)
sort(res$ind$contrib[,"Dim.2"],decreasing = TRUE)
```

Biarritz is far from the barycenter and has a big contribution on Axis 2 (33.6%). In order to verify if this city is an outlier, we remove it from the dataset and we re-compute the principal axes. If nothing changes (nearly), it is not an outlier.

In fact, we do not exactly remove Biarritz from the dataset, but we add it as a *supplementary individual*. It means that PCA function does not take it into account to compute the principal axes, but it still projects Biarritz on the plane. The row number of Biarritz is 5.

```
res2<-PCA(Dataset[,-1],scale.unit=TRUE,ind.sup=5)
```

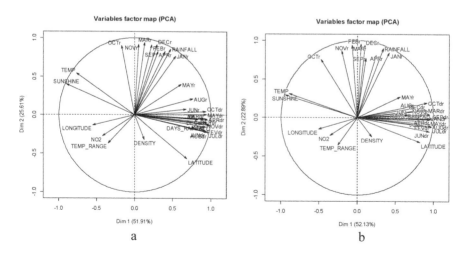

Figure 10.6. *Correlation circle (a) with or (b) without Biarritz*

We remark no change (eigenvalues and variable map are nearly the same, Figure 10.6). Finally, Biarritz is not an outlier and we can keep it in the study.

In order to understand the impact of an outlier, we use PCA with the dataset with the outlier Error (Dataset0). We note that only one data point can change the result (Figure 10.7).

```
Res3<-PCA(Dataset0[,-1],scale.unit=TRUE)
```

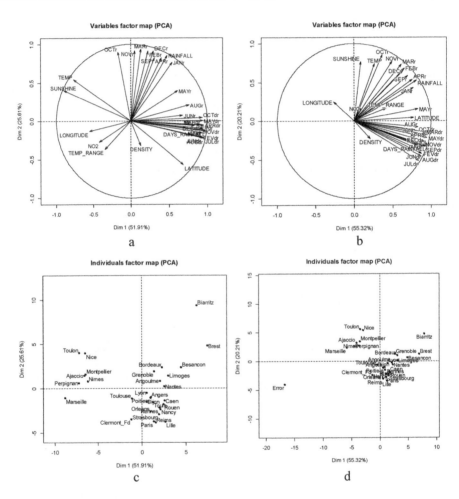

Figure 10.7. *PCA results with or without Error: (a) and (b) are correlation circles without Error, and (c) and (d) are individual maps without Error*

10.2.3. *Supplementary variables*

It is possible to add variables in the graphics. These variables are not taken into account to compute the principal axes, but only for the representation.

– *Supplementary quantitative variables.* We remove the 12 average monthly rainfall variables (columns 3–14) and the 12 average monthly number of rainy days (columns 16–27). We keep only RAINFALL and DAY_RAINFALL, and the other quantitative variables to compute the principal axes.

```
res4=PCA(Dataset[,-1],scale.unit=TRUE,quanti.sup =
c(3:14,16:27))
```

– *Supplementary categorical variables.* Each level of the supplementary categorical variable is considered as a point. The coordinates of this point are the averages of the data points which have the level. The column number of CLIMAT is 1.

```
res5=PCA(Dataset,scale.unit=TRUE,quali.sup = 1)
```

We note that Mediterranean climate is well projected on Axis 1. It means that the cities with this climate have a lot of sunny days and high temperature.

10.2.4. *Other representations*

Explor is a nice package to display interactive graphics for multivariate analysis results exploration. We have to install and load it in the session.

```
explor(res)
```

3D graphics are possible with two packages `rgl` and `plot3D`.

```
plot3d(res.PCA$ind$coord[,1:3],type="s",radius=0.2,col="blue")
# add text
rgl.texts(res.PCA$ind$coord[,1:3]+rbinom(nrow(data.scaled),1,0
.5)-0.5,text=row.names(Mydata), color =
"azure4",cex=0.8,font=2)
# save the picture
rgl.snapshot("plot3D_PCA.gif")
```

10.3. Multiple correspondence analysis

Since, there is only one categorical variable in FrenchCities dataset, we need to transform the quantitative variables into categorical variables. First, we suppress the 24 variables MONTH+r and MONTH+dr and the data point Error. Second, we build a categorical variable by dividing a quantitative variable into five categories according to its distribution: <20%, [20%-40%[, [40%-60%[, [60%-80%[, ≥80%.

```
Dataset=read.table("FrenchCities.csv",
header=T,sep=';',row.names=1)
Dataset$CLIMAT=as.factor(Dataset$CLIMAT)
Dataset=Dataset[-32,-c(4:15,17:28)]
Data.Factor=Dataset
for (i in 2:ncol(Dataset))
{
  cut.values=quantile(Dataset[,i],seq(0,1,0.2))
  Data.Factor[,i]=cut(Dataset[,i],cut.values,include.lowest =
T,
                                    labels =
c("1","2","3","4","5"))
}
```

The multiple correspondence analysis is run with MCA function and the results are displayed with explor package.

```
res=MCA(Data.Factor)
explor(res)
```

We obtain the same kind of results than with PCA: eigenvalues, coordinates, square cosines and contributions of variables and of data points (Figure 10.8).

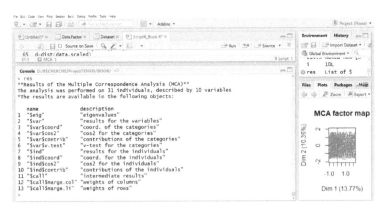

Figure 10.8. *Results of the multiple correspondence analysis. For a color version of this figure, see www.iste.co.uk/laffly/torus1.zip*

10.4. Clustering

Before to run clustering, we have to scale the quantitative variables, and remove the categorical variable CLIMAT and the Error point. The result of scale function is a matrix. It is necessary to transform it in a dataframe.

```
Dataset=read.table("FrenchCities.csv",
header=T,sep=';',row.names=1)
Dataset=Dataset[-32,-1]

Scaled.Data=scale(Dataset)
Scaled.Data=as.data.frame(Scaled.Data)
```

10.4.1. *k-means algorithm*

For the k-means algorithm, we use the R function kmeans

$$kmeans(x,centers,nstart,...)$$

where x is the dataset, center is the number of clusters (or the initial coordinates of the barycenters) and nstart is the number of times the algorithm is re-run.

```
res=kmeans(Scaled.Data,centers=2,nstart=5)
print(res)
```

kmeans returns an object with at least the following components:

cluster   A vector of integers (from 1:k) indicating the cluster to which each point is allocated.
centers   A matrix of cluster centers.
totss   The total sum of squares.
withinss   Vector of within-cluster sum of squares, one component per cluster.
tot.withinss Total within-cluster sum of squares, i.e. sum(withinss).
betweenss   The between-cluster sum of squares, i.e. totss-tot.withinss.
size   The number of points in each cluster.
iter   The number of (outer) iterations.

We can plot the data points with different colors per cluster and add the barycenters.

```
plot(Scaled.Data$LONGITUDE, Scaled.Data$LATITUDE, col =
res$cluster)
# Add the barycenters / pch=symbol,cex=size and lwd=line width
points(res$centers,col = 1:2,pch=8,cex=2,lwd=2)
# Add the point names with the cluster colors
text(Scaled.Data$LONGITUDE,
Scaled.Data$LATITUDE,row.names(Scaled.Data),col=res$cluster)
```

The percentage of total inertia explained by the clusters is displayed but it is not a component of the clustering result. We have to calculate it.

```
res$betweenss/res$totss
```

In order to select the number of clusters, we have to make vary the number of clusters and plot the R^2 coefficient.

```
R2=vector("numeric",length = 29)
for(k in 2:30)
{
   res=kmeans(Scaled.Data,centers=k,nstart=5)
   R2[k-1]=res$betweenss/res$totss
}
plot(2:30,R2,type="b",lwd=2)
```

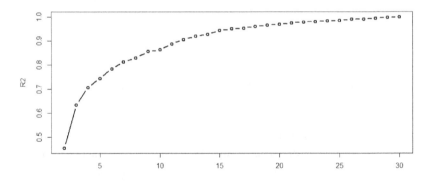

Figure 10.9. *R^2 vs number of clusters*

We note that the last significant gain of information is with three clusters (Figure 10.9).

10.4.1.1. *Agglomerative hierarchical clustering*

For AHC we use two functions. The first one is to build the tree with the clusters merged during the algorithm,

$$\texttt{hclust(d, method = "ward.D2",...)}$$

where `d` is an object with the pair distances between data points and `method` is the cluster dissimilarity criterion.

```
d=dist(Scaled.Data,method="euclidian") # compute the pair
distances
res=hclust(d,method="ward.D2")
plot(res) # plot the dendrogram
plot(res$height) # plot the criterion value during the
iterations
```

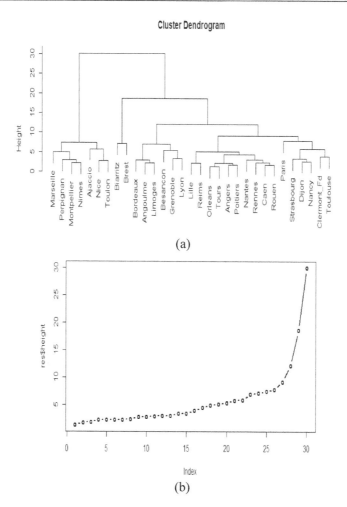

Figure 10.10. *Results of AHC: (a) dendrogram; (b) dissimilarity criterion vs. iterations*

We see that the last significant gain of information is also with three clusters (Figure 10.10). The second function is to build the three clusters,

```
cutree(tree, k = 2,…)
```

where `tree` is the object resulting from `hclust` and k is the number of clusters.

```
c=cutree(res,k=3)
print(c) # c is un vector with the number of the cluster

# plot the dendrogram with the 3 clusters
plot(res)
rect.hclust(res,k=3)

# plot the data points with the cluster color
plot(Scaled.Data$LONGITUDE, Scaled.Data$LATITUDE, col = c)
text(Scaled.Data$LONGITUDE,Scaled.Data$LATITUDE,row.names(Scal
ed.Data),col=c)
# add the point names with the cluster color
```

10.4.1.2. *Clustering and PCA*

There are two ways to use both methods together.

– PCA can help to provide meaning to clusters.

In the previous example, we plot the cities according to their longitude and latitude, but more variables are involved in the clustering algorithm. We can use PCA to represent the data points according to the two (or more) principal axes.

```
res.PCA=PCA(Scaled.Data)
plot(res.PCA$ind$coord[,1],res.PCA$ind$coord[,2], col=c)
text(res.PCA$ind$coord[,1],res.PCA$ind$coord[,2],
row.names(Scaled.Data), col=c)
```

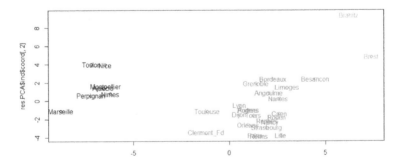

Figure 10.11. *Individual map for Axes 1 and 2 with three different colors for the clusters. For a color version of this figure, see www.iste.co.uk/laffly/torus1.zip*

By using the variable map, we can conclude that the cluster in black is constituted by warm and sunny cities, and the two cities in the green cluster have high rainfall (we can say nothing about the red cluster since it is in the middle).

– PCA can reduce the number of variables involved in the clustering.

Rather than running the algorithm with all variables, we can use the first principal components. We note that the two first components contained 78% of the information of the dataset. We can decrease the initial dimension D=31 to only D=2 for nearly the same result (Figure 10.12).

```
res.PCA$eig[1:10,]
Scaled.Data2=scale(res.PCA$ind$coord[,1:2])
d2=dist(Scaled.Data2)
res2=hclust(d2,method="ward.D2")
plot(res2)
rect.hclust(res2,k=4)
c2=cutree(res2,c=4)
plot(res.PCA$ind$coord[,1],res.PCA$ind$coord[,2], col=c2)
text(res.PCA$ind$coord[,1],res.PCA$ind$coord[,2],
row.names(Scaled.Data), col=c2)
```

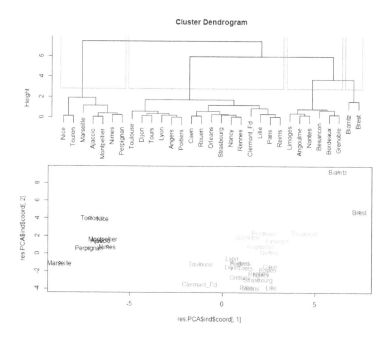

Figure 10.12. *Results for the clustering with the two first components. For a color version of this figure, see www.iste.co.uk/laffly/torus1.zip*

10.4.1.3. *Clustering and MCA*

Another way to make sense of the cluster is to cross them with other categorical variables. Here, we can interpret the clusters thanks to the climate.

```
Dataset=read.table("FrenchCities.csv",
header=T,sep=';',row.names=1)
Dataset=Dataset[-32,]# Remove the Error
# Combine the cluster vector c and CLIMAT variable by column
NewData=cbind(c,Dataset$CLIMAT)
# Transform the result into a dataframe
NewData=as.data.frame(NewData)
names(NewData)=c("CLUSTER","CLIMAT")
# Transform the variables into factor type
NewData$CLIMAT=as.factor(NewData$CLIMAT)
levels(NewData$CLIMAT)=c("CONT","MED","OCEAN","SEMI_OCEAN")
NewData$CLUSTER=as.factor(NewData$CLUSTER)

# Cross the two variables
table(NewData$CLIMAT,NewData$CLUSTER)
res=MCA(NewData)
explor(res)
```

We confirm (Table 10.3 and Figure 10.13) that Cluster 1 is entirely composed of Mediterranean cities and Cluster 2 of ocean cities. Group 2 is a mixture of different climates with the exception of the Mediterranean climate.

	1	2	3
CONT	0	9	0
MED	7	0	0
OCEAN	0	7	2
SEMI_OCEAN	0	6	0

Table 10.3. *Contingency table between CLIMAT and CLUSTER.*
For a color version of this table, see www.iste.co.uk/laffly/torus1.zip

Now, you can use the dataset countries.csv to perform PCA, MCA and clustering!

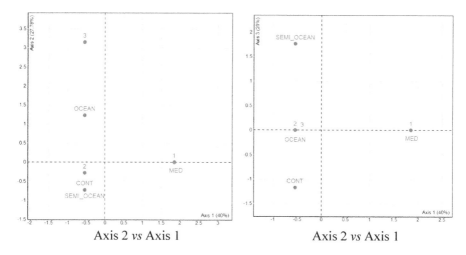

Axis 2 *vs* Axis 1   Axis 2 *vs* Axis 1

Figure 10.13. *MCA with CLIMAT and CLUSTER. For a color version of this figure, see www.iste.co.uk/laffly/torus1.zip*

10.5. References

Braun W.J. and Murdoch D.J.. *A First Course in Statistical Programming with R.* Cambridge University Press, 2007.

Everitt B., Hothorn T. (2011). *An introduction to applied multivariate analysis with R.* Springer.

James G., Witten D., Hastie T., Tibshirani R. (2013). *An Introduction to Statistical Learning with Applications in R.* Springer Texts in Statistics.

Husson F., Lê S, Pagès J. (2011). *Exploratoty multivariate analysis by example using R.* Computer Science and Data Analysis Series. CRC Press, Taylor & Francis Group.

## PART 3

Computer Science

High Performance and Distributed Computing

11.1. High performance computing

The recent developments in numerical modeling for geo-sciences are increasingly offering new approaches to study the complex and nonlinear processing involving Mother Earth, difficult or even impossible to scale down for studying in laboratory experiments. However, the developments of computer capabilities in terms of both computing resources and storage have opened the doors for large-scale parallel computations in Earth Sciences. This is leading to the use of increasing complex models where a greater number of tunable parameters can be taken into account.

High performance computing (HPC) most generally refers to the practice of aggregating computing power in a way that delivers much higher performance than we could get out of a typical desktop computer or workstation in order to solve large problems in science, engineering or business. In this section, we give an overview of the most common processor options used today for HPC.

The architecture of processors has changed dramatically during the last years, and this has a relevant impact not only on the hardware side and specially on the design of the processor itself, but also on the software side and in particular on how applications have to be programmed.

The evolution has been driven initially by the famous *Moore's Law*, an observation made in 1965 by Gordon Moore, co-founder of Intel, stating that the number of transistors double every 1.5 years (green line). This, combined with a

Chapter written by Sebastiano Fabio SCHIFANO, Eleonora LUPPI, Didin Agustian PERMADI, Thi Kim Oanh NGUYEN, Nhat Ha Chi NGUYEN and Luca TOMASSETTI.

constant shrinking of transistor size, translates in more hardware resources to integrate in a chip. Moreover, according to Dennard's law, as transistors get smaller, their power density stay constant, so that the power use stays in proportion with area, and both voltage and current scale downwards with the length of transistors. This roughly translates to the fact that decreasing the transistor size by a factor, the number of transistors increase by a factor of 2, the clock-speed increases by a factor and the energy used does not change. In summary, the increase in the performance comes from more hardware resources integrated into the chips and a constant increase in the clock frequency. However, Dennard's law is true as long as the leakage current is negligible. But, as the size of transistor becomes smaller and smaller, the leakage current becomes a relevant factor, and the chip can no longer dissipate the heat that accumulates when components operate shoulder-to-shoulder in a constricted area.

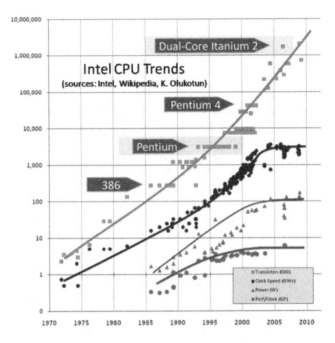

Figure 11.1. *Evolution of processors developed over the last decades. For a color version of this figure, see www.iste.co.uk/laffly/torus1.zip*

This happened around the year 2005, and has created the so-called power-wall limiting the operating clock frequency of chips to approximately 4 GHz. Since the computing performance of a processor is the result of the number of operations per clock cycle, times the frequency of the processor, this limitation seriously harmed the increase in computing performances. At this time, to overcome this limitation, the architecture of processors has been strongly changed introducing two important design changes: multi-core and vectorization. The first changes the architecture of processors from uni-core to multi-core. This means that into a single chip several full CPUs called core are integrated together, increasing the aggregate computing performance delivered. The latter change conversely introduces vector-units, giving to CPUs the capability to operate on vector operands increasing the number of operations performed in a clock cycle.

Recent development trends for multi-core processors are based on an increasing number of independent cores together with wider vector units within each core. Both changes allow us to increase the computing performance delivered by processors and to still scale according to the Moore's law.

High performance computing (HPC) has seen in recent years an increasingly large role played by general purpose graphics processor unit (GP-GPU or GPU). GPU are processors originally designed and specialized to accelerate the creation and manipulation of images to output to a display device. GPUs have been popularized by their inventor, the NVIDIA corporation, that has evolved the architecture of these devices to also include capabilities to support general purpose programming. The hardware architecture of GPUs follows that of CPUs, sharing a common multicore architecture together with wide vector units.

In the next two sections, we analyze the architecture of most common CPUs, and GPUs, and of programming frameworks required to develop codes for these systems.

11.2. Systems based on multi-core CPUs

The typical HPC system for scientific computing today is a large cluster of nodes based on commodity multi-core CPUs and interconnected by a high-speed switched network, such as InfiniBand.

In recent years, multi-core architecture has become the standard approach to develop high performance processors. Several cores are integrated on a single chip device; this has allowed peak performance at node level to scale according to Moore's law.

In many cases, the cores are x86-CPUs, usually including two levels of caches, and a floating-point unit able to execute vector instructions; the vector size increases steadily as newer processor versions are released.

Today, 256-bit and 512-bit vectors have been adopted in the Intel micro-architecture; cores within a device share a large L3-cache and external memory.

Many system vendors provide so-called multi-socket platforms, based on several multi-core CPUs. Typically, two, four or eight sockets can be installed on a motherboard; each socket has its own memory-bank and is connected to the other sockets by dedicated busses. Appropriate protocols allow us to share the global memory space and keep the content of caches coherent. From a programming point of view, these systems operate as symmetric multiprocessors (SMP), which means that they can be programmed as a single processor with Nc cores (Nc equal to the sum of cores of all sockets) sharing the full memory space and controlled by a single instance of the Linux operating system.

Effective performances heavily rely on the ability of programmers, compilers and run-time support to carefully exploit parallelism on all available hardware features, and are a combination of several factors:

$$P = f \times \#cores \times nInstrPerCycle \times nFlopPerInstr$$

where P is the performance, f the clock frequency, #cores the numbers of available cores, nInstrPerCycle the number of instructions executed per clock cycle and nFlopPerInstr the number of operations encoded on a single instruction.

Relevant optimization strategies to exploit performances of these systems are:

– core parallelism: the code should allow all cores to work in parallel exploiting MIMD or SPMD multi-task parallelism; in the first case, the application is decomposed in several sub-tasks and each one is executed by a different core; in the latter case, that can be also combined with the previous one, the data-set is typically partitioned among the cores, each one executing the same task;

– vector programming: each core has to process the data-set of the application using vector instructions and exploiting streaming-parallelism (SIMD). The number of data-items that can be processed by vector instructions depends on the architecture of the CPU; on the latest Sandybridge architecture the vector size is 256-bit, that is up to 8 single-precision or 4 double-precision floating point numbers;

– efficient use of caches: memory hierarchies of commodity systems are based on the concept of cache to minimize over-heads associated with accessing main memories. The application code has to exploit cache-reuse in order to save time in memory access; this may have a serious impact on the organization of the data-layout for the application;

– NUMA control: multi-socket platforms are non-uniform memory access (NUMA) systems; this means that the time to access data in memory is related to the allocation of the threads that perform the memory access; the time is shorter to access data stored onto memory attached to the socket where the thread is running.

11.2.1. *Systems based on GPUs*

GPUs are used as accelerators to upload and boost the execution time of some parts of applications. GPU devices are hosted into standard CPU cabinets and are physically attached to CPU processor through a PCI-e bus or more recently through the NVLINK bus developed by NVIDIA, one of major developers of GPUs.

NVIDIA GPUs are multi-core processors with each core capable of processing several operations in parallel. Core units are called streaming multiprocessors (SM) or extended streaming multiprocessors (SMX) on more recent systems, as they have enhanced capabilities. Each multiprocessor has several compute units called CUDA-cores in NVIDIA jargon. At each clock-cycle, multiprocessors execute multiple warps, with each warp being a group of operations called CUDA-threads processed in single instructions multiple threads (SIMT) fashion. SIMT execution is similar to SIMD but more flexible, and for example, different CUDA-threads of a SIMT group are allowed to take different branches at a performance penalty. At variance with CPU threads, context switches among active CUDA-threads are very fast, as these architectures maintain many thread states. Typically, one CUDA-thread processes one element of the data-set of the application. This helps exploit available parallelism of the algorithm, and hides latencies by switching between threads waiting for data coming from memory and threads ready to run. This structure has remained stable across all generations.

Table 11.1 summarizes only a few relevant parameters for several generations of NVIDIA GPUs.

	C2050 / C2070	K20X	K40	K80		P100	V100
GPU	GF100	GK110	GK110B	GK210	× 2	P100	V100
Number of SMs	16	14	15	13	× 2	56	80
Number of CUDA-cores	448	2688	2880	2496	× 2	3584	5120
Base clock frequency (MHz)	1.15	735	745	562		1328	1370
Base DP performance (Gflops)	515	1310	1430	935	× 2	4755	7000
Boosted clock frequency (MHz)	–	–	875	875		1480	1455
Boosted DP performance(Gflops)	–	–	1660	1455	× 2	5300	7500
Total available memory (GB)	3 / 6	6	12	12	× 2	16	16
Memory bus width (bit)	384	384	384	384	× 2	4096	4096
Peak mem. BW (ECC-off) (GB/s)	144	250	288	240	× 2	732	900
Max Power (Watt)	215	235	235	300		300	300

Table 11.1. *Some relevant parameters for several generations of NVIDIA GPUs*

The C2050 and C2070 boards based on the Fermi architecture differ in the amount of available global memory. The K20, K40 and K80 are boards based on Kepler processors. Several enhancements are available in the more recent Kepler and

Pascal architecture that have 256 32-bit registers addressable by each CUDA-thread (a 4X increase over Fermi) and each SMX has 65536 registers (a 2X increase). Kepler and Pascal GPUs are also able to increase their clock frequency beyond the nominal value (this is usually referred to as GPUBoost), if power and thermal constraints allow us to do so. The K40 processor has more global memory than the K20 and slightly improves memory bandwidth and floating-point throughput, meanwhile, the K80 has two enhanced Kepler GPUs with more registers and shared memory than K20/K40 and extended GPUBoost features. Up to now the only board based on the Pascal processor is the P100. The Tesla C2050 system has a peak performance of $\approx$ 1 Tflops in single-precision (SP), and $\approx$ 500 Gflops in double-precision (DP); on the Kepler K20 and K40, the peak SP (DP) performance is $\approx$ 5 Tflops ($\approx$ 1.5 Tflops), while on the K80 the aggregate SP (DP) performance of the two GPUs is $\approx$ 5.6 Tflops ($\approx$ 1.9 Tflops). The P100 delivers up to $\approx$ 10.5 Tflops (SP) and $\approx$ 5.3 (DP). Fast access to memory is strongly correlated with performance: peak bandwidth is 144 GB/s for the C2050 and C2070 processors, and 250 and 288 GB/s respectively for the K20X and the K40; on the K80, the aggregate peak is 480 GB/s, increased to 732 GB/s on the P100. The memory system has an error detection and correction system (ECC) to increase reliability when running large codes. This feature is usually always on, even though it slightly reduces available memory and bandwidth (e.g. on the Tesla C2050 available memory is reduced by $\approx$ 12 % and we measure a typical bandwidth cost $\approx$ 20 − 25%). The next generation NVIDIA GPU architecture Volta further increases the computing throughput to 7.5 Tflops DP, and the memory bandwidth to 900 GB/s, a factor 1.4X and 1.2X w.r.t. the Pascal architecture.

On GPUs, the native programming model is strongly based on data-parallel models, with one thread typically processing one element of the application data domain. The native language for NVIDIA GPUs is CUDA-C, together with OpenCL. Both languages have a very similar programming model, but use a slightly different terminology. For instance, on OpenCL the CUDA-thread is called work-item, the CUDA-block work-group, and the CUDA-kernel is a device program. A CUDA-C or OpenCL program consists of one or more functions that run either on the host, a standard CPU, or on a GPU. Functions that exhibits no (or limited) parallelism run on the host, while those exhibiting a large degree of data parallelism can go onto the GPU. The program is a modified C (or C++, Fortran) program including keyword extensions defining data parallel functions, called kernels or device programs. Kernel functions typically translate into a large number of threads, i.e. a large number of independent operations processing independent data items. Threads are grouped into blocks which in turn form the execution grid. The grid can be configured as a one-, two- or three-dimensional array of blocks. Each block is itself a one-, two- or three-dimensional array of threads, running on the same SM, and sharing data on a fast shared memory. When all threads complete their execution, the corresponding grid terminates. Since threads run in parallel with host CPU threads, it is possible to overlap in time processing on the host and on the accelerator.

```
#pragma acc data copyin(x), copy(y) {
  #pragma acc kernels present(x) present(y) async(1)
  #pragma acc loop vector(256)
  for (int i = 0; i < N; ++i)
    y[i] = a*x[i] + y[i];

  #pragma wait(1);
}
```

Box 11.1. *For a color version of this figure, see www.iste.co.uk/laffly/torus1.zip*

New programming approaches are now emerging, mainly based on directives, moving the coding abstraction layer at an higher level. These approaches should make code development easier on heterogeneous computing systems (OpenACC, 2016), simplifying the porting of existing codes on different architectures. OpenACC is one of such programming models, increasingly used by several scientific communities. OpenACC is based on pragma directives that help the compiler to identify those parts of the code that can be implemented as parallel functions and offloaded on the accelerator or divided among CPU cores. The actual construction of the parallel code is left to the compiler making, at least in principle, the same code portable without modifications across different architectures and possibly offering more opportunities for performance portability.

The listing below is a sample of OpenACC code computing a saxpy function on vectors x and y. The pragma clauses control data transfers between host and accelerator, and identify the code regions to be run on the accelerator.

The listing above shows an example of the saxpy operation of the Basic Linear Algebra Subprogram (BLAS) set coded in OpenACC. The pragma acc kernels clause identifies the code fragment running on the accelerator, while pragma acc loop specifies that the iterations of the for-loop should execute in parallel. The openACC standard defines many such directives, allowing a fine tuning of applications. As an example, the number of threads launched by each device function and their grouping can be tuned by the vector, worker and gang directives, in a similar fashion as setting the number of work-items and work-groups in CUDA. Data transfers between host and device memories are automatically generated, and occur on entering and exiting the annotated code regions. Specific data directives help to optimize data transfers, for example overlapping transfers and computation. For example, in listing 1, the clause copyin(ptr) copies the array pointed by ptr from host onto accelerator memory before entering the following code region; copy (ptr) copies it back to the host memory after leaving the code region. An asynchronous directive async instructs the compiler to generate asynchronous data transfers or device function executions; a corresponding clause (i.e. #pragma wait (queue)) awaits for completion. OpenACC is similar to the OpenMP (Open Multi-Processing) framework widely used to manage parallel codes on multi-core CPUs (Wienke *et al.* 2014); both frameworks are directive based, but OpenACC targets accelerators in general, while at this stage OpenMP targets mainly multi-core CPUs; the OpenMP4 standard has introduced directives to manage also accelerators, but currently, compiler support is still limited. Regular C/C++ or Fortran code, already developed and tested on traditional CPU architectures, can be annotated with OpenACC pragma directives (e.g. parallel or kernels clauses) to instruct the compiler to transform loop iterations into distinct threads, belonging to one or more functions to run on an accelerator. With the above-mentioned features, OpenACC is particularly well-suited for developing scientific HPC codes for several reasons: it is highly hardware agnostic, allowing us to target several architectures, GPUs and CPUs, allowing us to develop and maintain one single code version; the programming overhead to offload code regions to accelerators is limited to few pragma lines, in contrast to CUDA and, in particular OpenCL, verbosity; and the code annotated with OpenACC pragmas can still be compiled and run as plain C code, ignoring pragma directives.

Introduction to Distributed Computing

12.1. Introduction

When we face a problem due to lack of computing power (a calculation that requires more computing power than a single computer can provide), the "simple" solution is to link various computer resources. The network of computers is then used as a single, unique resource.

This solution is called distributed computing, and this term refers to just about any system where many computers solve a problem together.

Distributed computing systems are currently very common, but often they are not commonly well understood.

In this chapter, we provide a brief overview of distributed systems and their evolutions.

12.1.1. *A brief history*

Since 1945, at the very beginning of computer era, for about 35–40 years, computers were very large and very expensive. In addition, these computers did not communicate with each other.

Ethernet, the local area networking technology, was invented in the late 1960s [SPU 09]. ARPAnet (Advanced Research Projects Agency Network), the network predecessor of the Internet, was invented in the early 1970s.

Chapter written by Eleonora LUPPI.

Distributed evolved from the computational needs of "big science". At the beginning, the Internet was developed to cope with the need for a communication between large scientific computing centers. These communication links led to data and information sharing between these centers, and eventually to provide access to them for additional users. The standardization of the protocols used to communicate between different administrative domains was a consequence of this demand.

A proto-distributed systems date back to the early 1970s with the Distributed Computing System (DCS) [FAR 70] project at the University of California, Irvine. It was the first example of a set of computers connected to a network sharing computational capabilities.

Thanks to these communication technologies and to the invention of the first commercial personal computer [FAG 18], the era of distributed computing started.

The first Internet-based distributed computing project was started in 1988 by the DEC System Research Center [RIF 88].

Another milestone in information technology evolution was cluster computing. In 1994, two NASA scientists put some PCs together and made them to communicate to form a parallel, virtual supercomputer [STE 95]. The name of the first cluster, Beowulf, comes from an epic Nordic hero who killed a dragon. The "dragon" was the expensive mainframe. The success was beyond their imagination. All commercial companies now offer clusters of PCs as a standard solution.

During the last decade of 20th Century, cluster and distributed computing architecture increasingly became dominant. Since then, the development of new technologies and new network services has been very fast. Local-area networks (LANs) allow thousands of machines within a building or campus to be connected in such a way that data can be transferred at rates of billions of bits per second (Gbps). Wide-area networks (WANs) allow hundreds of millions of machines all over the world to be connected at speeds up to hundreds of millions of bits per second, and sometimes even faster.

In parallel to the development of increasingly powerful and networked machines, massively parallel computer architectures started rising and message passing interface (MPI) and other communication protocols started developing.

As a result of these developments, now it is possible to put together a computing system composed of many networked computers. These computers are generally geographically dispersed and, for this reason, they are called a distributed system. A distributed system may be composed of a few devices, as well as by millions of computers [VAN 16].

12.1.2. *Design requirements*

A loose definition is given by Van Steen and Tanenbaum [VAN 16]:

"A distributed system is a collection of autonomous computing elements that appears to its users as a single coherent system."

This definition underlines the two main characteristics of distributed systems. First, a distributed system is a collection of independent computing elements, generally called nodes. Second, users use it and "see" it as a single system.

More in details, we can distinguish two different families of distributed systems: network operating systems and *true* distributed systems.

Network operating systems consists of loosely coupled software running on loosely coupled hardware. As examples we can consider a network of workstations connected by LAN in which each machine has a high degree of autonomy or a files server where according to the client–server model, clients mount directories on file servers (NFS). This type of distributed systems has a few system-wide requirements: format and meaning of all the messages exchanged have to follow a standard.

For *true distributed systems* we mean having tightly coupled software running on loosely coupled hardware. It may provide a single-system image, and it needs a single, global, inter-process communication mechanism, process management, file system and the same system call interface everywhere. A single-system view is often too much difficult to reach, so we prefer the loose, weaker, definition of a distributed system, that it *appears to be coherent*. A system is coherent if it matches the expectations of the users. This goal is achieved if the whole collection of nodes behaves the same, regardless where, how and when the user interacts with the system.

To reach such a challenging result any distributed system model has to face the main design goals: transparency, reliability, flexibility, performance and scalability.

– *Transparency* is an essential design goal. A collection of computers must appear as a single computer. It requires that the end user does not have to know exactly on which computer a process is executing or if a part of a task has been entrusted to another process running on another node, perhaps far from the original process. Likewise, the end user does not need to know where data is stored, and neither if the system may be replicating data to improve performance. The users should be unaware of where the services are located and also the transferring from a local machine to a remote one should also be transparent. The main kinds of transparencies that a system must have to become truly transparent are:

- access transparency: hide differences in data representation and how a resource is accessed. Users are unaware of the distribution of files on specific servers or physical location; resources simply have to be available and accessible when required;

- location transparency: hide where a resource is located. User does not need to know the location of a resource in the system. The system presents a uniform namespace where files identifiers remain the same, even when they are relocated. A location transparent name should contain no information about the physical location;

- migration transparency: hide that a resource may move to another location. Information and processes can be moved from one physical server to another within the system, without the user's knowledge. This is often done for load balancing or to hide failures;

- replication transparency: hide that a resource may be replicated. Same data often is stored in the system in more than one copy (*replica*), for performances and security reason. Users do not need to know which replica he is using, how many copies are available and where they are;

- performance transparency: the system can be reconfigured to optimize the overall system performance, depending on load and availability of resources, but this process should be transparent to the user.

– *Reliability* of a distributed system is an important design parameter that can be described in terms of the reliability of computing elements and communication links, and also of the *redundancy* of processes and data files [WAS 13]. Distributed systems should be more reliable than single systems. In fact, if we consider a single machine having 95% of probability of being up, five machines will have a probability of being up of more than 99.999% (1-0.05^5, precisely). This improves system availability, namely, the fraction of time the system is usable. This goal is reachable with redundancy of resources, including communication links. In a redundant system maintaining consistency is very important, but impossible at an ideal level, so it is necessary to define the level of inconsistency compatible with the desired transparency level. A system consisting of many elements (nodes, links, etc.) can experience many faults and needs to be fault tolerant: this means that masking failures and errors recovering is needed.

– *Flexibility* makes it easier to let the system evolve, increase and match new requirements. There are two main operating system architecture models strictly related to the flexibility of distributed systems. In the first, each machine runs a traditional kernel that provides most services itself. In the second, the kernel should provide as little as possible, and the bulk of the operating system services are made available by user-level servers [VAN 07]. These component-based architectures are intrinsically more flexible than monolithic architectures, and are very attractive for distributed systems [GIE 91].

– Without gain on *performance*, there is no reason to deal with the tricky distributed systems. By using the combined processing power and storage capacity of many nodes, performance levels can be reached that are beyond the range of centralized machines. However, in a distributed system, we have to deal with *latency* (delay) in communications and data exchange between remote nodes. Another source of performance loss is the mechanisms implemented to make the system fault tolerant. More than for a single operating system, in the case of distributed systems performance is a particularly interesting challenge, since it directly conflicts with some other requirements like transparency, scalability (and security), which can easily be detrimental to performance [VAN 07].

– *Scalability* is one of the most important design requirements (and goals) for distributed systems. A distributed system can scale in three different dimensions: [NEU 94]:

- *Size*. A system can be increased adding more users and resources (nodes, links, etc.) to the system without any noticeable loss of performance.

- *Geography*. Users and resources may be spread over a very wide geographical area. A large distance generally results in large *latency* and potential for communication failures, but the fact that communication delays may be significant is hardly noticed.

- *Administrative organizations*. The number of organizations that exert administrative control over the system can grow. An administratively scalable system is still easily managed, even though it spans many independent administrative organizations.

Scalability problems have to be solved, maintaining transparency, hiding communication latency (using, for example, asynchronous communications – but not always), applying replication techniques (taking care of consistency, because with multiple copies of a resource, modifying one copy makes that copy different from the others) and increasing *distribution and decentralization* for system components, tables and *algorithms*. Any form of centralization can cause performance bottlenecks.

In a true distributed system, no algorithms has complete information about the system state, machines take decisions on local information, failure of one machine does not affect the algorithm and there is no strict assumption about a global clock.

Distributed systems are in essence different from traditional software because their components are dispersed across a large area network. It is essential taking this dispersion into account to design and implement an efficient distributed system.

12.1.3. Models

There are many types of distributed computing systems, a few of which are discussed below.

From the definition of distributed system, it follows that it implies both a hardware (independent computers are part of the system) and a software aspect (it can carry out a job and provide a service). From a hardware point of view, distributed systems are based on multi-computers, separate computing nodes connected over a network. The software architecture can be based on distributed operating systems or middleware (Figure 12.1).

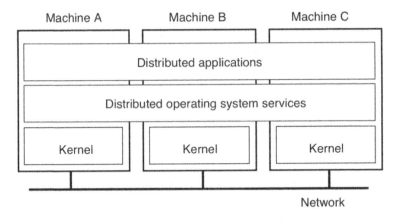

Figure 12.1. *Schematic view of a system based on a distributed operating system [VAN 07]*

A distributed operating system (DOS) is designed to provide distributed services and integrates distributed services into its architecture. An ideal DOS provides a single-system image, and users do not perceive that they are working on a distributed system. DOS generally assume a homogeneous multicomputer. Due to intrinsic limitation of network capability, they are more suited to LAN environments than to wide-area network environments.

Middleware primary aim is to create system-independent interfaces for distributed applications, and consists of a new *layer* of services placed between the regular network operative system and the user applications. Services provided by middleware are designed to simplify the implementation of distributed applications and to hide the heterogeneous hardware and software architectures of the underlying systems.

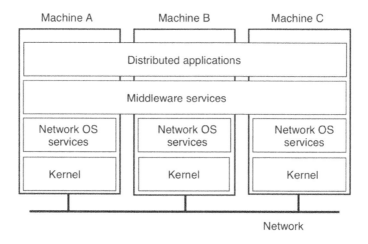

Figure 12.2. *Schematic view of a system based on a middleware [VAN 07]*

To reach this goal, communication mechanisms different from basic message passing are used, interfaces are independent of programming language, network protocol, and operating system of the single node, and specific middleware services are standardized [VAN 07].

In the family of distributed computing systems, we can make a distinction between two subgroups, cluster computing and grid (and cloud) computing.

In cluster computing, the hardware consists of a collection of similar workstations or PCs, tightly connected by means of a high-speed local-area network; moreover, each node runs the same operating system. Clusters can have different sizes. One of the main advantages of this solution is scalability: a cluster can be expanded simply by adding new PCs. The possible bottleneck is nodes communication that can be a challenge with large numbers of computers. Anyway, clusters of thousands of computers are common nowadays. The collection of computing nodes is usually controlled by a master node. The master runs the middleware necessary for the execution of programs and management of the cluster, while the compute nodes are equipped with a standard operating system extended with the minimum middleware functions permitting to communicate and execute master requests. Other cluster implementations try to give a single-system image of the cluster, appearing to be a single computer. This high level of transparency can be obtained by allowing processes to dynamically and preemptively migrate between the computer components of the cluster [AMA 04]. Nowadays, many cluster computers are more hybrid solutions in which the middleware is functionally partitioned across different nodes. Computing nodes with dedicated, lightweight operating systems can give better performance for compute-intensive applications, and other specially configured nodes can optimize management of important middleware service like storage, resource access and job management.

Cluster computing is typically used for parallel programming in which a compute intensive program is executed in parallel on multiple machines.

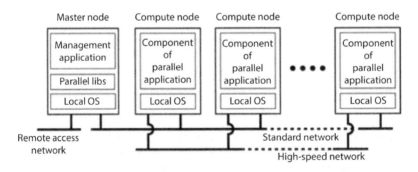

Figure 12.3. *A schematic view of Beowulf cluster architecture [VAN 16]*

The case of grid computing is more complex. This subgroup consists of distributed systems composed of a combination of computer systems, where each system may have different hardware, software and network technology and may be part of different administrative domains. Its main characteristic is its heterogeneity.

A key point in a grid computing system is that resources from different organizations are put together so that users of different institutions can collaborate and share their resources. A more detailed description of grid computing architecture is given in the next section.

Cloud computing can be seen as the logical step from grid computing for user communities that need compute-intensive applications, but do not have huge computing resources and organized technical and administrative infrastructures, as the *big science* collaborations have. Cloud computing provides the facilities to dynamically construct an infrastructure and compose, from offered services, what is needed for compute-intensive applications, simply outsourcing resources. A detailed description of cloud computing architecture is provided in the next chapter.

12.1.4. *Grid computing*

Grid computing is a distributed computing model aiming to provide a high-throughput computing system, consisting of many computers communicating over a wide area network, able to distribute jobs execution across a virtual parallel infrastructure. Grids use these resources to solve large-scale computation problems on large data sets, by breaking them down into many smaller ones. It also provides the ability to perform many more computations at once by modeling a parallel division of work between processes.

12.1.4.1. *Origins*

The computational grid was proposed by Ian Foster and Carl Kesselman at the end of last century [FOS 98]. The word "grid" was used in analogy to the electric power grid, which provides widespread access to the electrical power. The aim was to provide a widespread access to computational resources. In comparison with Word Wide Web, computing grid systems have to offer access not only to information, but also to computational power and storage space.

This means that grid middleware has to incorporate not just CPUs management, but also storage management, security provisioning, data movement, monitoring and a tool for developing additional services based on the same infrastructure.

There are many definitions of Grid computing. In 2002, Ian Foster [FOS 02] defined that the Grid system with a simple checklist according to the grid is a system that:

– coordinates resources that are not subject to a centralized control;

– uses standard, open, general purpose protocols and interfaces;

– delivers non-trivial qualities of service.

Taking into account these criteria, this definition eliminates computing systems (such as clusters and farms), single-purpose systems (such as SETI@home [SUL 96]) and peer-to-peer systems and any system that rely on cycle scavenging from individual processors.

Grid could, in principle, have access to parallel computers, clusters and farms, and would choose the appropriate resource for a given calculation. CERN, one of the largest institutions using the Grid technology, talks of the Grid as *a service for sharing computer power and data storage capacity over the Internet* [GRI 19]. Grid computing focuses on large-scale sharing, which goes beyond institutional boundaries.

Access to grid computing systems is realized using *virtual organizations* [FOS 01]. Users belonging to the same virtual organization have access rights to the resources that are provided to that organization. Typically, resources consist of compute servers, supercomputers, cluster systems, storage facilities and databases.

Given its characteristics, many efforts for developing grid computing concern providing access to resources from different administrative domains to users and applications that belong to a specific virtual organization.

12.1.4.2. *Grid architecture*

The grid computing system architecture consists of four layers.

The lowest *fabric* (or *network*) layer provides interfaces to local resources at a specific site, to allow sharing of resources within a virtual organization.

The next layer is *resources and connectivity* layer. Connectivity layer provides communication protocols for managing grid-specific transactions between computers and other resources of the grid. This includes communication protocols needed to move data between resources, or to access a resource from a remote site, and authentication and security protocols to authenticate users and resources. It is important to note that, in grid environment, not only users but also resources and processes are authenticated. Giving access rights to programs is a specific function that needs to be implemented in connectivity layer.

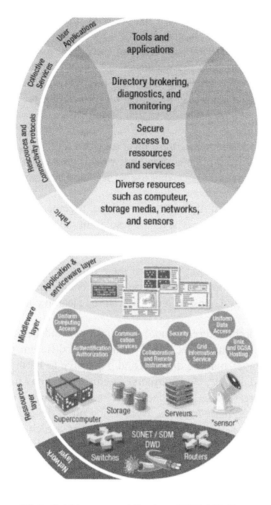

Figure 12.4. *Grid layers architecture [GRI 19]. For a color version of this figure, see www.iste.co.uk/laffly/torus1.zip*

At the resource layer level, management of a single resource is provided, using the functions made available by the connectivity layer and calling directly the interfaces made available by the fabric layer. The resource layer is responsible for access control to local resources, and relies on the authentication performed at connectivity layer.

The next level in the architecture hierarchy is the *collective* layer. It provides management protocols for managing the access to multiple resources and information protocols offering services for resource discovery, allocation and scheduling of tasks onto multiple resources, data replication and so on. While the connectivity and resource layer consists of a relatively small number of standard protocols, the collective layer may provide a lot of different protocols corresponding to the many services it may offer to a virtual organization.

On top of the stack, the *application* layer includes all the applications users want to execute within a virtual organization and which make use of the grid computing environment. This is the only layer that users "see" and have to deal with.

Sometimes, the connectivity and resource layer together with the collective layer are called the grid *middleware* layer. These joint layers provide access to and management of resources that are spread over multiple sites.

Scientists looking for a way to share their (often expensive) equipment have found the solution in computational grid. Grid computing is very attractive to geographically distributed non-profit collaborative research communities.

Despite the architecture model definition, independent grid system developments, in past years, have led to a number of different grid infrastructures. These grid technologies may be difficult and expensive to harmonize and integrate. To avoid this "grid babel", an alternative architecture known as the Open Grid Services Architecture (OGSA) has been developed to define Grid standards [FOS 06]. OGSA is trying to harmonize the work going on in developing grid computing as research and academic initiative, with Web services, which industry is pushing in order to provide a common standard for services offered over the World Wide Web.

The recent view is that Grid services could be a sub-class of Web services, still giving access to the sort of computing power that Grids enable.

12.1.4.3. *Evolution*

Grid implementation has been a success.

The Worldwide LHC Computing Grid (WLCG) [WLC 19] has been crucial in the data-analysis challenge of the CERN LHC physics experiments. Thanks to the Grid infrastructure, multiple copies of data can be kept at different sites, ensuring access for all scientists independent of geographical location; there is no single point of failure; computer centers in multiple time zones ease round-the-clock monitoring and the availability of expert support; resources can be distributed across the world, for funding and political reasons.

Users can make job requests from one of the many entry points into the system. A job request can be almost anything (storage, computing power, availability of analysis software, etc.). In response to the request, Grid infrastructure establishes the identity of the user, checks credentials and searches for available sites that can provide the resources requested. Users do not have to worry about where the computing resources are coming from – they can tap into the Grid's computing power and access storage on demand.

In spite of this successful history, there are some limitations on the horizon.

Grid systems are very complicated to build and use, and currently, users are required to have some level of expertise.

It works very well for large scientific collaboration with scientists ready to accept a 'not completely user-friendly' system and minded to develop directly part (sometimes a big part) of the software infrastructure. But grid computing had a very low impact outside the "hard science" research world and is generally only available for not-for-profit activities.

Moreover, while researchers were reflecting on how to organize computational grids that were more user-friendly and easily accessible, organizations in charge of managing data centers were facing the problem of opening up their resources to external customers.

It is obvious that researchers want to make scientific discoveries, while industry need to make profit, and when it comes to Grid technology, their views are not identical.

In general, commercial distributed computing technologies do not need to face broad scientific concerns, to manage flexible sharing relationships among different organizations and to deal with different hardware and software from different makers.

This led to the idea of utility computing by which a customer could request resources (i.e. computing power, storage) to a data center and be charged on a per-resource basis. Utility computing laid the foundation for what is called cloud computing.

12.2. References

[AMA 04] AMAR L., BARAK A., SHILOH A., "The MOSIX direct file system access method for supporting scalable cluster file systems", *Cluster Computing*, vol. 7, no. 2, pp. 141–150, 2004.

[FAG 18] FAGGIN F., "How we made the microprocessor", *Nature Electronics*, vol. 1, no. 88, 2018.

[FAR 70] FARBER D. and LARSON K., The Architecture of a Distributed Computer System – An Informal Description, Technical report no. 11, University of California, Irvine, 1970.

[FOS 98] FOSTER I. and KESSELMAN C., *The Grid: Blueprint for a New Computing Infrastructure*, Morgan Kaufman Publishers Inc., San Francisco, CA, 1998.

[FOS 01] FOSTER I., KESSELMAN C., TUECKE S., "The anatomy of the grid, enabling scalable virtual organizations", *International Journal of High Performance Computing Applications*, vol. 15, no. 3, pp. 200–222, 2001.

[FOS 02] FOSTER I., "What is the Grid? A three point checklist", *GRID today*, vol. 1, 2002.

[FOS 06] FOSTER I., KISHIMOTO H., SAVVA A., "The open grid services architecture, version 105", *GGF Informational Document*, GFD-I.080, 2006.

[GIE 91] GIEN M., "Next generation operating systems architecture", in KARSHMER A., NEHMER J. (eds), *Operating Systems of the 90s and Beyond: Lecture Notes in Computer Science*, vol. 563, Springer, 1991.

[GRI 19] GRIDCAFE, "The Grid Café – What is grid?", http://gridcafe.web.cern.ch/gridcafe, 2019.

[NEU 94] NEUMAN B., "Scale in distributed systems", in CASAVANT T., SINGHAL M. (eds), *Readings in Distributed Computer Systems*, IEEE Computer Society Press, Los Alamitos, 1994.

[RIF 88] RIFKIN G. and HARRAR G., *The Ultimate Entrepreneur: The Story of Ken Olsen and Digital Equipment Corporation*, McGraw-Hill, 1988.

[SPU 09] SPURGEON C.E., *Ethernet: The Definitive Guide*, O'Reilly Media Inc., 2009.

[STE 95] STERLING T., BECKER D.J. SAVARESE D. *et al.*, "Beowulf: A parallel workstation for scientific computation", *Proceedings of the 24th International Conference on Parallel Processing*, 1995.

[SUL 96] SULLIVAN III W.T., WERTHIMER D., BOWYER S. *et al.*, "A new major SETI project based on Project Serendip data and 100,000 personal computers", *Proceedings of the 5th International Conference on Bioastronomy*, IAU Colloquium no. 161, Capri, 1996.

[VAN 07] VAN STEEN M. and TANENBAUM A.S., *Distributed Systems: Principles and Paradigms*, Pearson Prentice Hall, Upper Saddle River, 2007.

[VAN 16] VAN STEEN M. and TANENBAUM A.S., "A brief introduction to distributed systems", *Computing*, vol. 98, no. 10, pp. 967–1009, 2016.

[WAS 13] WASEEM A. and YOUNG W.V., "A survey on reliability in distributed systems", *Journal of Computer and System Sciences*, vol. 79, no. 8, pp. 1243–1255, 2013.

[WLC 19] WLCG, "Welcome to the Worldwide LHC Computing Grid". Available at: https://wlcg.web.cern.ch/, 2019.

13

Towards Cloud Computing

13.1. Introduction

This chapter is a general presentation of cloud computing through its architecture and service offering. It deals with some basic cloud computing taxonomy and concepts to demonstrate how traditional IT usages are transformed.

13.1.1. *Generalities*

As defined in [MEL 11] by the US National Institute for Standards and Technology (NIST), "Cloud computing is a model for enabling ubiquitous, convenient, on-demand network access to a shared pool of configurable computing resources (e.g. networks, servers, storage, applications and services) that can be rapidly provisioned and released with minimal management effort or service provider interaction". It is an outsourced shared-computing model where resources are virtualized, distributed and pooled among external data centers as services, accessible by users through the Internet [VEN 12].

Its first introduction comes from *Amazon.com*, in the early 2000s. The company had servers suited to managing huge commercial activity during December and the Christmas period. For the rest of the year, they had a lot of machines available, and therefore decided to start business-renting services and servers for short-time usage: Amazon Web Services (AWS) and Elastic Cloud Compute (EC2). Other companies like Google also went into this economic model, providing storage capabilities, application development and hosting platform and online applications (Google App Engine [GOO 19a], Google Cloud Platform [GCP 19], Google Apps [GOO 19b], etc.). In early 2008, NASAs OpenNebula became the first open-source software for

Chapter written by Peio LOUBIÈRE and Luca TOMASSETTI.

deploying private and hybrid clouds, and for the federation of clouds [ROC 09]. In 2010, Rackspace Hosting and NASA jointly launched an open-source cloud-software initiative known as OpenStack. The OpenStack [OPE 19b] project intended to help organizations offering cloud-computing services, running on standard hardware. As an open-source offering and along with other open-source solutions such as CloudStack [CLO 19], Ganeti [GAN 19] and OpenNebula [OPE 19a], it has attracted attention from several key communities [KOS 13].

Now, a huge ecosystem of solutions provides, through the Internet, services to rent and use IT components from hardware to software.

13.1.2. *Benefits and drawbacks*

The main benefit of adopting a cloud computing solution is investment savings; such an outsourcing reduces the cost of investing in the infrastructure, its maintenance, security, software licenses, etc. Initial costs are reduced, pricing is pay-as-you-go, and therefore it is easier for a company to start a business or to explore a new technology. Furthermore it is easier for a university to share knowledge, conduct some heavy computation, share tools or programs and use eLearning.

There are some obstacles for cloud adoption: the legal aspect of where data is stored, how it will be used and its security. Providers respect security and data protection norms (such as ISO27001, ISO27018) and offer their own expertise in security processes. They also put quality of service and availability as basic contract clauses.

Another drawback of diving into a cloud solution is trust in solution stability and then the reversibility, compatibility and interoperability with other solutions. This can be a critical point; the customer does not manage where their data/services are hosted. The recent European Union General Data Protection Regulation (GDPR) [UNI 16], to ensure the control by users of their data, is balanced by the US government Clarifying Lawful Overseas Use of Data Act (CLOUD Act) [H.R 18], which can force US companies to provide requested data wherever it is stored.

13.2. Service model

This section presents three base-levels of IT outsourcing. On-demand services, "aaS" (as a Service), are remote consumables hosted by a cloud provider, accessible by a client through the Internet, according to an on-usage billing model (pay-as-you-go) and submitted to Service-Level Agreements (SLA) and Quality of Service (QoS) contracts. Figure 13.1 describes the level of outsourcing according to the service model.

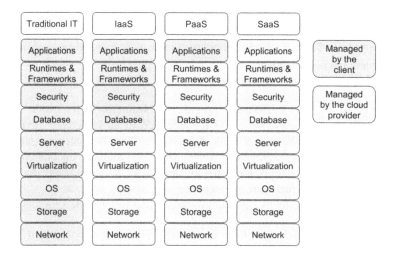

Figure 13.1. *Client/Provider repartition according to aaS models. For a color version of this figure, see www.iste.co.uk/laffly/torus1.zip*

13.2.1. *Software as a Service*

Software as a Service (SaaS) provides clients with the ability to use software applications remotely via an Internet web browser. Software as a Service is also referred to as "software on demand".

Clients can access SaaS applications from anywhere via the web because service providers host applications and their associated data at their location. The primary benefit of SaaS is a lower cost of use, since subscriber fees require a much smaller investment than that typically encountered under the traditional model of software delivery. Licensing fees, installation costs, maintenance fees and support fees, that are routinely associated with the traditional model of software delivery, can be virtually eliminated by subscribing to the SaaS model of software delivery.

In this delivery model, users have access to Service Provider Applications that execute on the cloud; applications are accessed via thin client interface such as a web browser or smartphone app; there is no control over the underlying cloud infrastructure and users have minimal control over application settings.

Examples of SaaS include Gmail (and equivalent email applications from other providers such as Yahoo! Mail, Hotmail, etc.), Google Docs, DropBox, Facebook, Evernote, etc.

13.2.2. *Platform as a Service*

Software as a Service (SaaS) provides clients with the ability to develop and publish customized applications in a hosted environment via the web. It represents a new model for software development that is rapidly increasing in its popularity.

Platform as a Service (PaaS) provides a framework for agile software development, testing, deployment and maintenance in an integrated environment. Like SaaS, the primary benefit of PaaS is a lower cost of use, since subscriber fees require a much smaller investment than what is typically encountered when implementing traditional tools for software development, testing and deployment. PaaS providers handle platform maintenance and system upgrades, resulting in a more efficient and cost-effective solution for enterprise software development.

In this delivery model users have access to a virtual development environment where they can develop and deploy applications for the cloud; there is no control over the underlying cloud infrastructure; users have complete control over the deployed application in terms of provisioning and access, for example.

Examples of PaaS include Google App Engine, Microsoft Azure, etc.

13.2.3. *Infrastructure as a Service*

Infrastructure as a Service (IaaS) allows clients to use IT hardware remotely and resources on a "pay-as-you-go" basis. It is also referred to as Hardware as a Service (HaaS). Major IaaS players include companies like IBM, Google and Amazon.com. IaaS employs virtualization, a method of creating and managing infrastructure resources in the "cloud". IaaS provides small start-up firms with a major advantage since it allows them to gradually expand their IT infrastructure, without the need for large capital investments in hardware and peripheral systems.

In this delivery model users have access to the virtualization of physical Compute Assets, such as Storage and Processing; there is no control over the underlying cloud infrastructure; users have complete control over the ability to deploy and run software, in terms of operating systems and applications, for example.

Examples of IaaS include AWS, OpenStack, CloudStack, etc.

13.2.4. *And many more: XaaS*

In recent years, many more services have become available in addition to those first three families, through the growth of new technologies around Internet of Things, web of things and industry 4.0 concepts [DUA 15, JUA 16]. They are categorized into small bricks of application development, such as security, billing, storage, network, etc., as well as marketing or business-oriented solutions such as device, decision or printing as a service.

13.3. Deployment model

In the taxonomy of cloud computing, there are three types of cloud infrastructures, according to where the cloud is installed and for whom the services are accessible (see Figure 13.2).

Figure 13.2. *Cloud taxonomy. For a color version of this figure, see www.iste.co.uk/laffly/torus1.zip*

13.3.1. *Public cloud*

Public cloud stands for resources and services provided through the public Internet. The services (from IaaS to SaaS) are replicable and scalable, and the billing model can refer to the bandwidth, CPU usage, a number of queries, of instances, etc.

Companies profit from public cloud as the hosting, management and maintenance of the system (physical and virtual) are devoted to the provider.

13.3.2. *Private cloud*

A private cloud aims to offer the same services as the public cloud, through the Internet or a private network, to a small group of users. According to privacy issues or to optimize an internal IT infrastructure, companies can take benefits from their own infrastructure to provide these kinds of services (with all the maintenance constraints), keeping their data/programs private and exposing them as services, or rent dedicated machines. Companies such as Rackspace or VMWare offer these kinds of services.

13.3.3. *Hybrid cloud*

Hybrid cloud aims to empower a system, an architecture, taking benefits from both public and private clouds. Several use-cases can take profits from such a hybrid architecture, for example:

– it can be used to split and deploy applications according to their business sensitivity. Core applications and sensitive data can be hosted in a private cloud, inside a company, and other services such as analytics, business intelligence, reporting, etc., can be outsourced in a public cloud;

– it can also be used as complementary computational resources. When all internal resources are busy or have to be kept available, additional computation can be sent toward a public cloud.

13.4. Behind the hood, a technological overview

There are many concepts underlying the term "cloud computing". This section introduces the most important ones, such as data centers, virtualization, scalability or service and Web Oriented Architecture (WOA).

13.4.1. *Structure*

A data center is hosted in specific configured rooms or floors, within buildings. Servers are stored in racks. There are different types of server; their requirements differ according to their usage: computation servers (with high computation capabilities: number of cores, large RAM memory) and storage servers (with large and fast hard drive capabilities). Figure 13.3 shows an example of the physical private cloud for the Torus project.

A data center requires efficient:

– power supply and inverters to prevent power outages;

– air-conditioning and cooling systems to manage heat and humidity levels;

– network connectivity for server communication to provide sufficient request flow capabilities;

– security access to rooms, hardware and software (e.g. firewall, Virtual Private Network (VPN), certificates, etc.).

Figure 13.3. *Hardware of Cloud Torus project. For a color version of this figure, see www.iste.co.uk/laffly/torus1.zip*

13.4.2. *Virtualization*

Virtualization is a key concept underlying cloud computing. As defined by Wikipedia, it refers to the creation of a virtual (rather than actual) version of something, including virtual computer hardware platforms, storage devices and computer network resources. It is a layer above a physical server that provides virtual components.

Virtualization models allows us to provide a well-suited Virtual Machine (VM) with the correct software, storage, CPU or RAM capabilities. Virtual machines can be replicated, turned on/off "on the fly" to adapt to computation or service requests or to recover from a server failure.

A virtual machine is hosted, on a server, by a virtual machine hypervisor (e.g. VMWare [VMW 19], KVM [LIN 19], Xen [XEN 19], Microsoft Hyper-V [MIC 19]). The hypervisor is a software running either directly on the hardware, or on a conventional Operating System (OS) called "host OS". Through the hypervisor, resources of a single physical server can be shared with multiple virtual machines running on it (see Figure 13.4).

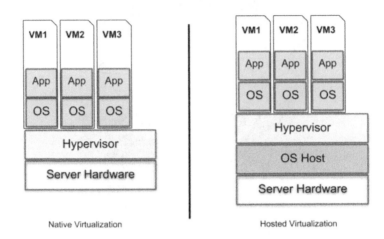

Figure 13.4. *Virtualization types. For a color version of this figure, see www.iste.co.uk/laffly/torus1.zip*

Each VM has its own virtual component specifications (hard drive and RAM size, number of cores, etc.) and hosts an OS and several defined software and libraries.

13.4.3. *Scalability*

Since the economic model of cloud computing is "pay-as-you-go", the costs fit the customer usage of resources. A hosted application must have the agility to grow when intense usage is requested, and shrink when there is less activity.

Scalability is the capacity to manage more data, more requests and more computation, without degrading application performances. There are two kinds of scalability according to workload:

– vertical scalability: add/retrieve computation/storage capabilities of a virtual machine (increase RAM, hard drive storage, number of cores, etc.);

– horizontal scalability: add/retrieve virtual machines to dispatch workload.

Through the possibility of configuring and provisioning virtual machines (with a delay), cloud providers or solutions for private cloud allow applicative architectures to scale according to their activity, and for the client, this maintains the same quality of service.

13.4.4. *Web-Oriented Architecture*

Taking scalability into account, a new way of designing applications has emerged. Introduced in early 2000, Service Oriented Architecture (SOA) is a new design pattern for building IT systems and applications. AOA separates application functionalities into autonomous, stateless, discoverable, composable and reusable units. The goal is to reduce specific development and integration. A system should be composed of different independent functional blocks, the services. Communication between them is assured by an exchange message system based on eXtensible Markup Language (XML) (Simple Object Access Protocol (SOAP)) or through HyperText Transfer Protocol (HTTP) requests (Representational State Transfer (REST)).

Based on SOA model and possibilities offered by the Internet, WOA stands for applications composed using web services, characterized by asynchronous communication. Detailed in Chapter 14, such an architecture has many benefits; one is that each functional part of an application is a single stateless instance. So each part of an application is independently scalable, heterogeneous in terms of language, data format, etc. In addition, an application can integrate external services instead of developing specific ones.

Through virtualization and a web services model, WOA allows applications to scale according to a workload on one of their parts. This aims to build systems that can face massive access or handle big computing workload.

13.5. Conclusion

Cloud computing is redefining application development and usages. It offers applications, whose functional part should be a service, that are able to scale quasi-infinitely. The virtualization and service architecture principles allow applications to fit properly to usage needs such as data space storage, computation nodes, web servers, etc. This implies a new way of building, managing, hosting and securing applications.

We have presented the three cloud models and many types of service offers. According to the usage, the customer audience, the investment budget or the existing infrastructure, there are many solutions available to build and host applications, understanding the costs. Private cloud allows us to profit from an existing infrastructure (that needs to be transformed to be cloud-ready) or renting dedicated machines to keep data and algorithms private for a small number of users. Public cloud allows us to benefit from the huge exposure of an application and hybrid cloud, to build mashup applications, taking the benefits from each type of cloud. Then, a choice of which service level responds to the needs. From infrastructure to application hosting, software usage and data storage, the outsourcing level implies the quantity of work that needs to be done to build a complete application.

This new paradigm drives new evolution in many solutions to build distributed applications, such as:

– distributed file systems to spread data across multiple servers: Google File System (GFS) [GHE 03], Haddop Distributed File System (HDFS) [HAD 19a] and Yet Another Resource Negotiator (YARN) [YAR 19];

– database management systems through new distributed and scalable databases: NoSQL databases (see section 13.7);

– distributed algorithms and frameworks: MapReduce [HAD 19b] and Spark framework (see section 13.6);

– distributed application design, based on asynchronous events: Reactive programming;

– mashup applications that are built using external services (e.g. Maps, Search engines, Weather, etc.) and personal development.

More than an economic benefit, it is a technological challenge to redesign IT systems. Such applications should face the growth of the data to manage and compute, in terms of inner size but also quantity and heterogeneity, or provide a service that could be used by a huge number of users.

13.6. References

[CLO 19] "Cloud Stack". Available at: https://cloudstack.apache.org/, 2019.

[DUA 15] DUAN Y., FU G., ZHOU N. *et al.*, "Everything as a Service (XaaS) on the cloud: Origins, current and future trends", *2015 IEEE 8th International Conference on Cloud Computing*, pp. 621–628, 2015.

[GAN 19] "Ganeti". Available at: http://www.ganeti.org/, 2019.

[GCP 19] "Google Cloud Platform". Available at: https://cloud.google.com/, 2019.

[GHE 03] GHEMAWAT S., GOBIOFF H., LEUNG S.-T., "The Google file system", *Proceedings of the 19th ACM Symposium on Operating Systems Principles*, Bolton Landing, NY, pp. 20–43, 2003.

[GOO 19a] "Google App Engine". Available at: https://cloud.google.com/appengine/, 2019.

[GOO 19b] "Google G Suite". Available at: https://gsuite.google.com/, 2019.

[HAD 19a] "Hadoop Distributed File System". Available at: https://hadoop.apache.org/docs/r1.2.1/hdfs_design.html, 2019.

[HAD 19b] "Hadoop Map reduce". Available at: https://hadoop.apache.org/docs/stable/hadoop-mapreduce-client/hadoop-mapreduce-client-core/MapReduceTutorial.html, 2019.

[H.R 18] "H.R.4943 - CLOUD Act". Available at: https://www.congress.gov/bill/115th-congress/house-bill/4943, 2018.

[JUA 16] JUAN-VERDEJO A., SURAJBALI B., "XaaS Multi-Cloud Marketplace Architecture Enacting the Industry 4.0 Concepts", CAMARINHA-MATOS L. M., FALCÃO A. J., VAFAEI N. *et al.* (eds), *Technological Innovation for Cyber-Physical Systems*, Springer International Publishing, pp. 11–23, 2016.

[KOS 13] KOSTANTOS K. AL., "OPEN-source IaaS fit for purpose: A comparison between OpenNebula and OpenStack.", *International Journal of Electronic Business Management*, vol. 11.3, 2013.

[LIN 19] "Linux KVM". Available at: https://www.linux-kvm.org/page/Main_Page, 2019.

[MEL 11] MELL P., GRANCE T., "The NIST definition of cloud computing", *Special Publication*, vols 800–145, NIST, 2011.

[MIC 19] "Microsoft Hyper-V". Available at: https://docs.microsoft.com/en-us/virtualization/index, 2019.

[OPE 19a] "Open Nebula". Available at: https://opennebula.org/, 2019.

[OPE 19b] "Open Stack". Available at: https://www.openstack.org/, 2019.

[ROC 09] ROCHWERGER B., BREITGAND D., LEVY E. *et al.*, "The Reservoir model and architecture for open federated cloud computing", *IBM Journal of Research and Development*, vol. 53, no. 4, pp. 4:1–4:11, 2009.

[UNI 16] UNION E., "Regulation (EU) 2016/679 of the European Parliament and of the Council of 27 April 2016 on the protection of natural persons with regard to the processing of personal data and on the free movement of such data, and repealing Directive 95/46/EC (General Data Protection Regulation) (Text with EEA relevance)". Available at: https://eur-lex.europa.eu/eli/reg/2016/679/oj, 2016.

[VEN 12] VENTERS W., WHITLEY E.A., "A critical review of cloud computing: Researching desires and realities", *Journal of Information Technology*, vol. 27, no. 3, pp. 179–197, 2012.

[VMW 19] "VMWare". Available at: https://www.vmware.com/, 2019.

[XEN 19] "XEN Project". Available at: https://www.xenproject.org/, 2019.

[YAR 19] "Hadoop YARN". Available at: https://hadoop.apache.org/docs/current/hadoop-yarn/hadoop-yarn-site/YARN.html, 2019.

14

Web-Oriented Architecture – How to design a RESTFull API

14.1. Introduction

Chronologically *SOA* are based on object-oriented architecture and then on component-based architecture. Object-Oriented Architecture were developed to define mechanisms for preventing code repetition. In this paradigm, objects are re-usable components (directly, or with partial modifications), which provide facilities to avoid code repetition. Exploring this paradigm deeply leads us to construct more and more complex applications/notions as Meyer notes in [MEY 97]. To allow the engineer/researcher to reason at a higher level of abstraction, the software community introduced component-based architecture (first introduced in [HÜR 95]).

SOA establishes an architectural model based on *Service Oriented Computing* (*SOC*). In this new paradigm, (web) services are the fundamental units. They are designed to make heterogeneous systems inter-operable and changed the way applications are designed [SHE 14]. Before *SOC*, technologies such as *Common Object Request Broker Architecture* (*CORBA*), and *Remote Procedure Call* (*RPC*) allowed systems to be inter-operable. However, the system was stuck in its own infrastructure, and components were often written in the same language. Web services were designed to overcome these problems, embedding description, invocation and publication in the same place.

Chapter written by Florent DEVIN.

There are two main types of web service: *SOAP* and *REST*. Both of them provide resources such as processing, database, storage and so on, and support inter-operability and loosely coupled architectures. *SOAP* were developed to ensure data transport over protocols such as *HTTP* in 1998, as a successor of XML-RPC, by sending data in *XML* format [SER 14].

REST was first introduced by Fielding in [FIE 00], where he wrote:

"The Representational State Transfer (REST) style is an abstraction of the architectural elements within a distributed hypermedia system. REST ignores the details of component implementation and protocol syntax ... "

This means that *REST* web services are not based on some standards (e.g. *XML* or *Web Services Description Language* (*WSDL*)). Thus, the effective cost of developing *REST* web services is reduced.

WOA is a new architectural style, based on *SOA*. In this new paradigm, each functionality is bound to a service. Each service communicates with other services using a lightweight communication protocol, usually *REST*. An application following this style consists of loosely coupled services [RIC 18]. These services have their own lifecycle from both development and deployment point of view. This new style was introduced to overcome the problem of monolithic applications, and with the emergence of cloud computing, many of those applications are not able to scale.

14.2. Web services

14.2.1. *Introduction*

Distributed applications can be built based on two models: Message passing and Request/Response. The latter can be implemented on a low-level implementation of the former. During the 1980s, *RPC* were used because of their large availability, and also because it fitted well with traditional programming techniques (imperative programming paradigm). In the 1990s, *Object Request Broker* (*ORB*) was proposed and adopted because it followed the up-to-date programming paradigm (object oriented), and also because it provided a way to do real remote call (i.e. on other systems). Some *ORB* implementations are *Distributed Component Object Model protocol* (*DCOM*) and *CORBA*. Those two protocols are good for server-to-server communication, but they are not convenient for client-to-server communication, especially for clients spread over the Internet (particularly for security reasons) [HAL 13]. At the end of the 1990s, business applications started to grow, and this brought two new requirements [DON 13]:

– the applications must work over the Internet, across boundaries (network, organization, etc.);

– security must be considered, to protect organizations and consumers.

These two requirements can be satisfied neither with *RPC* nor with *ORB*. To communicate between business applications, *XML* and *HTTP* were used. With the momentum of IBM, Microsoft and then the *World Wide Web Consortium* (*W3C*), *SOAP* was standardized, and then widely used.

14.2.2. *SOAP web services*

SOAP was inspired by XML-RPC, Dave Winer participated in both specifications, but only *SOAP* is a widely accepted standard. The basic idea behind *SOAP* is to do remote procedure call over the Internet protocols (not only *HTTP*, but all protocols like *Simple Mail Transfer Protocol* (*SMTP*), *File Transfer Protocol* (*FTP*), etc.). A *SOAP* message is an *XML* document containing an envelope, a body, and possibly a header and a fault. The envelope identifies the *XML* document as a *SOAP* message. This is potentially followed by a header, which contains some header about application-specific information. Then the body follows which contains all mandatory information to run the required web services (method and parameters). Finally, a fault part can be found (to manage errors). This serialization allows the *SOAP* message to overcome Internet firewalls.

The *W3C* provides this definition in [HAA 04]:

"A Web service is a software system identified by a URI [RFC 2396], whose public interfaces and bindings are defined and described using XML. Its definition can be discovered by other software systems. These systems may then interact with the Web service in a manner prescribed by its definition, using XML based messages conveyed by Internet protocols."

To fully respect this definition, additional standards were developed: *WSDL* and *Universal Description Discovery and Integration* (*UDDI*) to support (respectively) the description and discover aspects.

14.2.2.1. *WSDL*

A *WSDL* file is a formal interface similar to *Interface Definition Language* (*IDL*) in *CORBA*, specified in *XML* format. It describes the available interfaces (supported operations, and parameters[1] for each one) and also describes the binding of the abstract method to concrete address:

```
<definitions>
  <types>
    data type definitions........
  </types>
  <message>
    definition of the data being communicated....
  </message>
  <portType>
    set of operations......
  </portType>
  <binding>
    protocol and data format specification....
</binding>
  <service>
    name given to the web service
  </service>
  </definitions>
```

Code 14.1. *For a color version of this code, see*
www.iste.co.uk/laffly/torus1.zip

The three first parts are the definition part describing the data types (type), the input/output of the service (message) and a set of operations (portType) which encapsulates messages, and types. The binding part is where the method is located in the system, and service part is how it is exposed to the world outside. A real example can be found in section 14.4.

14.2.2.2. *UDDI*

UDDI is a registry containing published web services. With this directory, services and service providers can be discovered (and described). *UDDI* is also responsible for determining the security and transport protocols. It can store information about the company and services provided by a company as well. With all of this information, users can search in different ways in a *UDDI* registry.

From an *SOA* point of view, *UDDI* is a critical component. However, dynamic search and binding rarely occurs today, for several reasons [CHE 03] including: there is no active effort of building web service standards, and there is no public *UDDI*.

---

1 Name and type.

Figure 14.1 shows how these three standards interact. First the web service provider describes their own service with *WSDL*, and publishes it in *UDDI* (Description part). The web service consumer searches for a specific service on *UDDI*, which reply with the appropriate *Uniform Resource Identifier* (*URI*) of where to find the web service (Discovery part). With that address, the web service consumer asks for the *WSDL* from the web service producer (Specification part). And finally the web service consumer can invoke the web service (Invocation part).

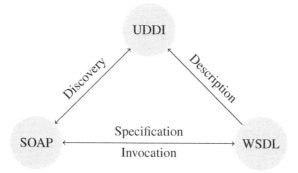

Figure 14.1. *Global architecture of a SOAP System*

14.2.3. *REST web services*

REST web services are web services that provide resources across the Internet like *SOAP* web services. They are less strongly typed than *SOAP*, and rely on the *HTTP* verbs to add some semantic on resources[2] manipulation. It does not need a particular format like *SOAP*, so sending data or parsing response is not required. According to [MUM 13], the message size is 9–10 times smaller, and processing is at least five times quicker. The keystone of the *REST* system is the *Application Programming Interface* (*API*) design. Following the *REST* principle leads to clear identification of exposed resources, operations provided to manipulate these resources, and to be stateless. As *HTTP* is the underlying protocol, every service should fully respect this protocol. This means the system should use the good *HTTP* verbs for the good actions and return a coherent status code associated with the delivered message.

In [RIC 07], Richardson identifies six properties of *REST* services:

– URI: each exposed resource should have a URI, and those should be descriptive;.

---

2 In a such system, resources are everything that can be identified using a *URI*.

– addressability: each resource should have at least one *URI*;

– statelessness: there is no dependence between two requests and the same request always produce the same result;

– representation: the same data could be serve in different format if it needs;

– links: returned document should contain links to other resources;

– uniform interface: *HTTP* provides this uniform interface.

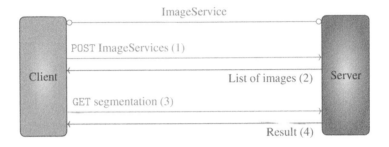

Figure 14.2. *REST level 0. For a color version of this figure, see*
www.iste.co.uk/laffly/torus1.zip

In [FOW 10], Fowler identifies four levels of *REST* usage.

– **Level 0** – The swamp of *Plain Old XML (POX) HTTP* is used as a transport system, without any other consideration. This generally comes from a direct translation of an *RPC* system, where the invocation is the principle. There is only one entry point for the services. *HTTP* verbs are used without meaning, as shown in Figure 14.2. In this figure, the client wants to get a list of images that are available on the server, and then invoke specific processing on a particular one. So they ask for a list of images (1) from the Image Services, the server responds to the client with the list of all available images (2). Then the client selects a particular one and asks the same service to run a segmentation on the selected image (3). The server launches the computation and responds to the client.

– **Level 1 – Resources:** at this level, the client has more than one service to call. *HTTP* verbs are still meaningless. For the same scenario as before, the client calls a specific *URI* to get the list of images (1), and then calls another one to launch process (3), as shown in Figure 14.3. This allows the service to be run on different system, because they do not have to share anything. The server could be split into two parts, one for serving the catalog, and another one for the image's processing. Another consequence is that the client can directly call the wanted process on a specific image, if they know the *URI*.

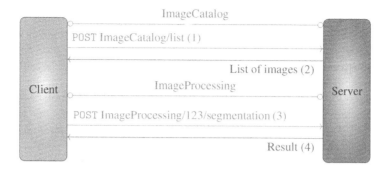

Figure 14.3. *REST level 1. For a color version of this figure, see www.iste.co.uk/laffly/torus1.zip*

– **Level 2 – *HTTP* Verbs:** in the previous scenarios, the client uses *POST* or *GET* equally and it has no impact on the operation. In level 2, verbs have to be used for their specific meaning, and resources should also be used. Moreover, the server has to answer according to the *HTTP* codes. Using the same scenario leads to a slightly different schema, shown in Figure 14.4. It is interesting to note that here, in this context, the verbs are meaningful. For example, *GET* means a safe operation (and idempotent), and does not cause any change on the server. To process, we need to indicate that this operation may alter resources, and that is the role of *POST* (or *PUT*). The more important thing to note however, is that the server responds with a code. Every code has its own meaning. Answering with code allows the client and server to automatically build scenarios depending on the previous request's result.

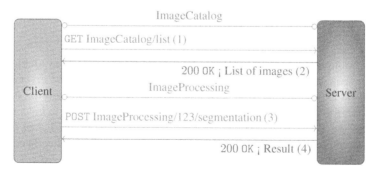

Figure 14.4. *REST level 2. For a color version of this figure, see www.iste.co.uk/laffly/torus1.zip*

– Level 3 – Hypermedia controls: this is the final level of *REST* usage, and can be achieved by adding hypermedia controls to the response from the server. In [FIE 00], this is known as *Hypertext As The Engine Of Application State* (*HATEOAS*). It is important to note that Fielding considers this level as the only "legal" level of *REST*. These controls allow the client to know what to do with a particular resource, allowing the discovery of new services, and the construction of complex workflows. Hypermedia tells the client what to do next, how to manipulate the resources, and the *URI*. The *World Wide Web* (*WWW*) can be considered the first *RESTful* application [JAC 04].

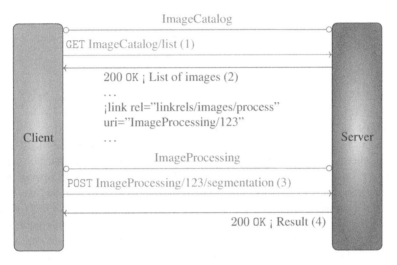

Figure 14.5. *REST level 3. For a color version of this figure, see www.iste.co.uk/laffly/torus1.zip*

In this example, (Figure 14.5), the client wants to have a list of available images, so asks the `ImageCatalog` service for the list of images (1). The server responds with a 200 *HTTP* code meaning that the request has been successfully processed. In this response, the server also sends the list of images, and all possible links the client might use if they want to launch some processing (2). Usually, the list of images is split into several pages, and the client can ask for a specific page, when needed. With this response, the client is able to call the right web service (`ImageProcessing`), using the good *URI* (3).

14.3. Web-Oriented Applications – Microservice applications

Before using microservice applications, web applications were built as monolithic applications. The only way to scale is to replicate the entire application on different servers, bringing its share of complexity (like managing a session on multiple servers, for example). Moreover, if only one component is overloaded, the application has to scale, no matter if the others components are vacant.

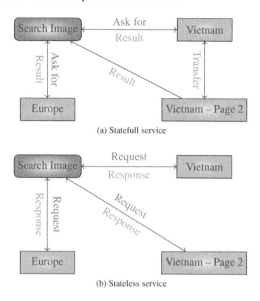

(a) Statefull service

(b) Stateless service

Figure 14.6. *Different kind of services. For a color version of this figure, see www.iste.co.uk/laffly/torus1.zip*

REST was designed to improve the performance of web applications. This design leads to a new architectural design where every service is gathered into a small package. Packaging services into small pieces allows the system to be scalable, by replicating, on another computer, the service which is overloaded and only that one. *WOA* comes from this design, where each service takes into account this scalability. It also embraces the fact that the service will be failed. In a monolithic application, the Information Technology (IT) does everything possible to avoid failure. In a *WOA* the amount of small services, and the possible replication of each one leads to a paradox: for sure, the service will fail, or will be unreachable. So each service is built in such a way as to embrace the failure. This awareness of failure demands that all services should be idempotent and stateless. Conceiving a stateless service needs special effort when designing the service (see Figure 14.6), especially by providing the good *API*.

14.3.1. *Stateless and scalabilty*

HTTP is a stateless protocol, and as *REST* use it as the transport layer, a *REST* microservice is by nature stateless. For breaking this, the developer needs to do something. The easiest thing to do, for breaking the stateless property, is to implement a session. A session is a memory space on the server, where it stores some "useful" information about the previous request of the client. Sessions are often used, as they are convenient for tracking user activity and other information. The point is, sessions do not scale well.

When a service needs to scale, the service is started on another server, but the session is not replicated on this new server (see Figure 14.7). As shown in the figure, if a user wants to connect to a service, there is no problem if the service is running on one server. However, if the service is running on two different servers, the user is effectively connected to one server. As the session is not replicated on the second server, the user is not connected. This scenario is worst if there is a load balancer between the user and the service [DES 00].

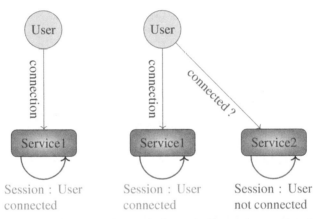

(a) Connection from user to a service   (b) Connection from user to a replicated service

Figure 14.7. *Scalability's problem. For a color version of this figure, see www.iste.co.uk/laffly/torus1.zip*

14.3.2. *API*

Everything processing can be represented as *Create Read Update Delete* (*CRUD*) operations, even complex processing needs data taken from data sources. Designing an *API* is abstracting the data source and exposing some (not all) of the processing to the user, using an entrypoint. This entrypoint should be as simple as possible, like *https://cloud-torus.com/api*   or   *https://api.cloud-torus.com,*   and   use   secure communications. Accessing the root of your *API* should return a list of usable endpoints, like GitHub (an extracted sample is shown in Code 14.2).

```
{
"current_user_url": "https://api.github.com/user",
"current_user_authorizations_html_url":
 ↪   "https://github.com/settings/connections/applications
 ↪   {/client_id}",
"authorizations_url": "https://api.github.com/authorizations",
"code_search_url":
 ↪   "https://api.github.com/search/code?q={query}
 ↪   {&page,per_page,sort,order}",
"commit_search_url":
 ↪   "https://api.github.com/search/commits?q={query}
 ↪   {&page,per_page,sort,order}",
"emails_url": "https://api.github.com/user/emails",
"emojis_url": "https://api.github.com/emojis",
"events_url": "https://api.github.com/events",
 .../...
}
```

Code 14.2. *Example of root content entrypoint. For a color version of this code, see www.iste.co.uk/laffly/torus1.zip*

14.3.3. *HTTP Methods*

The *W3C* defines, in [W3C 14], the methods (verbs) that can be used when using *HTTP*, and their behavior. Following their definition leads to mapping these methods to *CRUD* operations.

The *GET* method, which is considered safe (meaning that this method should not alter the server state), is for retrieving a specific/collection from a server. It could be mapped on `read` operations, like SQL `SELECT`. The *GET* method is idempotent. The response may be cached to serve the resources efficiently.

The *POST* method has no particular semantics, because *POST* should react according to the resource semantics. However, it is not an idempotent method, and is often used to create a new resource on the server. This is often mapped on `create` operations, like an SQL `INSERT`.

The *PUT* method is idempotent and is used to update a resource on the server. The resources should be entirely provided in the request, if the aim is to only change some part of the resources, the *PATCH* method should be used. These two methods act like SQL `UPDATE`.

The *DELETE* method (considered idempotent) is used for deleting a resource on the server, like SQL `DELETE`.

14.3.4. *Example of an API*

As an example, if we want to build an *API* to serve images, these endpoints should be used:

HTTP verbs	endpoint	meaning
GET	/api/images	List all images
POST	/api/images	Create (or upload) an image
GET	/api/images/{img_id}	Get a specific image
PUT	/api/images/{img_id}	Update an image (all its parts)
PATCH	/api/images/{img_id}	Update an image (partially)
DELETE	/api/images/{img_id}	Delete an image

Table 14.1. *Example of endpoints*

14.4. WSDL example

```
 1  <definitions
 2      xmlns:tns="fr.eisti.wsdl"
 3      xmlns:soap="http://schemas.xmlsoap.org/wsdl/soap/"
 4      xmlns:xsd="http://www.w3.org/2001/XMLSchema"
 5      xmlns:xsd1="fr.eisti.xsd"
 6      xmlns:soapenc="http://schemas.xmlsoap.org/soap/encoding/"
 7      xmlns:wsdl="http://schemas.xmlsoap.org/wsdl/"
 8      xmlns="http://schemas.xmlsoap.org/wsdl/"
 9      name="GetCapabilites (example)"
10      targetNamespace="fr.eisti.wsdl">
11  <!-- data type definitions  -->
12  <types>
13    <schema xmlns="http://www.w3.org/2000/10/XMLSchema"
14            targetNamespace="fr.eisti.xsd">
15      <element name="nickname">
16        <complexType>
17          <all>
18            <element name="value" type="string"/>
19          </all>
20        </complexType>
21      </element>
22      <element name="message">
23        <complexType>
24          <all>
25            <element name="value" type="string"/>
26          </all>
27        </complexType>
28      </element>
29      <element name="void">
30        <complexType>
31          <sequence/>
32        </complexType>
33      </element>
34    </schema>
35  </types>
36  <!-- definition of the data being communicated : response messages
    ↳ -->
37  <message name="returns_message">
38    <part name="message" type="xsd:message"/>
39  </message>
40  <!-- definition of the data being communicated : request messages
    ↳ -->
41  <message name="sayHello">
42    <part name="nickname" type="xsd:nickname"/>
43  </message>
44  <message name="sayHelloWorld">
45    <part name="void" type="xsd:void"/>
46  </message>
47  <!-- set of operations  -->
```

```
48    <portType name="Example">
49      <operation name="sayHello">
50        <input message="tns:sayHello"/>
51        <output message="tns:returns_message"/>
52      </operation>
53      <operation name="sayHelloWorld">
54        <input message="tns:sayHelloWorld"/>
55        <output message="tns:returns_message"/>
56      </operation>
57    </portType>
58    <!-- protocol and data format specification -->
59    <binding name="Example_webservices" type="tns:Example">
60      <soap:binding style="rpc"
61                    transport="http://schemas.xmlsoap.org/soap/http"/>
62      <operation name="sayHello">
63        <soap:operation
          ↪ soapAction="urn:xmethods-delayed-quotes#sayHello"/>
64        <input>
65          <soap:body
66              use="encoded"
67              encodingStyle="http://schemas.xmlsoap.org/soap/encoding/"/>
68        </input>
69        <output>
70          <soap:body
71              use="encoded"
72              encodingStyle="http://schemas.xmlsoap.org/soap/encoding/"/>
73        </output>
74      </operation>
75      <operation name="sayHelloWorld">
76        <soap:operation
          ↪ soapAction="urn:xmethods-delayed-quotes#sayHelloWorld"/>
77        <input>
78          <soap:body
79              use="encoded"
80              encodingStyle="http://schemas.xmlsoap.org/soap/encoding/"/>
81        </input>
82        <output>
83          <soap:body
84              use="encoded"
85              encodingStyle="http://schemas.xmlsoap.org/soap/encoding/"/>
86        </output>
87      </operation>
88    </binding>
89    <!-- name given to the web service -->
90    <service name="research">
91      <port name="research_0" binding="Example_webservices">
92        <soap:address location="http://127.0.0.1./test_soap/"/>
```

```
93      </port>
94    </service>
95  </definitions>
```

Code 14.3. *For a color version of this code, see*
www.iste.co.uk/laffly/torus1.zip

14.5. Conclusion

In this chapter, we have seen how to build a *REST API*. Building such an *API* is mandatory when creating cloud applications. Cloud applications have to consider scalability and resilience. Microservice architectures allow the users to scale efficiently, and as these applications do not manage state, it is easier to take resilience into consideration. We also covered the different usage levels of *REST*. Cloud applications should consider building at least a level 2, as it allows some other features like composition.

14.6. References

[CHE 03] CHEN M., CHEN A.N., SHAO B.B., "The implications and impacts of web services to electronic commerce research and practices.", *J. Electron. Commerce Res.*, vol. 4, no. 4, pp. 128–139, 2003.

[DES 00] DESHPANDE S., "Clustering: Transparent replication, load balancing, and failover", *Building Scalabe and Highly Available E-Commerce Applications with the Inprise Application Server*, CustomWare, San Carlos, 2000.

[DON 13] DONG L., Restful service composition, PhD thesis, University of Saskatchewan, Canada, 2013.

[FIE 00] FIELDING R.T., *Architectural Styles and the Design of Network-based Software Architectures*, University of California, Irvine, 2000.

[FOW 10] FOWLER M., "Richardson maturity model". Available at: https://martinfowler.com/articles/richardsonMaturityModel.html, March 2010.

[HAA 04] HAAS H., BOOTH D., NEWCOMER E. *et al.*, Web services architecture, W3C Note, W3C, February 2004. Available at: http://www.w3.org/TR/2004/NOTE-ws-arch-20040211/.

[HAL 13] HALPIN H., "Architecture of the World Wide Web", *Social Semantics*, vol. 2, Springer US, 2013.

[HÜR 95] HÜRSCH W.L., LOPES C.V., Separation of concerns, Report , College of Computer Science Northeastern University, 1995.

[JAC 04] JACOBS I., WALSH N., Architecture of the World Wide Web, Volume One, W3C Recommendation, W3C, December 2004. Available at: http://www.w3.org/TR/2004/REC-webarch-20041215/.

[MEY 97] MEYER B., *Object-Oriented Software Construction (Second Edition)*, vol. 2, Prentice Hall, Englewood Cliffs, 1997.

[MUM 13] MUMBAIKAR S., PADIYA P., "Web Services Based On SOAP and REST Principles", *International Journal of Scientific and Research Publications*, vol. 3, no. 5, May 2013.

[RIC 07] RICHARDSON L., RUBY S., HANSSON D.H., *RESTful Web Services*, O'Reilly, 2007.

[RIC 18] RICHARDSON C., "Microservice Architecture", 2018.

[SER 14] SERRANO N., HERNANTES J., GALLARDO G., "Service-Oriented Architecture and Legacy Systems", *IEEE Software*, vol. 31, no. 5, pp. 15–19, 2014.

[SHE 14] SHENG Q.Z., QIAO X., VASILAKOS A.V. *et al.*, "Web services composition: A decade's overview", *Information Sciences*, vol. 280, pp. 218–238, 2014.

[W3C 14] W3C, "HTTP - Hypertext Transfer Protocol Overview". Available at: https://www.w3.org/Protocols/, 2014.

15

SCALA – Functional Programming

15.1. Introduction

Wikipedia defines programming as:

> Computer programming is the process of designing and building an executable computer program that carries out a given computing task.

It means that programming is a more complex word than it may sound. The aim of programming is to compute a problem on *a computer*. Turing provides a formalism of the concept of algorithm and computation in [TUR 37], and Church in [CHU 40].

In [VON 30], von Neumann introduces the *von Neumann* architecture[1]. This architecture introduces four functional blocks: Memory, Control Unit, Arithmetic and Logic Unit and an Input/Output Unit. This could be represented as in Figure 15.1. This general architecture, which is still used for modern computer, was influenced by the work of Alan Turing.

Program and data are stored in the memory part. the arithmetic and logic unit is in charge of doing small computation, and the control unit has to execute the instructions of the program.

Chapter written by Florent DEVIN.

1 Even though von Neumann uses the work of John William Mauchly and John Eckert, we still use the name of von Neumann architecture.

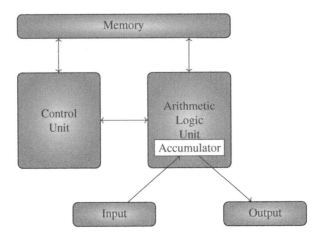

Code 15.1. *Von Neumann architecture (from wikipedia).*

15.1.1. *Programming languages*

On top of this theoretical model, computer scientists built some "high-level" languages (see Figure 15.2), to be able to run a program without knowing exactly how the computer works (i.e. without knowing physical details of the computer). The very first language was FORTRAN, created by IBM's team to be able to run a program on the IBM 704, in 1957. FORTRAN led to C (in 1972), and also to Simula (in 1962). Both of these languages introduced a major offspring:

– C for the type system, and also for the syntax writing;

– Simula for the use of classes [HOA 65].

One year later, in 1958, John McCarthy invented LISP (based on both [CHU 36] and [TUR 37]); the full implementation came in 1962. This language introduced the functional offspring.

15.1.2. *Paradigm*

Choosing a programming language is very difficult, as you have to know all, to make the good choice. But the choice can be made using some criteria; for example, which paradigm we want to use, which language is supported on the computer/platform, where the code will be executed and so on.

For illustrating this, an example is used: the generation of a login's list from an employees' list. This list should be a comma-delimited string. Each login has to be in lower case. The rule to build a login from an employee is to use the first letter of the first name, the first letter of the last name, and the last letter of the last name.

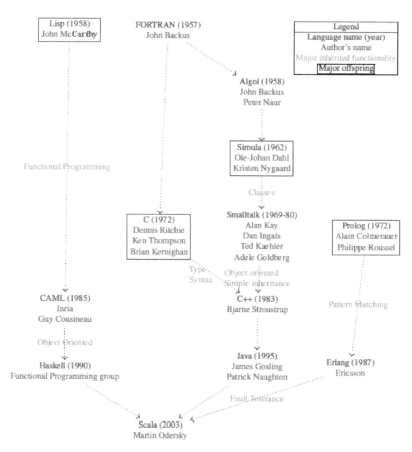

Code 15.2. *Brief history of languages. For a color version of this figure,*
see www.iste.co.uk/laffly/torus1.zip

For example, the list "'Minda Courser", "Bailey Ickes", "Kaleigh Severance", "Elijah Ferber", "Levi Gordan", "Tu Hinnenkamp", "Laronda Kleiber", "Eva Freshwater", "Sasha Aguilar", "Eustolia Conte", will generate the list: "`mcr, bis, kse, efr, lgn, thp, lkr, efr, sar, ece`"

15.1.2.1. *Procedural example*

To do this in a procedural style, we have to explain to the computer how to do. Given a list of employees (`List<Employee> listOfEmployee`), and considering the existence of a class that represents an employee (and all methods already implemented), code 15.1 is a valid answer when using Java.

```
1   public String generateLogin (List<Employee> listOfEmployee) {
2     StringBuilder result = new StringBuilder();
3     for (int i=0; i < listOfEmployee.size(); i++) {
4       String name = listOfEmployee.get(i).getLastName();
5       String firstName = listOfEmployee.get(i).getFirstName();
6       result.append(firstName.charAt(0)).toLowerCase()
7       .append(name.charAt(0)).toLowerCase()
8       .append(nam.charAt(name.length() - 1)).toLowerCase()
9       .append(",");
10    }
11    return result.substring(0, result.length()-1).toString();
12  }
```

Code 15.1. *Procedural processing for generating a list of login in Java. For a color version of this code, see www.iste.co.uk/laffly/torus1.zip*

This listing deserves some explanations. On line 2, in Java for performance, when you need to build a String, you need to use the StringBuilder. The processing occurs from line 3 to line 10. In this processing, we express that we need to iterate[2] over the collection (here a list). Note that you have to know how the collection is implemented. A LinkedList is a collection, that starts at 0. Lines 4–5 are here to avoid repetitions on the next lines. Lines 6–8 are used to express how we can build a login from an employee. Line 6 extracts the first letter of the first name (in Java the first letter is located at position 0), line 7 is for the first letter of the surname and line 8 is for the last letter. Note that for each extracted letter the function toLowerCase is used, to put each character in lower case. On line 9 after each login generation, a comma is inserted. At the end of the processing, the final String is built. As there is a final comma, which is unwanted, before returning the full string, the last comma is removed. In this listing, the overall process is expressed in a sequential way, without any other consideration. More precisely, the usage of a variable (line 2, and the subsequent) prevent using this algorithm, as it is, for parallel processing.

15.1.2.2. *Functional example*

In *Functional Programming (FP)*, rather than express how to process, the processing is focused on the user needs. Code 15.2 is an answer for processing the

---

2 In Java, we can iterate in different ways, but this way is the one which is close to others languages.

login list. In this code, a simple function (generateLogin) is created for generating a login from an employee's name (lines 1–5). take(1) means take only one character in the beginning, and takeRight, is for taking from the end. Then on each element of the list of employee, the generateLogin function is called, and all of this login are assembled in a string (mkString) to generate the wanted list. As there is nothing expressed on the way to achieve the process, and also as there is no variable in this code, it could be easily turned into parallel processing.

```scala
1  def generateLogin (employee : Employee) : String = {
2    (employee.firstName.take(1) +
3    employee.lastName.take(1) +
4    employee.lastName.takeRight(1)).toLowerCase
5  }
6  listOfEmployee.map(generateLogin(_)).mkString(",")
```

Code 15.2. *Functional processing for generating a list of login in Scala. For a color version of this code, see www.iste.co.uk/laffly/torus1.zip*

15.1.2.3. *Logical example*

Logical programming is quite the same as *FP*, as they are both declarative language.

```prolog
1   listOfLogin(ListEmployees,StringLogin):-
2   maplist(emp_to_log,ListEmployees,ListLogin),
3   atomic_list_concat(ListLogin,',',StringLogin).
4   emp_to_log(Employee,Login):-
5   member(firstname(FirstName),Employee),
6   member(lastname(LastName),Employee),
7   sub_atom(FirstName,0,1,_,FirstLetter),
8   sub_atom(LastName,0,1,_,SecondLetter),
9   sub_atom(LastName,_,1,0,ThirdLetter),
10  atomic_list_concat([FirstLetter, SecondLetter, ThirdLetter],
11  Login).
```

Code 15.3. *Logical processing for generating a list of login in Prolog. For a color version of this code, see www.iste.co.uk/laffly/torus1.zip*

15.2. Functional programming

15.2.1. *Introduction*

Before mentioning what *FP* is, it is necessary to tell what *FP* is not. *FP* is not programming using functions, because on almost each language functions exist. Many programs are using functions (or methods) and they are not written using functional paradigms. *FP* has nothing to do with recursion, because recursion is used in other paradigm. Of course, recursion can be used when using the functional paradigm, but this is not mandatory. As Alvin Alexander says in [ALE 17], recursion is a by-product of *FP*.

The definition of "functional programming", by Wikipedia, is:

> In computer science, functional programming is a programming paradigm –a style of building the structure and elements of computer programs– that treats computation as the evaluation of mathematical functions and avoids changing-state and mutable data. It is a declarative programming paradigm, which means programming is done with expressions or declarations instead of statements.

This definition emphasizes that *FP* is more related to pure functions. The pure functions have no side effect, they avoid changing-state, and mutable data. They manipulate values. Rosy Mary Cook, in [COO 16], emphasized this.

15.2.2. *Why now?*

The most important question, is why now? Why is it important to learn a new paradigm today? Nowadays modern application have to deal with concurrency. Concurrency is mandatory when the amount of data is huge. It allows applications to process faster, or to process bigger data. Concurrency is also useful for scalability, as the process is naturally design for. The scalability is also requested when there is a need of high availability for an application.

With classical[3] approach the scalability is hard to achieve. Classical application runs on a web container using session, for example, to manage the global state. But managing a session in a distributed application might be tricky. Several options are possible:

– configuring a load balancer to route all incoming request from the same location to the same server;

---

3 By classical, we mean "old" traditional web server.

– storing the session on a database, and referring to this database when the session is needed;

– replicating all the sessions on all servers.

Most of the time, avoiding the usage of session is the best way to manage replication. As *FP* avoid changing state, they do not manage session. The application does not take session into account, and managing session is useless.

More generally, using mutable variables, prevents or discourages the usage of multi-core processors. As a mutable variable can be modified simultaneously by a multiple processor, the variable's modification has to be put in critical section, which means that only one processor should modify this variable at once. Code 15.20 presents two distinct ways to compute the number of prime number lesser than a value. Both try to compute the value using parallel sequences. The first uses a pure functional approach, and the second uses mutable variables. It is interesting to note that the functional approach always answers the same response for the same value, which is expected (e.g. there are 1,230 prime numbers less than 10,000). The second approach does not answer the same number (it varies from 1,226 to 1,230), which is unexpected, and especially false (most of the time). This happens only because of the usage of mutable variables in conjunction with multiple processors.

Using *FP*, it is easy to change the data representation. For example, if the representation needed is *JavaScript Object Notation (JSON)*, a `JSONTransformer` is used. If there is a need for an *XML* representation, a `XMLTransformer` is used. So, for generating both representation, the application has just to change the transformer function. A modern application provides interfaces for both people and other applications.

Finally, as *FP* use "only" pure functions, modification of a function only affect the result of this function. When using other languages like `C`, `C++`, `Java`, function's modification can impact more than one function. It is very hard to know the exact impact of a modification. This leads to time-consuming modification, and it is harder and harder to deliver an application.

15.2.3. *High order function*

Firstly *FP* treats functions as other type. This means that functions can be used as an input parameter or as an output.

For example, to compute the sum of the integers between `bInf` and `bSup`, an answer could be code 15.4. To compute the sum of the *square* of the integers between `bInf` and `bSup`, an answer could be code 15.5. To compute the sum of the *cube* of the integers between `bInf` and `bSup`, an answer could be code 15.6.

```
1  def sumInts          (bInf: Int, bSup: Int): Int = {
2    if (bInf > bSup) 0
3    else
4    sumInts            (bInf + 1, bSup) + bInf
5  }
```

Code 15.4. *Computation of* $\sum_{i=bInf}^{bSup} i$. *For a color version of this code,*
see www.iste.co.uk/laffly/torus1.zip

```
1  def sumSquareInts (bInf: Int, bSup: Int): Int = {
2    if (bInf > bSup) 0
3    else
4    sumSquareInts (bInf + 1, bSup) + bInf * bInf
5  }
```

Code 15.5. *Computation of* $\sum_{i=bInf}^{bSup} i^2$. *For a color version of this code,*
see www.iste.co.uk/laffly/torus1.zip

These answers do the same thing:

$$\sum_{i=bInf}^{bSup} f(i), \text{ with } f(x) = x, f(x) = x^2, f(x) = x^3, \dots$$

In *FP*, we can build this pattern, and then, use it with the good function, like done on code 15.7. This ability of taking a function, as a parameter, is called *high order function*. The term *high order function* is also used when the result of a function is a function. *High order function* allows conciser programs, and builds some useful patterns. This concept is mainly used with basic functional blocks.

A direct application of high-order function is the chance of defining a 'function in a function'. As a function is considered as a classical type, they can be defined inside another function, like any variable. This makes encapsulation of code simpler, like on code 15.8.

```
1  def sumSquareInts (bInf: Int, bSup: Int): Int = {
2    if (bInf > bSup) 0
3    else
4    sumSquareInts (bInf + 1, bSup) + bInf * bInf * bInf
5  }
```

Code 15.6. *Computation of* $\sum\limits_{i=bInf}^{bSup} i^3$. *For a color version of this code,*
see www.iste.co.uk/laffly/torus1.zip

```
1  // Define the pattern (f is a parameter)
2  def sum (bInf: Int, bSup: Int, f: Int => Int): Int = {
3    if (bInf > bSup) 0
4    else
5    sum (bInf + 1, bSup, f) + f (bInf)
6  }
7  // And then
8  def sumInts       (bInf: Int, bSup : Int) = sum(bInf, bSup, x
   ↪  => x)
9  def sumSquareInts (bInf: Int, bSup : Int) = sum(bInf, bSup, x
   ↪  => x*x)
10 def sumCubeInts   (bInf: Int, bSup : Int) = sum(bInf, bSup, x
   ↪  => x*x*x)
11 // Or
12 def square(x : Int) = x * x
13 def sumSquareInts2 (bInf: Int, bSup : Int) = sum(bInf, bSup,
   ↪  square)
```

Code 15.7. *Computation of* $\sum\limits_{i=bInf}^{bSup} f(i)$, *and its usage . For a color*
version of this code, see www.iste.co.uk/laffly/torus1.zip

15.2.4. *Basic functional blocks*

In *FP*, the most important thing is to identify the functional blocks that are traditionally used. These are common patterns in *FP* and they work on collections. A collection is a container (data structure) that sticks together some data items. Collections in *FP* are important and a good programmer should know what the collections are for. Linus Torvalds says:

Bad programmers worry about the code. Good programmers worry about data structures and their relationships.

```scala
1   import scala.annotation.tailrec
2
3   def facto (value: BigInt): BigInt = {
4     require(value > 0, s"first paramater should no be negative")
5
6     @tailrec
7     def factRT (value: BigInt, acc: BigInt = 1): BigInt = {
8       if (value < 2) acc
9       else factRT(value-1, acc * value)
10    }
11    factRT(value)
12  }
```

Code 15.8. *Recursive computation of factorial. For a color version of this code, see www.iste.co.uk/laffly/torus1.zip*

Of course, this quote is more global that just for the collection, but it also fits well.

In *FP*, collections have some specific methods, but some are global to all collections. Three are very common:

– map: apply a function on each item of the data structure;

– filter: apply a predicate on each item of the collection, and keep only those where the predicate is true;

– fold: apply a function on each item, and apply a reducer on each call.

15.2.4.1. *filter*

The function filter is the first functional block. Given a collection and a predicate, apply the latter on each item of the collection and keep only those that satisfy the condition. This can be represented like shown in Figure 15.3, and written as code 15.9.

15.2.4.2. *map*

For a map function, take a collection and apply a function on each item of the collection. This could be represented like shown in Figure 15.4, and written as code 15.10.

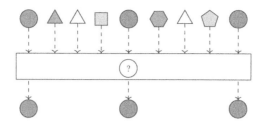

Figure 15.3. *Filter . For a color version of this figure, see*
www.iste.co.uk/laffly/torus1.zip

```
1   val ll : List[Int] = List.range(0,10)
2
3   ll.filter(_%2 == 0) // => List(0, 2, 4, 6, 8)
```

Code 15.9. *Filter function in Scala. For a color version of this code, see*
www.iste.co.uk/laffly/torus1.zip

15.2.4.3. *fold*

A `fold` function is slightly different from the previous one. [fold] takes a "reducer" function and applies this function on each item, with the result of the previous call. This could be represented like shown in Figure 15.5, and written as code 15.11.

As it can viewed on code 15.11, the `fold` function takes two parameters. This first one is the initial value and the second one is a function with two parameters. This function takes the first parameter and reduces it with the initial value. The result becomes the new initial value and so on till the end.

15.3. Scala

Scala is a language designed by Martin Odersky. The main functionalities of Scala are:

– functional programming, see section 15.2;

– strong statically typed, see 15.3.1;

– object oriented;

– UTF-8 by default;

– works on *Java Virtual Machine (JVM)*;

– easily extensible.

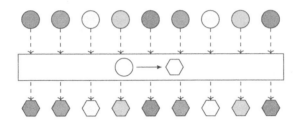

Figure 15.4. *Map. For a color version of this figure, see www.iste.co.uk/laffly/torus1.zip*

```
1   val l1 : List[Int] = List(1, 2, 3, 4, 5, 6, 7)
2
3   l1.map(_ + 10)     // => (11, 12, 13, 14, 15, 16, 17)
```

Code 15.10. *Map function in Scala. For a color version of this code, see www.iste.co.uk/laffly/torus1.zip*

There are many tutorials on how to install Scala, so this part will not be covered in this chapter. Many functionalities are explained in this chapter, some others are not covered by this chapter, like object-oriented, UTF-8 and so on. Scala programs are run on the *JVM*, which means that they could be run wherever Java could run. For a good comprehension of the *JVM*, readers should also read [BLO 17] and [GOE 06].

15.3.1. *Types systems*

A type defines a set of values a variable can possess. It also defines a set of usable functions on these values. Type coherence can be checked at compile time (when writing the code), and values are checked at run time (when a code is in progress). Scala is a strong statically-typed language.

A statically-typed language is a language where types are checked at the compile time. For the opposite (dynamic-typed language), types are checked at the run time (i.e. on the fly). Statically-typed languages are not error prone, because as types are checked, the compiler (or the interpreter) catches type error instead of finding them at run time.

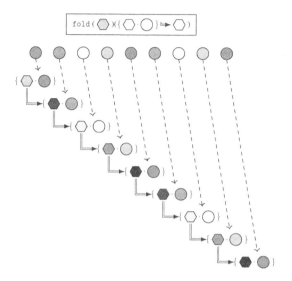

Figure 15.5. *Fold. For a color version of this figure, see www.iste.co.uk/laffly/torus1.zip*

```
1    val l1 : List[Int] = List(1, 2, 3, 4, 5, 6, 7)
2
3    l1.fold(1)(_ * _)      // => 5040
4    l1.fold(0)(_ + _)      // => 29
5
6    def f(accumulator : String, value : Int) : String = {
7      accumulator + value.toString
8    }
9
10   l1.foldLeft("")(f)      // "12345"
```

Code 15.11. *Fold function in Scala. For a color version of this code, see www.iste.co.uk/laffly/torus1.zip*

Strong typing languages impose having a type for every variable/expression. A type cannot be used where another one is needed, unless using a transforming function.

All exceptions to type rules cause a compilation error. For a complete description of type system, Cardelli provides a full explanation in [CAR 96].

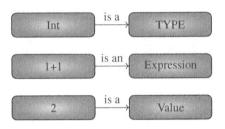

Figure 15.6. *Difference between type, value and expression*

When using a strong statically-typed language, the users should try to use the type system as much as possible to avoid error. A simply thing to do is to define type aliases to avoid some errors. For example, to add two distances, many programmers will write the function add, as on code 15.13. Writing this code is error prone, if this code is used by people using metrics system and imperial system. A better code, to prevent error, is shown in code 15.14. In this code, there are two definitions of type aliases, and the function add is quite different.

In Scala, a function is defined by using the keyword def. Code 15.12 defines a function that takes two parameters (of type Int), and returns an Int.

```
1  def min(x:Int, y:Int) : Int = {
2    if (x < y) {
3      x
4    } else {
5      y
6    }
7  }
```

Code 15.12. *Simple example of function's definition. For a color version of this code, see www.iste.co.uk/laffly/torus1.zip*

The second step of type's definition is to provide its own class. A class is a formal description of a type, and is composed of *fields* and *methods*. This means a type describes the global shape (with fields) and also behaviour (with methods).

A first approach to define a class that represents Rational number ($\mathbb{Q}$) could be class Rational (p: Int, q: Int). But this definition does not provide, neither some behavior on rational, nor something useful, as the following short example shows (code 15.15).

```
1    def addDistances(d1 : Double, d2 : Double) : Double = {
2      d1 + d2
3    }
```

Code 15.13. *Addition of two distances. For a color version of this code, see www.iste.co.uk/laffly/torus1.zip*

```
1    type Centimeter = Double
2    type Inches = Double
3
4    def addDistances(d1 : Centimeter, d2 : Centimeter) : Centimeter
     ↪  = {
5      d1 + d2
6    }
7    def addDistances(d1 : Inches, d2 : Inches) : Inches = {
8      d1 + d2
9    }
10   def addDistances(d1 : Centimeter, d2 : Inches) : Centimeter = {
11     d1 + toCentimeter(d2)
12   }
```

Code 15.14. *Addition of two distances using a typed system. For a color version of this code, see www.iste.co.uk/laffly/torus1.zip*

The equality is not possible because most of languages test the equality on references in memory. The addition is not possible because we have not defined the behavior of addition. In Scala, there is a keyword case class that transform the behavior of a class. So the definition case class Rational2(p: Int, q: Int) provides many things, like equality on value rather on reference, a way to access to fields. To provide some behaviors to a class, function must be defined inside the class. A "complete" code of a rational's class implementation can be found in section 15.4.

The description of a type can be modeled with logical *and* (which are product types) and logical or (which are sum types). Product types are used when the type can be described like an A has a B *and* C. In this case, the Scala equivalent code is case class A(b : B, c : C). Sum types are for modeling the pattern an A is a B or a C. Code 15.16 translates this pattern.

```
1    //This is the definition of a new type (class)
2    class Rational1 (p : Int, q : Int)
3
4    // Here we will create new instances of Rational1 (this means
     ↪ new value)
5    val r1 = new Rational1(1,3)
6    val r2 = new Rational1(1,3)
7
8    // Lets use them
9    // Will print false
10   println("Equality : " + (r1 == r2))
11   //r1 + r2 this can not compile !!!
12   //r1.p this does not compile, because you do not have direct
     ↪ access to the numerator, neither the denominator
```

Code 15.15. *First declaration of a type. For a color version of this code, see www.iste.co.uk/laffly/torus1.zip*

```
1    sealed trait A
2    case class B() extends A
3    case class C() extends A
```

Code 15.16. *Pattern to use for a sum type. For a color version of this code, see www.iste.co.uk/laffly/torus1.zip*

The term case to define a class is not mandatory, but it provides many facilities, like equality on "values" rather on references, an easy way to access to (public) fields, a pretty printer and so on. The term sealed is not mandatory when defining sum types, but it is a good habit to undertake. It indicates that all the subtypes are defined in the same file, and there is no other place where subtype's definitions will be found.

Finally, a function can be polymorphic. This can be achieved like it is shown on code 15.17. In this listing, T represent an abstracted type, which will be used later.

15.3.2. *Basic manipulation of collection*

There are many ways to compute the sum of a vector in Scala. Some of them are shown on code 15.18. Functional style is preferred as it is more readable and it could also easily be run on multiple cores, as section 15.2.2 emphasizes.

```scala
def mergeSort[T] (l: List[T])(implicit ord: Ordering[T]):
    List[T] = {
  val middle = l.length / 2
  if (middle == 0) l
  else {
    def merge (l1: List[T], l2: List[T]): List[T] = (l1, l2)
        match {
      case (Nil, _) => l2
      case (_, Nil) => l1
      case (x :: i, y :: i1) if ord.lt(x, y) => x :: merge(i,
          l2)
      case _ => l2.head :: merge(l1, l2.tail)
    }
    val split = l splitAt middle
    merge(mergeSort(split._1)(ord), mergeSort(split._2)(ord))
  }
}
```

Code 15.17. *Polymorphic function. For a color version of this code, see www.iste.co.uk/laffly/torus1.zip*

Looking carefully at code 15.18, the Scala way uses some specific functions to compute the sum. In fact, there are many[4] other functions that may be used:

– drop: remove the n first elements;

– dropRight: remove the n last elements;

– find: finds the first value that satisfy a condition (return an Option type);

– count: counts the number of elements that satisfy a condition;

– union: produces a new collection with all elements of the first and the second collection;

– sortWith: sorts a collection with a comparison function;

– zip: produces a collection formed from this collection and another iterable collection by combining corresponding elements in pairs;

– takeWhile: takes longest *prefix* of elements that satisfy a predicate;

---

4 A complete description can be found at scala-lang.org

– dropWhile: drops longest *prefix* of elements that satisfy a predicate;

– splitAt: splits this collection into two at a given position;

– zipWithIndex: zips this collection with its indices.

```scala
// Procedural way
var sum = 0
for (i <- 0 until vector.length) { // or i <- vector.indices
  sum = sum + vector(i)            // or sum += vector(i)
}

var sum = 0
for (i <- vector) {
  sum += i
}

// Functional way
val sum = vector.fold(0)(_+_)

// Scala way
val sum = vector.sum
```

Code 15.18. *Computation of the sum of a vector. For a color version of this code, see www.iste.co.uk/laffly/torus1.zip*

15.4. Rational

We present here a partial definition of a new rational type. This implementation lacks complete integration, in the Scala system types, as it is not the point of this code. Note that, because Scala is UTF-8 by default, function names can begin with symbols such as +. This allows the class Rational to be used like any other numeric types, providing operator +, *, ...

15.5. Why immutability matters?

Immutability matters, especially when using multiple processor architecture. Code 15.20 presents a code to compute the number of prime number lesser than a value (bounds in the code). For the value 10,000, there are 1,230 prime numbers. As count is a mutable variable, each time two processors have to increment count at the same time, only one processor will increment the variable. This leads to inconsistent computation.

```scala
import scala.annotation.tailrec
// Using denominator : Int = 1, is a way to define default
↪   value, if user does not provide some
case class Rational (numerator: Int, denominator: Int = 1) {
  require(denominator != 0, "denominator must be nonzero")
  // val or def (you choose)
  private val gcd: Int = {
    @tailrec
    def gcdRec (x: Int, y: Int): Int = {
      if (y == 0) x else gcdRec(y, x % y)
    }
    gcdRec(numerator, denominator)
  }
  // Here we use the simplify representation,
  // but the number does not change
  val numer: Int = numerator / gcd
  val denom: Int = denominator / gcd
  override def toString = numer + "/" + denom
  def + (that: Rational) = {
    Rational(that.numer * denom + numer * that.denom, denom *
    ↪   that.denom)
  }
  def - (that: Rational) = this + -that
  // The special keyword unary_ allow to use the - sign
  // as a unary operator like -a
  def unary_- = new Rational(-numer, denom)
  def * (that: Rational) = Rational(numer * that.numer, denom *
  ↪   that.denom)
  def / (that: Rational) = Rational(numer * that.denom, denom *
  ↪   that.numer)
  def > (that: Rational) = !(this < that)
  def max (that: Rational) = if (this < that) that else this
  def < (that: Rational) = numer * that.denom < that.numer *
  ↪   denom
  // We have to define this equality because 1/3 == 2/6
  def == (that: Rational) = {
    that.numer == numer && that.denom == denom
  }
  // If you want to make addition possible with Int,
  // you should define or extends a trait (later):
  def + (a: Int): Rational = this + Rational(a)
}
```

Code 15.19. *Concrete implementation of a class. For a color version of this code, see www.iste.co.uk/laffly/torus1.zip*

```
1    val bounds = 10000
2
3    def isPrime(x: Int): Boolean = {
4      (2 to Math.sqrt(x).toInt).forall(p => x % p != 0)
5    }
6    def countPrimesPure(lim: ParSeq[Int]) = {
7      lim.filter(isPrime).length
8    }
9    def countPrimesImpure(lim: Int) = {
10     var count = 0
11     val l : ParSeq[Int] = (1 to lim).par
12     l.map(x => if (isPrime(x)) count = count + 1)
13     count
14   }
15
16   val s =  countPrimesPure(
17   Stream.from(1).takeWhile(p => p < bounds).par)
18
19   println(s"Pure way : number of prime number lesser than
      ↪ ${bounds} : ${s}")
20   println(s"Using a var : number of prime number lesser than
      ↪ ${bounds} : ${countPrimesImpure(bounds)}")
```

Code 15.20. *Computation on the number of prime number less than
10000. For a color version of this code, see
www.iste.co.uk/laffly/torus1.zip*

15.6. Conclusion

Mastering collections and functions that can be applied are a key point for using *FP*. This chapter has presented a quick introduction to *FP*, some interesting features like *monads*, or *future* may require attention. However, this introduction allows the reader to start reading the chapter on SPARK (a general purpose cluster computing framework), and using it. There is a great gain in using *FP*, as it can be used on multi-processors architecture. It is also easy to scale, by using some features of the language, or by using some dedicated platform, like SPARK. Of course, changing of paradigm is hard, but it is time to shift as computer and applications are changing radically.

15.7. References

[ALE 17] ALEXANDER A., *Functional Programming, Simplified: (Scala Edition)*, CreateSpace Independent Publishing Platform, October 2017.

[BLO 17] BLOCH J., *Effective Java*, 3rd edition, Addison-Wesley Professional, 2017.

[CAR 96] CARDELLI L., "Type systems", *ACM Comput. Surv.*, vol. 28, no. 1, pp. 263–264, ACM, March 1996.

[CHE 03] CHEN M., CHEN A.N., SHAO B.B., "The implications and impacts of web services to electronic commerce research and practices", *J. Electron. Commerce Res.*, vol. 4, no. 4, pp. 128–139, 2003.

[CHU 36] CHURCH A., "A note on the Entscheidungs problem", *Journal of Symbolic Logic*, vol. 1, pp. 40–41, 1936.

[CHU 40] CHURCH A., "A formulation of the simple theory of types", *Journal of Symbolic Logic*, vol. 5, pp. 56–68, June 1940.

[COO 16] COOK M.R., "A practical introduction to functional programming". Available at: https://maryrosecook.com/blog/post/a-practical-introduction-to-functional-programming, 2016.

[DES 00] DESHPANDE S., "Clustering: Transparent replication, load balancing, and failover", *Building Scalabe and Highly Available E-Commerce Applications with the Inprise Application Server*, CustomWare, San Carlos, CA, 2000.

[DON 13] DONG L., Restful service composition, PhD thesis, University of Saskatchewan, Canada, 2013.

[FIE 00] FIELDING R.T., *Architectural Styles and the Design of Network-based Software Architectures*, University of California, Irvine, January 2000.

[FOW 10] FOWLER M., "Richardson maturity model". Available at: https://martinfowler.com/articles/richardsonMaturityModel.html, March 2010.

[GOE 06] GOETZ B., PEIERLS T., BLOCH J. *et al.*, *Java Concurrency in Practice*, Addison-Wesley Professional, May 2006.

[HÜR 95] HÜRSCH W.L., LOPES C.V., Separation of Concerns, Report, College of Computer Science Northeastern University, 1995.

[HAA 04] HAAS H., BOOTH D., NEWCOMER E. *et al.*, Web services architecture, W3C Note, W3C. Available at: http://www.w3.org/TR/2004/NOTE-ws-arch-20040211/, February 2004.

[HAL 13] HALPIN H., "Architecture of the World Wide Web", *Social Semantics*, vol. 2, Springer US, 2013.

[HOA 65] HOARE C.A.R., "Record handling", *ALGOL Bull.*, vol. 21, pp. 39–69, November 1965.

[JAC 04] JACOBS I., WALSH N., Architecture of the World Wide Web, Volume One, W3C Recommendation, W3C. Available at: http://www.w3.org/TR/2004/REC-webarch-20041215/, December 2004.

[MEY 97] MEYER B., *Object-Oriented Software Construction*, 2nd edition, vol. 2, Prentice Hall, New York, 1997.

[MUM 13] MUMBAIKAR S., PADIYA P., "Web services based on SOAP and REST principles", *International Journal of Scientific and Research Publications*, vol. 3, no. 5, May 2013.

[RIC 07] RICHARDSON L., RUBY S., HANSSON D.H., *RESTful Web Services*, O'Reilly, 2007.

[RIC 18] RICHARDSON C., "Microservice Architecture", 2018.

[SER 14] SERRANO N., HERNANTES J., GALLARDO G., "Service-oriented architecture and legacy systems", *IEEE Software*, vol. 31, no. 5, pp. 15–19, September 2014.

[SHE 14] SHENG Q.Z., QIAO X., VASILAKOS A.V. *et al.*, "Web services composition: A decade's overview", *Information Sciences*, vol. 280, pp. 218–238, October 2014.

[TUR 37] TURING A.M., "On computable numbers, with an application to the entscheidungsproblem", *M. Davis Edition*, vol. 43, pp. 116–151, 1937.

[VON 30] VON NEUMANN J., First Draft of a Report on the EDVAC, IEEE, June 30, 1945.

[W3C 14] W3C, "HTTP – Hypertext transfer protocol overview". Available at: https://www.w3.org/Protocols/, 2014.

16

Spark and Machine Learning Library

16.1. Introduction

Due to the increasing amount of available data in environmental science (remote sensing, in-situ sensing, *Internet Of Things (IOT)*, etc.), it is no longer possible to process machine learning on single node computers. In the last five years, two main distributed solutions have emerged. The convolution networks use *Deep Learning (DL)* algorithms like Tensor Flow, specialized in image recognition and classical machine learning that can combine heterogeneous data, like *Spark*. We will consider all of the interesting algorithms from the *Spark Machine Learning (ML)* library that can be useful in environmental science.

Spark is a distributed framework in which we can build our own distributed algorithms, based on distributed data types or use a distributed library like *ML*, Stream or GraphX. To use distributed framework efficiently, we need to understand the two main types of action that can be used to build distributed algorithms, the transformations and the actions. In *Spark* framework, we can use Java, Python or Scala language. In the first part, we will focus on *Resilient Distributed Dataset (RDD)*. *RDD* is the main type of *Spark*, in which all data has to be stored, before proceeding to distributed computation. In the second part, we will focus on *ML* library, and all its existing algorithms for classification and regression. All the parts will be presented by mixing definitions and practical sub-parts. Practice will be done on *Spark-shell* using the Scala language explained in Chapter 15.

Chapter written by Yannick LE NIR.

16.2. Spark

16.2.1. *Spark introduction*

A *Spark* program can be seen as a router that launches parallel operations on a cluster. The SparkContext object is the entry point to the cluster. It describes how many nodes you can use and other specific parameters that will be used during the processing. In a spark-shell or a spark-notebook, it is automatically created and accessible with the variable sc. Once created, you can use sc to build and manipulate *RDD*. The code will be the same on a single machine or on the cluster. According to the SparkContext, the distribution of the processing will be performed directly by the framework.

As an example, in code 16.1, we create an instance of SparkContext using spark-shell, on four local nodes.

In the following code examples, the Path value should be replaced by the directory containing your data, for example /home/torus for a local user torus.

```
-sh-4.2$ spark-shell --master local[4]
Welcome to
      ____              __
     / __/__  ___ _____/ /__
    _\ \/ _ \/ _ `/ __/  '_/
   /___/ .__/\_,_/_/ /_/\_\   version 1.6.0
      /_/

Using Scala version 2.10.5 (Java HotSpot(TM) 64-Bit Server VM,
 ↪    Java 1.7.0_67)
Spark context available as sc (master = local[4], app id =
 ↪    local-1542293651704).
scala>
```

Code 16.1. *Instantiate a spark-shell session on 4 local nodes*

16.2.2. *RDD presentation*

RDD is an immutable distributed collection of arbitrary objects. Each collection is divided into partitions, which can be distributed on different nodes of the cluster. There are many ways to create *RDD* collections.

16.2.2.1. *Creation from external data-set*

In *Spark* (code 16.2), you can create *RDD* from external data-sets supported by *Hadoop*: localFile, *HDFS, Amazon Simple Storage Service (Amazon S3)*:

```
sc.textFile("file://Path/my_local_file")
sc.textFile("hdfs://my_hdfs_file_url")
sc.textFile("s3://my_s3_file_url")
```

The input file will be parsed as a text file into *RDD* collections of string lines:

```
org.apache.spark.rdd.RDD[String]
```

```
scala> val rdd = sc.textFile("file://Path/data.txt")
rdd: org.apache.spark.rdd.RDD[String] = data.txt
↪   MapPartitionsRDD[1] at textFile at <console>:27
```

Code 16.2. *Read text file into* RDD. *For a color version of this code, see www.iste.co.uk/laffly/torus1.zip*

16.2.2.2. *Creation from Scala collection*

In *Spark* (code 16.3), you can also create *RDD* explicitly paralleling a collection of objects:

16.2.3. *RDD lifecycle*

There are two types of operations on *RDD*. The first to proceed are transformations, taking an *RDD* and creating a new *RDD*. Transformations are only recorded by *Spark*. Their execution is delayed until the second type of operation, named actions, proceed. Actions take *RDD* and return classical scala-typed variables. Actions can be dangerous operations, since they rebuild the entire variable on one single node (the driver). You have to be certain that the computed value is not too big for this single node.

```
sc.parallelize(objectCollection)
```

```
scala> val scalaCollection = Array(1, 2, 3, 4, 5)
scalaCollection: Array[Int] = Array(1, 2, 3, 4, 5)

scala>    val rdd = sc.parallelize(scalaCollection)
rdd: org.apache.spark.rdd.RDD[Int] = ParallelCollectionRDD[0]
 ↪  at parallelize at <console>:29
```

Code 16.3. *Parallelize scala collection to* RDD. *For a color version of this code, see www.iste.co.uk/laffly/torus1.zip*

16.2.4. *Operations on RDD*

16.2.4.1. *Actions on RDD*

The more important actions, to understand exercises from section 16.2.5, are presented in codes 16.4, 16.5, 16.6 and 16.7.

collect() : return to the driver node the elements of *RDD*

```
scala> val rdd = sc.parallelize(Array(1, 2, 3, 4, 5))
rdd: org.apache.spark.rdd.RDD[Int] = ParallelCollectionRDD[1]
 ↪  at parallelize at <console>:27

scala> val array = rdd.collect()
array: Array[Int] = Array(1, 2, 3, 4, 5)
```

Code 16.4. *collect action. For a color version of this code, see www.iste.co.uk/laffly/torus1.zip*

collect() : return to the driver node the aggregation of all elements of RDD using an associative and commutative function

```
scala> val rdd = sc.parallelize(Array(1, 2, 3, 4, 5))
rdd: org.apache.spark.rdd.RDD[Int] = ParallelCollectionRDD[1]
 ↪  at parallelize at <console>:27

scala> val sum = rdd.reduce((x,y)=>x+y)
sum: Int = 15
```

Code 16.5. *reduce action. For a color version of this code, see*
www.iste.co.uk/laffly/torus1.zip

collect() : return to the driver node the number of elements in RDD

```
scala> val rdd = sc.parallelize(Array(1, 2, 3, 4, 5))
rdd: org.apache.spark.rdd.RDD[Int] = ParallelCollectionRDD[2]
 ↪  at parallelize at <console>:27

scala> val count = rdd.count()
count: Long = 5
```

Code 16.6. *count action. For a color version of this code, see*
www.iste.co.uk/laffly/torus1.zip

saveAsTextFile(path) : write the *RDD* as text file, calling to String on each
element

```
scala> val rdd = sc.parallelize(Array(1, 2, 3, 4, 5))
rdd: org.apache.spark.rdd.RDD[Int] = ParallelCollectionRDD[10]
 ↪  at parallelize at <console>:27

scala> val file = rdd.saveAsTextFile("file://Path/data")
file: Unit = ()
```

Code 16.7. *saveAsTextFile action. For a color version of this code,*
see www.iste.co.uk/laffly/torus1.zip

16.2.4.2. *Transformations on RDD*

Before applying actions on *RDD*, you can make transformations (including creation) on it. They will be recorded in Spark and lazy executed when actions will be called. In codes 16.8, 16.9, 16.10, 16.11 and 16.12, we present the main transformations needed to understand exercises from section 16.2.5.

`map(func)` : apply a function to an *RDD*

```
scala> val rdd = sc.parallelize(Array(1, 2, 3, 4, 5))
rdd: org.apache.spark.rdd.RDD[Int] = ParallelCollectionRDD[5]
↪   at parallelize at <console>:27

scala> val newrdd = rdd.map(x => x+1)
newrdd: org.apache.spark.rdd.RDD[Int] = MapPartitionsRDD[6] at
↪   map at <console>:29

scala> val array = newrdd.collect()
array: Array[Int] = Array(2, 3, 4, 5, 6)
```

Code 16.8. *map transformation. For a color version of this code, see www.iste.co.uk/laffly/torus1.zip*

`flatMap(func)` : apply a function returning a sequence of value to an RDD

```
scala> val rdd = sc.parallelize(Array(1, 2, 3, 4, 5))
rdd: org.apache.spark.rdd.RDD[Int] = ParallelCollectionRDD[15]
↪   at parallelize at <console>:27

scala> val newrdd = rdd.flatMap(x => Seq(x,x+1))
newrdd: org.apache.spark.rdd.RDD[Int] = MapPartitionsRDD[16] at
↪   flatMap at <console>:29

scala> val array = newrdd.collect()
array: Array[Int] = Array(1, 2, 2, 3, 3, 4, 4, 5, 5, 6)
```

Code 16.9. *flatMap transformation. For a color version of this code, see www.iste.co.uk/laffly/torus1.zip*

`filter(func)` : select elements from *RDD*

```
scala> val rdd = sc.parallelize(Array(1, 2, 3, 4, 5))
rdd: org.apache.spark.rdd.RDD[Int] = ParallelCollectionRDD[20]
↪   at parallelize at <console>:27

scala> val newrdd = rdd.filter(x => x > 3)
newrdd: org.apache.spark.rdd.RDD[Int] = MapPartitionsRDD[21] at
↪   filter at <console>:29

scala> val array = newrdd.collect()
array: Array[Int] = Array(4, 5)
```

Code 16.10. *filter* transformation. For a color version of this code,
see www.iste.co.uk/laffly/torus1.zip

`union(rdd)` : union of two *RDD*

```
scala> val rdd = sc.parallelize(Array(1, 2, 3, 4, 5))
rdd: org.apache.spark.rdd.RDD[Int] = ParallelCollectionRDD[22]
↪   at parallelize at <console>:27

scala> val rdd2 = sc.parallelize(Array(4, 5, 6, 7))
rdd2: org.apache.spark.rdd.RDD[Int] = ParallelCollectionRDD[23]
↪   at parallelize at <console>:27

scala> val rdd3 = rdd.union(rdd2)
rdd3: org.apache.spark.rdd.RDD[Int] = UnionRDD[24] at union at
↪   <console>:31

scala> val union = rdd3.collect()
union: Array[Int] = Array(1, 2, 3, 4, 5, 4, 5, 6, 7)
```

Code 16.11. *union* transformation. For a color version of this code, see
www.iste.co.uk/laffly/torus1.zip

`intersection(rdd)` : intersection of two RDD

```
scala> val rdd = sc.parallelize(Array(1, 2, 3, 4, 5))
rdd: org.apache.spark.rdd.RDD[Int] = ParallelCollectionRDD[25]
↪  at parallelize at <console>:27

scala> val rdd2 = sc.parallelize(Array(1, 2, 6, 7))
rdd2: org.apache.spark.rdd.RDD[Int] = ParallelCollectionRDD[26]
↪  at parallelize at <console>:27

scala> val rdd3 = rdd.intersection(rdd2)
rdd3: org.apache.spark.rdd.RDD[Int] = MapPartitionsRDD[32] at
↪  intersection at <console>:31

scala> val intersection = rdd3.collect()
intersection: Array[Int] = Array(1, 2)
```

Code 16.12. *intersection* transformation. For a color version of this
code, see www.iste.co.uk/laffly/torus1.zip

16.2.5. *Exercises for environmental sciences*

16.2.5.1. *Counting*

After a year of field observation using pollution loggers, we have a database with more than one terabyte of data (many loggers, high frequency). We have collected all the logs in a hadoop cluster in hdfs. Write a program that counts the number of pollution logs we have collected.

16.2.5.2. *Average*

The computed logs from previous exercises are JSON strings. It contains a value field with the observed pollution value. Write a program that computes the average of pollution values we have collected.

16.2.5.3. *Normalization*

The loggers use different levels of calibration. To efficiently compare the values, we need to normalize them. Write a program that computes the maximum pollution value of loggers and normalize all the values between 0 and 1.

16.2.5.4. *Filtering*

The computed logs in JSON format also have a date field. Write a program that selects the logs with dates in August 2018.

16.3. Spark machine learning library

In section 16.2, we have presented the *RDD* data structure and its associated operations. It allow us to process huge amounts of data, using a cluster, an *HDFS* storage and *RDD* computation in Scala. *ML* library implements many *ML* algorithms in a distributed way, using *RDD* data as the main datatype. We will present three implementations of famous algorithms (linear regression, random forest and gradient-boosted trees). They belong to the category of supervised learning algorithms and will thus manipulate labeled points as input data.

16.3.1. *Local vectors*

To define a labeled point, we need first to define local vectors. A local vector can store double values on a single node. It can be dense or sparse.

```
scala> import org.apache.spark.mllib.linalg.{Vector, Vectors}
import org.apache.spark.mllib.linalg.{Vector, Vectors}


scala> val dense = Vectors.dense(1,0,2,0,0,3)
dense: org.apache.spark.mllib.linalg.Vector =
↪  [1.0,0.0,2.0,0.0,0.0,3.0]

scala> val sparse = Vectors.sparse(6,Array(0,2,5),Array(1,2,3))
sparse: org.apache.spark.mllib.linalg.Vector =
↪  (6,[0,2,5],[1.0,2.0,3.0])
```

Code 16.13. *Dense and sparse local vector declaration. For a color version of this code, see www.iste.co.uk/laffly/torus1.zip*

16.3.2. *Labeled points*

Labeled points are data types used in supervised learning algorithms, defined from local vectors. It adds a label to the sparse or dense vector, which can be integers (for classification) or doubles (for regression).

```
scala> import org.apache.spark.mllib.regression.LabeledPoint
import org.apache.spark.mllib.regression.LabeledPoint

scala> import org.apache.spark.mllib.linalg.{Vector, Vectors}
import org.apache.spark.mllib.linalg.{Vector, Vectors}

scala> val dense = Vectors.dense(1,0,2,0,0,3)
dense: org.apache.spark.mllib.linalg.Vector =
↪  [1.0,0.0,2.0,0.0,0.0,3.0]

scala> val labeledpoint = LabeledPoint(1,dense)
labeledpoint: org.apache.spark.mllib.regression.LabeledPoint =
↪  (1.0,[1.0,0.0,2.0,0.0,0.0,3.0])
```

Code 16.14. *Labeled point declaration. For a color version of this code,
see www.iste.co.uk/latfly/torus1.zip*

16.3.3. *Learning dataset*

The learning dataset is a set of observations we can distribute on the nodes of the cluster in two ways:

16.3.3.1. *Parallelize labeled points*

The first method involves parallelizing labeled points

16.3.3.2. *Using MLUtils library*

The second method consists of using a predefined function `loadLibSVMFile` from `MLUtils` library. It constructs an *RDD* of labeled points from lines of a file in the following format:

```
label index1:value1 index2:value2 ...
```

where the indices numbered from one represent, in ascending order, the non-zero values of a sparse vector.

16.3.4. *Classification and regression algorithms in Spark*

In Chapter 15, classification and regression models are defined. In this section, we will present the implementation and use of three of them, Linear regression in code 16.17, random forest in code 16.18 and gradient-boosted trees in code 16.19. Once the different models have been built, you have to evaluate their accuracy on testData set, different to the learning dataset, as in code 16.20.

```
scala> import org.apache.spark.mllib.linalg.Vectors
import org.apache.spark.mllib.linalg.Vectors

scala> import org.apache.spark.mllib.regression.LabeledPoint
import org.apache.spark.mllib.regression.LabeledPoint

scala> val dense = Vectors.dense(1,0,2,0,0,3)
dense: org.apache.spark.mllib.linalg.Vector =
↪   [1.0,0.0,2.0,0.0,0.0,3.0]

scala> val sparse = Vectors.sparse(6,Array(0,2,5),Array(1,2,3))
sparse: org.apache.spark.mllib.linalg.Vector =
↪   (6,[0,2,5],[1.0,2.0,3.0])

scala> val labeledpoint1 = LabeledPoint(1,dense)
labeledpoint1: org.apache.spark.mllib.regression.LabeledPoint =
↪   (1.0,[1.0,0.0,2.0,0.0,0.0,3.0])

scala> val labeledpoint2 = LabeledPoint(0,sparse)
labeledpoint2: org.apache.spark.mllib.regression.LabeledPoint =
↪   (0.0,(6,[0,2,5],[1.0,2.0,3.0]))

scala> val rdd =
↪   sc.parallelize(Array(labeledpoint1,labeledpoint2))
rdd:
↪   org.apache.spark.rdd.RDD[....mllib.regression.LabeledPoint]
↪   = ParallelCollectionRDD[1] at parallelize at <console>:39
```

Code 16.15. *Create learning data set from scala collection of labeled points. For a color version of this code, see www.iste.co.uk/laffly/torus1.zip*

16.3.5. *Exercises for environmental sciences*

To end this chapter, we will apply all the previous concepts in two exercises for environmental sciences: exercise 16.3.5.1 to manipulate a regression model for pollution prediction and exercise 16.3.5.2 to manipulate a classification model for plant classification.

```scala
scala> //content of sample_libsvm_data.txt (2 lines)
scala> //1 2:2.0 4:3.0
scala> //0 1:2.0 3:1.0

scala> import org.apache.spark.mllib.regression.LabeledPoint
import org.apache.spark.mllib.regression.LabeledPoint

scala> import org.apache.spark.mllib.util.MLUtils
import org.apache.spark.mllib.util.MLUtils

scala> import org.apache.spark.rdd.RDD
import org.apache.spark.rdd.RDD

scala> val examples: RDD[LabeledPoint] =
  ↪ MLUtils.loadLibSVMFile(sc,
  ↪ "file:///home/torus/sample_libsvm_data.txt")
examples:
  ↪ org.apache.spark.rdd.RDD[....mllib.regression.LabeledPoint]
  ↪ = MapPartitionsRDD[8] at map at MLUtils.scala:108

scala> examples.collect()
res0: Array[org.apache.spark.mllib.regression.LabeledPoint] =
  ↪ Array((1.0,(4,[1,3],[2.0,3.0])), (0.0,(4,[0,2],[2.0,1.0])))
```

Code 16.16. *Create learning data set from LIBSVM text format. For a color version of this code, see www.iste.co.uk/laffly/torus1.zip*

```scala
// Building the model
val numIterations = 100
val stepSize = 0.00000001
val model = LinearRegressionWithSGD.train(trainingData,
  ↪ numIterations, stepSize)
```

Code 16.17. *Linear regression model with SGD. For a color version of this code, see www.iste.co.uk/laffly/torus1.zip*

16.3.5.1. *Pollution prediction*

Consider the dataset of pollution logs from previous exercises. In the dataset in JSON, we have collected different values at the same time as pollution values. Let us consider the fields representing the temperature, the wind and the hour that have all been normalized between zero and one. Write a program that creates a random forest regression model from this dataset with 70% of the dataset for learning and 30% to test.

```scala
// Building the model.
// Empty categoricalFeaturesInfo indicates all features are
↪   continuous.
val numClasses = 2
val categoricalFeaturesInfo = Map[Int, Int]()
val numTrees = 3 // Use more in practice.
val featureSubsetStrategy = "auto" // Let the algorithm
↪   choose.
val impurity = "gini"
val maxDepth = 4
val maxBins = 32

val model = RandomForest.trainClassifier(trainingData,
↪   numClasses, categoricalFeaturesInfo,
  numTrees, featureSubsetStrategy, impurity, maxDepth, maxBins)
```

Code 16.18. *Random forest model. For a color version of this code, see www.iste.co.uk/laffly/torus1.zip*

16.3.5.2. *Plant classification*

Consider a dataset we have built in the field in an arctic area, where plant classification has to be built from remote and *in situ* sensing data. The dataset contains the observation with 10 values for description of the field and the category of the plant (6 classes) that occurs the most in a squared meter area. Write a program that creates a gradient-boosted trees classification model from this dataset with 70% of the dataset for learning and 30% to test.

```
// Building the model.
val boostingStrategy =
↪   BoostingStrategy.defaultParams("Classification")
boostingStrategy.numIterations = 3 // Note: Use more iterations
↪   in practice.
boostingStrategy.treeStrategy.numClasses = 2
boostingStrategy.treeStrategy.maxDepth = 5
// Empty categoricalFeaturesInfo indicates all features are
↪   continuous.
boostingStrategy.treeStrategy.categoricalFeaturesInfo =
↪   Map[Int, Int]()
val model = GradientBoostedTrees.train(trainingData,
↪   boostingStrategy)
```

Code 16.19. *Gradient-boosted trees model. For a color version of this code, see www.iste.co.uk/laffly/torus1.zip*

```
// Evaluate the model.
// Evaluate model on test instances and compute test error
val labelAndPreds = testData.map { point =>
  val prediction = model.predict(point.features)
  (point.label, prediction)
}

val testErr = labelAndPreds.filter(r => r._1 !=
↪   r._2).count.toDouble / testData.count()
println(s"Test Error = $testErr")
```

Code 16.20. *Model evaluation. For a color version of this code, see www.iste.co.uk/laffly/torus1.zip*

16.4. Conclusion

In this chapter, we have presented the tools and methods to create a distributed program in Scala language for *Spark*. These programs can be executed on a *Spark* cluster to process environmental logging data from every *IOT* that will record numeric or categorical values. In the area of big datasets, it is an easy and efficient solution to store and compute environmental data, with minimum syntactic programming effort, like if you were on your usual single node laptop. The next step is to include non-*IOT* values, like remote sensing data. This will be explained using a similar approach to that in Chapter 5, Volume 2 about image processing in *Spark*.

17

Database for Cloud Computing

17.1. Introduction

NoSQL stands for Not only *Standard Query Language (SQL)*. *NoSQL* represents database families characterized by highly scalable databases through replication and distribution concepts. The first database, Bigtable, appeared from Google in the early 2000s [CHA 06] to respond to new storage issues and application architectures attached to the Cloud Computing model. For Google, the challenge was to provide a storage system that was able to index all the web content and perform read/write operations very efficiently. This chapter contextualizes the issues that allowed the emergence of *NoSQL* databases.

It characterizes the concepts underlying *NoSQL* and the taxonomy of the different storage paradigms.

17.2. From myGlsrdbms to *NoSQL*

Relational Database Management Systems (RDBMS) are characterized by centralized data and processing, efficiency through data normalization (according to normal forms) and indexing. For querying the data, they provide a standardized, rich, intuitive and tooled language: *SQL*. They can handle complex queries using inner/outer joins and aggregations, and ensure data integrity with locks, transactions and integrity constraints.

RDBMS are an efficient answer to a majority of industrial problems but optimization operations as replication or parallelization are expensive. The "one size fits all" proverb is suitable for most of the industrial problems and needs since the

Chapter written by Peio LOUBIÈRE.

1980s but *RDBMS* cannot extend infinitely. In [STO 05], the authors argued that while this model still continues to be successful, it cannot adapt to emerging usages.

Many solutions that improve data management, such as object-oriented or XML-formatted data, have been integrated, but they do not address any scalability issue efficiently.

Since the advent of Cloud Computing, new usages are questioning the use of traditional *RDBMS* to manage data:

– indexing all the web content is heavy;

– providing an efficient online shopping service 365 days/year is exhausting;

– storing and retrieving billions of friends' friends' (friends'...) opinions and advice and analyzing them is challenging.

Such usages imply dealing with storing extremely large volumes of data and also managing a huge amount of queries. Since applications are services available from the Internet, this has to be done with an immediate or at least fast constant response time.

But how? As the processing is distributed, the data follows the same way. A huge amount of data is split toward many servers. It must also be replicated to provide high availability or to perform failure/recovery processes. However, as will be detailed in 17.2.2, such mechanisms imply that they are more tolerant about the data consistency.

17.2.1. *CAP theorem*

The CAP theorem [BRE 00, BRE 12] states that it is impossible, for a distributed system, to respect all the three following constraints at the same time:

– *Consistency*: all nodes see the same data at the same time.

– *Availability*: data are available for all users, with constant response time.

– *Partition tolerance*: network failures do not affect the results.

As described in Figure 17.1, traditional *RDBMS* respect consistency and availability constraints. Their logic is to always provide the database at a stable state, with the latest version of the data. *NoSQL* databases respect the partition tolerance constraint (which is obvious since they are distributed databases) and then they are dispatched in two groups, according to the second constraint. If they choose to provide a stable database, ensuring that write and replication operations are correctly done, they respect the consistency constraint; if they prefer to expose the data, even though it is not their latest version, they are close to the availability constraint.

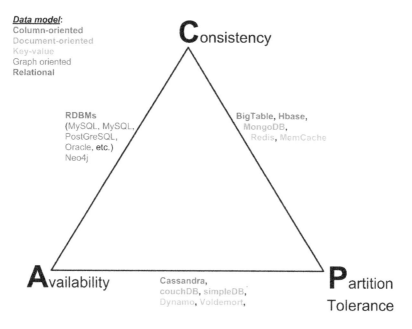

Figure 17.1. *CAP theorem and database distribution map. For a color version of this figure, see www.iste.co.uk/laffly/torus1.zip*

Although this theorem has a big influence on introducing *NoSQL* database systems, in [KLE 15a, KLE 15b], Kleppmann criticizes the CAP theorem. He argues consistency and availability constraints are a simplified version of all the constraints that should face a distributed database. He proposes that this theorem should be relegated to history and not used any more for the design of distributed databases.

In a recent article [BRE 17], Google announced an online *SQL* database (Spanner) in which architecture and performances are presented as being consistent, available and distributed, due to a very short replication and availability latency time.

17.2.2. *From ACID to BASE*

In order to fit to correct constraints, *NoSQL* databases have to relax one of the properties that qualifies traditional *RDBMS*, which choose between availability or consistency. *RDBMS* databases respect data normalization and transactions of ACID properties:

– *Atomicity*: a set of instructions that are globally accepted or globally refused. If one of them fails to be applied, then the whole transaction is rejected;

– *Consistency*: guarantees the consistent state of the database after a transaction is completed. A set of rules (integrity constraints, triggers, stored procedures, etc.) are defined to control the state of the database;

– *Isolation*: manages concurrent transaction interference;

– *Durability*: the modifications of a committed transaction which are permanently saved into the database.

These properties describe a system where every user sees the same data at the same time. BASE is a new acronym which has emerged to describe distributed database properties:

– *Basically Available*: most of the time, the data is available;

– *Soft state*: guarantees the database state but not the latest version;

– *Eventual consistency*: has the updates that will be exposed with enough time.

These properties describe a system with a scalable goal, where the partition tolerance is prime. Therefore, they have to make compromises. On the one hand, they choose to provide consistency and cannot guarantee that data is the same for all connected users; on the other hand, they choose to provide data, even though there are some failures with the read/write/replication process. But in all cases, the database is always in a soft state. Figure 17.1 shows examples of database repartition according to which constraint they respect.

17.3. NoSQL database storage paradigms

NoSQL storage paradigms decline themselves into four categories. Each category is related to a specific use case and groups several databases that aim similar usages.

Nevertheless, these different paradigms have common properties and goals, such as:

– schema-less storage system, providing heterogeneous data structure: each piece of data does not have the same number of attributes;

– sharded and replicated storage system: takes benefits of the cloud infrastructure;

– data redundancy (dependent data is embedded in/closest to its parent), to avoid external joins and integrity constraints.

To illustrate each storage concept, Table 17.1 is an example of data dependency in a *RDBMS* database. This is a simple and usual (1-N) relationship between the entities of the database where:

– each line has the same number of attributes even though there are null ones;

– data dependency is represented by an integrity constraint between the "idCar" belonging to "Employee" table and the "Car" table one.

lastname	firstname	office	age	city	#idCar
Doe	John		57	Toulouse	2
Diaz	Ana	4		Madrid	1
Eguy	Michel	1	42	Bayonne	2
Martin	Kurt	7		Berlin	

idCar	brand	model	color
1	Renault	Twingo	Blue
2	Toyota	Yaris	Orange

Table 17.1. *Example of data relationship between employees and cars. For a color version of this figure, see www.iste.co.uk/laffly/torus1.zip*

17.3.1. *Column-family oriented storage*

In this storage system, data is not stored in lines, as shown in Table 17.1, but the whole data is split into blocks, according to attribute families. Each part of the data belongs to a column family, and an index is used to reconstruct the whole data.

```
columnFamily lastName ((id1,"Doe"), (id2,"Diaz"))
columnFamily firstName ((id1,"John"), (id2,"Ana"))
columnFamily office ((id2, 4))
columnFamily age ((id1, 57))
columnFamily city ((id1,"Toulouse"), (id2,"Madrid"))
```

Code 17.1. *Column family storage example*

This is used when computation of a part of the data is more useful than retrieving the complete data. It allows efficient aggregations (sum, average, count, etc.) by column. Sharding can be managed by column family or according to indexed key values. Examples of column family databases are Google's Bigtable, Cassandra and Amazon's SimpleDB.

17.3.2. *Key/value-oriented storage*

This database family stores the data in a (key, value) format, as a hashmap or associative array structure. The key is unique, to retrieve one data. Querying a key retrieves the whole data, with all its attributes. Each attribute is also a (key, value) pair.

```
(usr1: (lastName: "Doe", firstName: "John", age: 57, city:
 ↪  "Toulouse", car:car2))
(usr2: (lastName: "Diaz", firstName: "Ana", office: 4, city:
 ↪  "Madrid", car:car1))
...
(car2 : (brand:"Toyota", model:"Yaris", color:"Orange"))
```

Code 17.2. *Key/value family storage example*

In this paradigm, data can also have a heterogeneous structure. According to the implementation, data dependency can be done by embedding (key, value) pairs or matching keys as done with integrity constraints in classic *RDBMS*.

Sharding is managed by indexes on key ranges. Example of key/value family databases are Redis, Oracle NoSQL Database and Amazon's Dynamo.

17.3.3. *Document-oriented storage*

Document store-oriented family is an extension of the key/value paradigm. A key makes it possible to retrieve a value formatted as a document. Different formats are encoded, such as *XML, YAML Ain't Markup Language (YAML)* or *JSON*. The unique key returns the whole document.

```
{usr1: {lastName: "Doe",
        firstName: "John",
        age: 57,
        city: "Toulouse",
        car : {brand:"Toyota",
               model:"Yaris",
               color:"Orange"} }}
{usr2: {lastName: "Diaz",
        firstName: "Ana",
        office: 4,
        city: "Madrid",
        car : {brand:"Renault",
               model:"Twingo",
               color:"Blue"} }}
```

Code 17.3. *Document store family storage, JSON example. For a color version of this code, see www.iste.co.uk/laffly/torus1.zip*

Data can have a heterogeneous structure. Documents belong to collections for which join possibilities are reduced or impossible. Data dependency can be done by embedding the dependent document into its parent data. Examples of document store database families are MongoDB, DocumentDB and CouchDB.

17.3.4. *Graph-oriented storage*

The database is represented as a graph. It contains data as nodes and relationships between them as edges. A node contains the data attributes. The specificity is that an edge, representing a relation between two nodes, can store advanced information such as attributes, direction or weight. This structure makes it possible to use graph theory algorithms, semantic queries, etc.

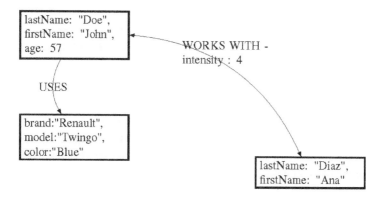

Code 17.4. *Graph family storage example*

Examples of graph database families are graphDB and Neo4j.

17.4. SQL versus NoSQL, the war will not take place

Underlying the term *SQL* there are all *RDBMS*. Both are designed to store data. They are alternatives, with arguments that make it possible to choose between technologies. Several criteria can orientate the choice:

– *Replication, sharding and scalability*: powerful built-in procedures to automate such operations in *NoSQL* databases. However, usually the database system needs many machines to manage sharding and replication efficiently.

– *A strongly relationship-based model*: it is difficult or impossible to perform join operations with *NoSQL* databases. Usually, it is filtering post-treatments or requests executed sequentially to provide the same result as a single *SQL* request. Merise or *Unified Markup Language (UML)* methods do not apply any more in a *NoSQL* context; denormalization and redundancy are the norm. There is a new way of thinking and building the data model. Such databases perform very well when the data modeling is weakly relational.

In the opposite case, *RDBMS* are much more efficient on such use cases:

– *Transactions*: even though some *NoSQL* databases try to include this concept into their behavior (as MongoDB); most databases do not guarantee a transaction system. It is due to the partition paradigm and the asynchronous-based operations.

– *Performance*: this is not a correct evaluation point. Despite all the benchmarks that a user will find on the Internet, performance will depend on all the points described above.

RDBMS should be chosen in cases where the data is hardly structured and very relational, complex queries are needed, and integrity and transactions are essential.

NoSQL would be preferred when the data model is not entirely defined, simple, evaluative and the database should be scalable. Even in this case, the choice of the correct database family should be done according to the project context.

In other cases, both technologies can cohabit in the technical stack. Hybrid/mashup technologies, for example: the business logic is stored in a *RDBMS* and applicative logs, functional flows could be stored in a *NoSQL* database. Users can also benefit from the *newSQL* movement with *SQL*-based *RDBMS* with very low-latency replication (such as Google's Spanner, Hstore and CockroachDB). Such databases offer scaling capabilities with all classical querying and transaction mechanisms. Finally, to make a clear choice in this dense ecosystem, there is no best justification than the use case: use the correct tool for the correct job.

17.5. Example: a dive into MongoDB

In this section, MongoDB concepts and basics are detailed. The current version used in this chapter is version 4.0.

Through this *NoSQL* database system, one of the most widely used, the aim is to illustrate capabilities in terms of storing/retrieving data and using powerful queries such as aggregation and geospatial queries. This scope focuses on presenting data structure and query capabilities; it does not include understanding the database architecture for replication/sharding storage, and this should be done personally, according to your usage.

17.5.1. *Presentation*

MongoDB[1] was released in 2009 by 10gen. It implements a schema-less, web-ready, document-oriented storage system using a derivative *JSON* format: *Binary JSON (BSON)* (see Code 17.5, taken from openaq api[2]). It provides horizontal scalability capabilities with data auto-partitioning across different servers and replication through a master/slave infrastructure.

The taxonomy, which is linked to *RDBMS* basic concepts, is the following: a server (or many) hosts a database. A database is composed of *collections* (i.e. tables), storing *BSON documents* (representing the data, limited to 16 MB, i.e. rows). A data is composed of *attributes* (i.e. columns). Several *RDBMS* concepts are implemented in MongoDB such as indexes, stored procedures (using JavaScript language), cursors and roles.

```
{"_id": 86452384,
  "location":"Aranyaprathet",
  "city":"Sa Kaeo",
  "country":"TH",
  "comments":"Everything OK",
  "last-check-up": "2017/01/03",
  "measurements":[
{"param":"pm10","value":40,"unit":"g/m","updt":"2019-02-19"},
{"param":"so2","value":0.017,"unit":"ppm","updt":"2017-01-08"},
{"param":"no2","value":0.053,"unit":"ppm","updt":"2018-02-22"}
  ],
  "loc":{
      "type": "Point",
      "coordinates": [102.50621, 13.689029]}
  }
}
```

Code 17.5. *Example of a* JSON *document of air quality sensor data. For a color version of this code, see www.iste.co.uk/laffly/torus1.zip*

A rich ecosystem of drivers[3] for managing interactions with MongoDB is available (Scala, Java, Python, PhP, C++, etc.). To illustrate the concepts, we will not use a specific driver but the JavaScript syntax used in the client console. The reader is

1 https://www.mongodb.com/.

2 https://api.openaq.org.

3 https://docs.mongodb.com/ecosystem/drivers/.

advised to explore each driver's own documentation to describe the syntax of each further example in their favorite client language.

For further concepts, explanations and examples, the concerned reader will find an exhaustive user manual available at https://docs.mongodb.org/manual.

In the following, symbols $<...>$ stand for an attribute to be replaced (such as database or collection names).

17.5.2. *First steps*

A single database server instance can be launched using the `mongod` command in a terminal. Parameters (such as ip, port, replication, sharding, storage options) can be defined in the configuration file `mongod.conf`[4].

Once the database server is up, a shell client instance to connect to database is launched by: `mongo --host <host>:<port>`. At first connection, the shell is connected to a default `test` database. To list existing databases, there are several commands such as: *show databases* and *show dbs*.

17.5.3. *Database level commands*

Specific database commands are used to manage databases (connection, information, deletion, etc.).

The keyword *db*, that prefixes all these commands and those further, is a defined generic term that represents the current database (by default, database `test`).

db command displays the current database.

`use <db-name>` command switches to another database. One important concept is that it is not necessary to use explicit commands to create databases or collections. Everything is created implicitly at first document insertion.

There are many commands[5] at the database level such as: help and info (`db.help()`, `db.stats()`), list collections (`db.getCollectionNames()`), logout (`db.logout()`), drop database (`db.dropDatabase()`) and many more operations.

`db.runCommand(...)` runs a specific command (administration commands, specific requests) at the database level, not from a collection, as seen in the following subsections. The reader should look forward to this command, to evaluate all its capabilities.

---

4 https://docs.mongodb.com/manual/reference/configuration-options/.

5 https://docs.mongodb.com/manual/reference/method/#database.

```
// start a mongoDB instance
mongod --port 27017 --dbpath /var/lib/mongodb

// connect to client, from another terminal
mongo --port 27017

// from the client, choose a database to work with
> use airDB
```

Code 17.6. *First client connection. For a color version of this code, see www.iste.co.uk/laffly/torus1.zip*

17.5.4. *Data types*

MongoDB manages a large number of atomic and complex types with specific operators to manage them. Code 17.5 illustrates several type usages.

– atomic type: string, double, integer, Boolean;

– complex types: date, *JSON* document, arrays.

17.5.5. *Modifying data*

In this section, insert, update and delete commands are presented. These commands are launched at the collection level (db. *collection_name.command*).

17.5.5.1. *Inserting data*

There are two ways for inserting data: one by one or several in an array. When inserting, an automatic id property, "_id", is added to the data.

Code 17.7 illustrates an insertion example. In this code, after connection to a client (mongo command into a terminal), the user switches to his/her database (use airDB). The first time, the database and *sensors* collection will be created at first insert. Then the user executes an insertion command of one piece of data in the collection *sensors*. The command returns an OK code with the generated _id value for this data.

17.5.5.2. *Deleting data*

Deletion of data is done by targeting one collection. The same pattern as insertion is used:

Code 17.8 deletes all documents from the "sensors" collection where the "city" attribute has the value "Sa Kaeo". *Note that the filter is formatted as a* JSON *document.* How to write filters is detailed in 17.5.5.6.

```
// insert one data
db.<collection>.insertOne({JSON Object})

// insert an array of many data
db.<collection>.insertMany([JSON Object Array])
```

```
> use airDB        // switch to specific DB

> db.sensors.insertOne(
  { "location":"Aranyaprathet",
    "city":"Sa Kaeo",
    "country":"TH",
    "measurements": [],
    "loc":{
         "type": "Point",
         "coordinates": [102.50621, 13.689029]},
    "active":true
  }
)

returns :

{
  "acknowledged" : true,
  "insertedId" : ObjectId("5c8f76702b5024fb2a2f6fdd")
}
```

Code 17.7. *Example of an insertion of one* JSON *document in collection "sensors". For a color version of this code, see www.iste.co.uk/laffly/torus1.zip*

17.5.5.3. *Updating data*

Updating follows the same pattern:

Code 17.9 renames the "country" attribute of all sensors, when the attribute "city" has the value "Vietnam", to "VN". In this case, note that both the action (with the $set command) and the value to be modified are formatted as *JSON* documents.

```
// delete first data that checks the filter
db.<collection>.deleteOne({JSON filter})

// delete all data that check the filter
db.<collection>.deleteMany({JSON filter})
```

```
> db.sensors.deleteMany({"city":"Sa Kaeo"})
```

Code 17.8. *Example of deletion of all sensors located in city "Sa Kaeo".*
For a color version of this code, see www.iste.co.uk/laffly/torus1.zip

```
// update first data that checks the filter with action
db.<collection>.updateOne({JSON filter}, {action})

// update all data that check the filter with action
db.<collection>.updateMany({JSON filter}, {action})
```

```
> db.sensors.updateMany({"country":"Vietnam"},{$set:
↪   {country:`VN`}})
```

Code 17.9. *Example of renaming the country of a sensor. For a color*
version of this code, see www.iste.co.uk/laffly/torus1.zip

$set command indicates that the value is changed (as in *SQL*). Be aware that
this is different from code 17.10, which will replace all the documents, by the new
document containing only {country:'VN'}, i.e. the other attributes (location, city,
etc.) will be lost.

```
> db.sensors.updateMany({"country":"Vietnam"},{country:`VN`})
```

Code 17.10. *Example of badly renaming the country of a sensor*
(because of replacement). For a color version of this code, see
www.iste.co.uk/laffly/torus1.zip

17.5.5.4. *Updating operators*

Many operators make it possible to modify any document attributes according to:

– Attributes: $rename, $inc, $min, $max, $set, $unset, etc. These operators make it possible to modify attributes, names, values, etc.

– Array: $push, $pushall, $pop, $pull, $pullall, $addToSet, $slice, $sort, etc. These operators make it possible to add/delete elements in an array, or set.

17.5.5.5. *Querying data*

In this section, basic data retrieving commands are presented. The f ind command makes it possible to execute classical queries:

```
db.<collection>.find({<restriction>},{<projection>})
```

A restriction is a constraint to retrieve a subpart of the documents in the collection (same as a "line" selection). A projection is the selection of a specific subset of document attributes (same as a "column" selection). Those parameters are optional. Code 17.11 is an illustration of how to retrieve all documents and their attributes.

```
// retrieves all documents from sensors collection,
// with all attributes.
> db.sensors.find()
```

Code 17.11. *Example of simple query. For a color version of this code, see www.iste.co.uk/laffly/torus1.zip*

For a better understanding of restrictions and projections, an *SQL* selection syntax is the following:

```
SELECT <projection attributes>
FROM <tables>
WHERE <restriction constraints>
```

Code 17.12. *Simple SQL query architecture. For a color version of this code, see www.iste.co.uk/laffly/torus1.zip*

The following sections detail the restriction and projection capabilities.

17.5.5.6. Restriction

The restriction is an optional parameter. If no restriction is specified, all documents are returned by the find query. To add restriction constraints, the parameter is a *JSON*-formatted document, with all restrictions defined. If there is more than one restriction, it will be understood as an "AND" operator (each document must verify all constraints).

```
// retrieves docs from Vietnam country
> db.sensors.find({"country":"VN"})

// retrieves docs, from Ha No city which are active.
> db.sensors.find({"city":"Ha No", "active":true})

// retrieves docs from Vietnam country and all the inactive
↪   ones
> db.sensors.find({$or : [{"country":"VN"}, {"active":false}])

// retrieves docs, from Ha No or Da Nang cities which are
↪   active.
> db.sensors.find({"city":{$in:["Ha No", "Da Nang"]},
↪   "active":true})
```

Code 17.13. *Example of restrictions. For a color version of this code, see www.iste.co.uk/laffly/torus1.zip*

The two last queries from Code 17.13 introduce operators ($or: which adds a matching constraint, $in: which scans a value in an array). For an overview of operators, please refer to section 17.5.5.8.

17.5.5.7. Projection

The projection is an optional parameter. If no projection is specified, all attributes are returned by the find query. To retrieve/not retrieve some attributes, the parameter is a *JSON*-formatted document, with all desired/non-desired attributes with the flag 1/0. By default, the internal attribute "_id" is always returned. If not needed, it has to be removed explicitly.

To write more powerful restrictions, there are many operators available.

```
// retrieves docs, with "city", "country", "loc" and "_id"
↪  attributes.
> db.sensors.find({},{"city":1, "country":1, "loc":1})

// retrieves docs, with "city", "country", "loc" attributes.
> db.sensors.find({},{"city":1, "country":1, "loc":1, "_id":0})

// retrieves docs, with all attributes, but "_id".
> db.sensors.find({},{"_id":0})

// retrieves docs, with all attributes, but "_id" and
↪  "country"
> db.sensors.find({},{"_id":0, "country":0})
```

Code 17.14. *Example of simple queries with projections. For a color version of this code, see www.iste.co.uk/laffly/torus1.zip*

17.5.5.8. *Restriction operators*

The restriction operators can be sorted according to attribute data types:

– comparison: $gt, $gte, $lt, $lte, $eq, $neq, $in, $nin. These operators make it possible to restrict on alphanumerical values, to check (not) belonging in sets, etc.;

– logical: $and, $or, $xor, $not, etc. These operators make it possible to restrict Boolean expressions and values;

– array: $all, $elemeMatch, $size. These operators make it possible to check constraints on all/any elements in an array, its size, etc.;

– element: $exists, $type, etc. These operators make it possible to check an attribute existence in a document, its type, etc.;

– evaluation: $regex, $text, etc. These operators make it possible to search in text attributes using regular expressions, text indexation, etc.;

– geospatial operators: $geoWithin, $geoIntersects, $near, etc. (see section 17.5.5.11 for more). These operators make it possible to execute geographical zone membership, according to latitude/longitude or Euclidean coordinates.

The use of an operator is embedded in a *JSON*-formatted value. The *JSON* formatting depends on the operator (e.g. in Code 17.15); for more detailed information, the reader should refer to the official reference page[6].

6 https://docs.mongodb.com/manual/reference/operator/query/.

```
// all sensors located in Ha No, which has 3 measurements
↪    capabilities,
// returns all attributes but internal id
> db.sensors.find({"city":"Ha No",
↪    "measurements":{$size:3}},{"_id":0})

// all sensors located in Ha No, where attribute measurements
↪    is defined
// and which measure only 1 or 2 values
> db.sensors.find({"city":"Ha No",
        {$and:[{"measurement":{$exists:true}},
        {"measurement":{$size:{$lte:2}}}]}})

// all sensors which have "loc" attruibute
> db.sensors.find({"loc":{$exists:true}})

// all sensors which are not located in France, Belgium, Italy
> db.sensors.find({"country":{$nin:["FR","BE","IT"]}})
```

Code 17.15. *Example of queries with operators. For a color version of this code, see www.iste.co.uk/laffly/torus1.zip*

17.5.5.9. *Sorting*

Sorting a simple query is a post-treatment, applying a sort function with an ordering constraint to the result of a request. The sorting constraint is *JSON*-formatted. The direction of sorting is defined by 1/–1 values. Cumulative sorting is available, appending attributes (e.g. 17.16).

```
// sort by country name ascending
> db.sensors.find().sort({country:1})

// sort by country name descending, then city name ascending
> db.sensors.find().sort({country:-1, city:1})
```

Code 17.16. *Example of sorting. For a color version of this code, see www.iste.co.uk/laffly/torus1.zip*

17.5.5.10. *Paging*

Paging is a post-treatment, which can be applied after a simple query or a sort operation. It is used to limit the number of results returned by the query and to adapt to web pages rendering. There are two functions (e.g. Code 17.17), which can be used independently:

– skip(*nb*): rejects the first *nb* results;

– limit(*nb*): take the next *nb* results.

```
// the first 100 sensors from Thailand and Vietnam, sorted by
↪  country
> db.sensors.find({country: {$in:["TH", "VN"]}})
            .sort({country:1}).skip(0).limit(100)

// the next 100 sensors
> db.sensors.find({country: {$in:["TH", "VN"]}})
            .sort({country:1}).skip(100).limit(100)
```

Code 17.17. *Example of paging. For a color version of this code, see www.iste.co.uk/laffly/torus1.zip*

Facing other *NoSQL* databases, an advantage of working with MongoDB is its capability of building complex queries that can handle geospatial queries and aggregations.

17.5.5.11. *Geospatial queries*

MongoDB provides functionalities to store and query geospatial data. It stores GeoJSON[7] objects, dealing with *Euclidean* or *WGS84*[8] *longitude/latitude* coordinate systems. It can handle queries such as "is near", "is inside" or "intersects" defined shapes. As an example, a sensor defined in Code 17.5 owns a "loc" attribute that is a GeoJSON point object.

17.5.5.12. *GeoJSON object*

A MongoDB GeoJSON object owns two required attributes: type and coordinates. The type describes the shape of the object (point, polygon, line, etc.), coordinates defines the shape location. Each point is an array defined as: **[longitude, latitude]**. Code 17.18 illustrates an example of GeoJSON objects.

---

7 http://geojson.org/.
8 http://spatialreference.org/ref/epsg/4326/.

The different objects are:

– a Point: this defines a single point located at specified coordinates;

– a MultiPoint: this defines a set of single points;

– a LineString: this defines a broken line constituted of an array of at least two points;

– a MultiLineString: this defines a set of LineStrings, and its coordinates are an array of LineStrings;

– a Polygon: this is almost the same as LineString apart from the fact that it contains at least four points and that the line is closed (i.e. the first and last point coordinates are the same).

In addition, a polygon can own multiple rings, and this means that the coordinates attribute is an array of many polygons; each polygon, the exterior polygon, must be included completely in the next one.

– a MultiPolygon: this defines a set of polygons.

```
// Ppoint
{ type: "Point",
  coordinates: [-0.3667,43.3] }

// LineString
{ type: "LineString",
  coordinates:[[-0.33357,43.30675], [-0.33357,43.30675],
               [-0.33365,43.30674], [-0.33370,43.30672]] }

// Polygon
{ type: "Polygon",
  coordinates: [[[-73.958,40.8003], [-73.9498,40.7968],
               [-73.9737,40.7648], [-73.9814,40.7681],
               [-73.958,40.8003]]] }
```

Code 17.18. *Examples of GeoJSON objects according their types. For a color version of this code, see www.iste.co.uk/laffly/torus1.zip*

To specify which system of coordinates and to efficiently query this kind of data, geospatial indexes must be defined on the GeoJSON object attribute. Code 17.19 provides the two ways to define an index, according to the coordinates system used. 2d is used when dealing with an Euclidean coordinates system; 2dsphere is used when using the WGS84 coordinate system. From the sensor example (Code 17.5), the collection is *sensor* and the location field is *loc*. For more information on indexes, please refer to section 17.5.5.15.1.

```
// 2d index for euclidean
db.<collection>.createIndex( {<location field> : "2d"} )

// 2dsphere index for GPS coordinates
db.<collection>.createIndex( {<location field> : "2dsphere"} )
```

Code 17.19. *GeoJSON indexes according their system. For a color version of this code, see www.iste.co.uk/laffly/torus1.zip*

17.5.5.13. *Queries*

There are four operators to process geospatial queries:

– `$geoIntersects`: this returns all documents which geometry intersects the given geometry. It accepts 2dsphere index only;

– `$geoWithin`: this returns all documents that belong within the given geometry. This given geometry can be a box, polygon, circle, etc. It accepts 2d and 2dsphere indexes;

– `$near` and `$nearSphere`: these return all documents which geometry is in proximity of a given point, with min/max distance. The difference between the two methods is the distance computation. They return matching documents ordered from the nearest to the farthest and accept 2d and 2dsphere indexes.

Code 17.20 illustrates the use of geospatial operators to query the sensors' collection.

```
db.<collection>.aggregate( [
  { <operation 1> },
  ...
  { <operation n> }
] )
```

17.5.5.14. *Aggregation pipeline*

17.5.5.14.1. Definition

Aggregations make it possible to chain projections, restrictions, grouping functions (such as counts, average, min, max) and so on. They can be seen as an equivalent of the *SQL* group by having instructions. To understand the syntax and the behavior of this powerful command, it can be compared to the Unix pipelining system: a set of commands will be executed in a defined order and the result of the nth command is the entry parameter of the $(n + 1)^{th}$ one. Such commands apply many filters and transformations to a collection data, step by step, to provide a result document.

```
// select all sensors defined in a zone
> db.sensors.find( {
    loc: {
      $geoWithin: {
        $geometry: {
          type : "Polygon" ,
          coordinates: [[[-73.958,40.8003], [-73.9498,40.7968],
                  [-73.9737,40.7648], [-73.9814,40.7681],
                  [-73.958,40.8003]]]
      } } } } )

// select all sensors in proximity (from 200m to 3 km) of a
  ↪  point
> db.sensors.find( {
    loc: {
      $near: {
        $geometry: {
          type: "Point",
          coordinates: [ -73.9667, 40.78 ]
        },
        $minDistance: 200,
        $maxDistance: 3000
      } } } )
```

Code 17.20. *Geospatial queries examples. For a color version of this code, see www.iste.co.uk/laffly/torus1.zip*

17.5.5.14.2. Classical aggregations

This section describes how to write simple aggregations corresponding to usual *SQL* aggregation queries (Code 17.21).

In the aggregation framework, this can be used using the following operators:

– $project: to return only desired attributes;

– $match: to add restrictions as in where or having statements (according to the position);

– $group: to add aggregation functions (sum, average, min, count, etc.);

– $sort: to add order operations.

```
SELECT <projection fields>, <aggregation function>
FROM <tables>
WHERE <restrictions and joins>
GROUP BY <grouping fields>
HAVING <restrictions on aggregation result>
ORDER BY <sorting>
```

Code 17.21. *SQL aggregation query pattern. For a color version of this code, see www.iste.co.uk/laffly/torus1.zip*

For example, to count all sensors by country, ordered by decreasing number of sensors:

```
// SQL like :
// SELECT country, count(sensor_id) as total FROM sensors
// GROUP BY country ORDER BY total DESC;
db.sensors.aggregate( [
{ $project: { _id : 0, country : 1 }  },
{ $group: { _id : "$country", total : { $sum : 1 } } },
{ $sort: {total: -1} }
] )
```

Code 17.22. *Request for all sensors by country, ordered by decreasing number of sensors. For a color version of this code, see www.iste.co.uk/laffly/torus1.zip*

In this example, first only country attribute is selected from all sensor documents. Then, the grouping function counts "1" and sums them for each same country name in the field names "total" (note that the $ symbol before "country" attribute is used to reference previous attribute). Then, the decreasing sorting function is applied to "total" attribute.

Restrictions can be added in the pipeline, for example to count sensors, by city, in a given country; then return only the cities that own less than 20 sensors.

In the aggregation pipeline, the order of each operation has a huge importance. Be aware that the matching operator must be used BEFORE the project operator. Indeed, after the project operator is applied, there is no more the attribute "country". Note also that the $match operator stands for both the "WHERE" and "HAVING" *SQL* operators, according to where it is used.

```
// SQL like :
// SELECT city, count(sensor_id) as total FROM sensors
// WHERE country = "VN" GROUP BY city HAVING total < 20;
db.sensors.aggregate( [
{ $match: { country : "VN" }  },
{ $project: { _id : 0, city : 1 }  },
{ $group: { _id : "$city", total : { $sum : 1 } } },
{ $match: { total : {$lt: 20} }
] )
```

Code 17.23. *Request to count sensors, by Vietnamese city; for the cities that own less than 20 sensors. For a color version of this code, see www.iste.co.uk/laffly/torus1.zip*

Another framework can be used to process more complex treatments for aggregations. The curious interested reader can discover more about MongoDB MapReduce framework at: https://docs.mongodb.com/manual/core/map-reduce/.

Many more operators are available in pipeline framework, such as averages, array transformations, string concatenation, date, time, arithmetic or join operators. An exhaustive list is available at: https://docs.mongodb.com/manual/reference/operator/aggregation/.

17.5.5.15. *A few more*

Before ending this MongoDB presentation, three more concepts are detailed, inherited from relational databases that are important when dealing with *NoSQL* databases: indexes, users/roles management and third part application connection.

17.5.5.15.1. Indexes

To improve database performances, correct indexing of data is a crucial point of configuration. Indexing data purpose is to accelerate queries executions by performing efficient collection scans. The objective is to index the mostly used restriction criteria to improve the reading performances. As used in most of database systems, indexes are built using B-Trees. This avoids scanning all the data and provides a logarithmic complexity when retrieving data.

```
// create a simple index on city name, in decreasing order
> db.sensors.createIndex( { city: -1 } )

// create a compound index on city and country names
> db.sensors.createIndex( { country:1, city: 1 } )

// create a multikey index on measurement name
> db.sensors.createIndex( { measurements.param:1} )

// create a geospatial index
> db.sensors.createIndex( { loc: "2dsphere" } )

// create a text index
> db.sensors.createIndex( { comments: "text" } )
```

Code 17.24. *Index definition examples. For a color version of this code, see www.iste.co.uk/laffly/torus1.zip*

By default, the internal field "_id" is indexed. However, a user can create their own indexes to improve search performances. Several different indexes can be used for particular needs:

– single value index: to index an often restricted value;

– compound index: to index a tuple of values. Valid only if all attributes of the tuple are restricted together;

– multikey index: to index a content of an array;

– geospatial index: to index a GeoJSON object or coordinates array to perform geospatial queries;

– text index: to convert powerful text queries into strings, with pertinence computation;

– hash index: to use collection sharding according to specific attributes and hash functions (advanced feature).

17.5.5.15.2. Users and roles

By default, it is possible to connect and use MongoDB without authentication. As all databases, MongoDB provides users/password connections and roles to restrict usage. The simplified standard command, focusing on login, password and roles, is illustrated by Code 17.25. This section illustrates how to simply use user authentication and role management.

```
// select all sensors defined in a zone
> db.createUser( {
  user: "<name>",
  pwd: "<cleartext password>",
  customData: { <any information> },
  roles: [
    { role: "<role>", db: "<database>" } | "<role>",  ...
  ],
  writeConcern: { <write concern> },
  digestPassword: <boolean>
} )
```

Code 17.25. User/roles definition. For a color version of this code, see www.iste.co.uk/laffly/torus1.zip

To create access rights and roles for users, an administration user must be created from a MongoDB client instance (Code 17.26). Only an admin user can create other users. In this example, the admin user created can manage users on the database "airDB" and can read or write data on all the database instances.

```
// start an instance
mongod --port 27017 --dbpath /var/lib/mongodb

// connect to client and database
mongo --port 27017
> use airDB

// create admin user
> db.createUser( {
    user: "myAdmin",
    pwd: "admin0001",
    roles: [ { role: "userAdmin", db: "airDB" },
    ↪ "readWriteAnyDatabase" ]
  } )
```

Code 17.26. Create administration user. For a color version of this code, see www.iste.co.uk/laffly/torus1.zip

Then disconnect the client and restart the database instance, adding an --auth option to enable authentication. Code 17.27 illustrates first authentication with the newly created admin user "myAdmin" on the database "airDB" and how it can create a user that can access "airDB" with read-only permission.

```
// start an instance
mongod --auth --port 27017 --dbpath /var/lib/mongodb

// connect to client and database "airDB", then create a new
↪  user
mongo --port 27017 -u "myAdmin" --authenticationDatabase
↪  "airDB" -p

> db.createUser( {
    user: "myUser",
    pwd: "userpass0001",
    roles: [ { role: "read", db: "airDB" } ]
  } )
```

Code 17.27. *First admin authentication and user creation. For a color version of this code, see www.iste.co.uk/laffly/torus1.zip*

Then, the administration user will be able to create users and give them roles to read/write data in specific databases/collections.

There are many built-in roles. Each role offers several privileges at the database level. The following list presents basic roles for admin and common users. For administration roles, appending AnyDatabase to the role name gives privileges for almost all databases of the MongoDB instance.

– read: this allows a user to only read into a database (use find, aggregate and many other listing commands);

– readWrite: this allows a user to read and write into a database (use find, aggregate, insert, update, remove data and indexes commands);

– dbAdmin: this allows a user to do database administration commands (such as create/drop collections, databases, indexes);

– userAdmin: this allows a user to manage users and to create/delete, etc.;

– dbOwner: this owns the three last roles;

– root: this is the highest privilege role, which owns all administration privileges, on any database.

New roles can be defined (db.createRole() command) to add specific privileges/roles on a specific database level or even at collection level.

As an example, Code 17.28 illustrates how to create a new role, which allows only find privilege on the collection "sensors" from the "airDB" database. Then, Code 17.29 shows how this new role is granted to the user.

```
// create Role
> db.createRole(
   {
     role: "sensorsReadOnly",
     privileges: [
       {
         actions: [ "find" ],
         resource: { db: "airDB", collection: "sensors" }
       }
     ],
     roles: []
   }
```

Code 17.28. *Create specific role at collection-level. For a color version of this code, see www.iste.co.uk/laffly/torus1.zip*

Admin users can modify users/roles *a posteriori*, adding or revoking a role, changing a password (e.g. Code 17.29).

A last useful illustration of how privileges and user update can be used is to allow a user to update their own password. Code 17.30 summarizes this process.

Since the concepts presented in this chapter are a slight overview of MongoDB capabilities, such complex user and role management should be dealt with in depth in the MongoDB reference manual[9].

Many actions related to core database administration, clustering, sharding and replication and also simple data management are fully customizable in users' roles/privileges.

---

9 https://docs.mongodb.com/manual/reference/method/#role-management-methods.

```
// update user password
> db.changeUserPassword("myUser", "71t2voC1r")

// revoke role read
> db.revokeRolesFromUser(
    "myUser", [ role: "read", db: "airDB" } ]
)

// grant role read on sensors collection
> db.grantRolesToUser(
    "myUser", [ role: "sensorsReadOnly", db: "airDB" } ]
)
```

Code 17.29. *Update user example. For a color version of this code, see www.iste.co.uk/laffly/torus1.zip*

```
// Create a role for own password update (connected as
↪  admin)
> db.createRole(
  { role: "changeOwnPass",
    privileges: [
    {
        resource: { db: "", collection: ""},
        actions: [ "changeOwnPassword" ]
    } ],
    roles: []
  }
)
// grant this role to existing user (connected as admin)
> db.grantRolesToUser(
    "myUser", [ role: "changeOwnPass", db: "airDB" } ]
)

// Now, user can now change its password (connected as
↪  "myUser")
> db.updateUser( "myUser", { pwd: "71t2voC1r" } )
```

Code 17.30. *Allow user to update their password. For a color version of this code, see www.iste.co.uk/laffly/torus1.zip*

17.5.5.15.3. Drivers

The syntax presented so far is the inner database javascript-based syntax. Usually, the users will send requests to the database from a client application written in a specific language. As far as MongoDB is a widely used *NoSQL*, many language drivers are available (such as Scala, Python, C#, Java, PHP). The curious reader will be able to explore them at: https://docs.mongodb.com/ecosystem/drivers/.

17.6. Conclusion

NoSQL and *RDBMS* are alternatives according to problem modeling and usage. Working with MongoDB first implies rethinking the data model. Since there are no simple join queries, a document structure must contain all the information needed. This is a key point to understand how to correctly use a document-based *NoSQL* database.

Other classical database features, such as users/roles, indexes, *CRUD* and aggregations work just the same, modulo in javascript-based syntax. This last point is not a crucial point. This has been explained in this chapter, for a generic purpose. It is obvious that all the presented features should be used in a client application language. Therefore, we encourage readers to discover more about their favorite language driver syntax to work with a MongoDB database (especially Scala or Python as languages hosted in the HUPI SaaS platform).

This chapter focuses on the use of MongoDB as a single instance database. It is important to note that the purpose of a *NoSQL* database is to manage scalability. We also encourage readers interested in database administration and configuration to look for replication and sharding concepts.

17.7. References

[BRE 00] BREWER E.A., "Towards robust distributed systems", *Symposium on Principles of Distributed Computing*, ACM, p. 7, New York, USA, 2000.

[BRE 12] BREWER E.A., "CAP twelve years later: How the "rules" have changed", *Computer*, vol. 45, no. 2, pp. 23–29, 2012.

[BRE 17] BREWER E.A., Spanner, TrueTime and the CAP Theorem, Report, Google, 2017.

[CHA 06] CHANG F., DEAN J., GHEMAWAT S. *et al.*, "Bigtable: A distributed storage system for structured data", *7th USENIX Symposium on Operating Systems Design and Implementation*, pp. 205–218, 2006.

[KLE 15a] KLEPPMANN M., "A critique of the CAP theorem", *CoRR*, vol. abs/1509.05393, 2015.

[KLE 15b] KLEPPMANN M., "Please stop calling databases CP or AP". Available at: https://martin.kleppmann.com/2015/05/11/please-stop-calling-databases-cp-or-ap.html, 2015.

[STO 05] STONEBRAKER M., CETINTEMEL U., "One size fits all: An idea whose time has come and gone", *21st International Conference on Data Engineering*, pp. 2–11, April 2005.

WRF Performance Analysis and Scalability on Multicore High Performance Computing Systems

Weather Research and Forecast (WRF) is one of the most commonly used numerical weather prediction models that has superior scalability and computational efficiency. Its performance and scalability was tested on the Computing on Kepler Architecture (COKA) cluster, a recent multicore high-performance computing (HPC) system installed at the University of Ferrara, Italy. Two major experiments were designed: single domain with varied grid size (E1) and nesting domain (E2) WRF configuration. As expected, simulation speed decreased when domain grid size increased, while an increase in the number of computing nodes used in the simulation would increase the simulation speed under E1. We run WRF with several combinations of Message Passing Interface (MPI) tasks and threads per MPI task. Optimum performances for E1 and E2 were achieved either using 4 computing nodes with 8 MPI per node (MPN) and 2 threads per MPI (TPM) or 4 nodes with 2 MPN and 8 TPM. Most often, time was spent on computational processing (89–99%) rather than other processes such as input processing and output writing. The WRF model domain configuration was an important factor for simulation performance: for example, the nesting domain would slow down the simulation by 100 times in comparison to the single domain configuration. Further works can be done for testing the performance and scalability for other WRF applications, forecasting and air quality simulation on the newly installed TORUS cloud at the Asian Institute of Technology.

Chapter written by Didin Agustian PERMADI, Sebastiano Fabio SCHIFANO, Thi Kim Oanh NGUYEN, Nhat Ha Chi NGUYEN, Eleonora LUPPI and Luca TOMASSETTI.

18.1. Introduction

The Numerical Weather Prediction (NWP) model is an important tool for both research and operational forecast of meteorology which can be used for various other purposes such as weather aviation, agriculture, air pollution dispersion modeling, etc. A fundamental challenge is to understand how increasingly available computational power can improve modeling processes, in addition to the reliability of the NWP output itself [MIC 08]. The Weather Research and Forecast (WRF) model is one of the most commonly used NWP that is designed to run on a variety of platforms, either serially or in parallel, with or without multi-threading [SKA 07]. In light of the rapid development of the WRF model, a successor of the previously well-known mesoscale meteorological model (MM5), other NWP models exist such as the Regional Atmospheric Modeling (RAMS) System, the Regional Climate Model (RegCM), etc.

WRF model performance benchmarking has been done within different environments to demonstrate the scalability of the computational environment and considerations for higher productivity [HPC 15]. It is well understood that the WRF model is widely adopted for the assessment for at least the following two reasons: 1) its superior scalability and computation efficiency [CHU 17] and 2) the last generation of the NWP which is equipped with current developments in physics, numerics and data assimilation [POW 17]. We conducted WRF performance analysis and scalability on multicore a High Performance Computing (HPC) system using our own benchmarking configuration. We used WRF version 3.7 for testing its application for a tropical domain in Southeast Asia (SEA), dominated by convective meteorology conditions. First, we tested performance and scalability using a WRF single domain configuration for different grid sizes, followed by a two-way nesting configuration. In this study, we have run the code enabling both Message Passing Interface (MPI) to exploit parallelism among different node-processors, and Open-MPI to exploit parallelism within each node-processor.

18.2. The weather research and forecast model and experimental set-up

18.2.1. *Model architecture*

WRF, a mesoscale NWP, is designed for both atmospheric and forecasting research. It was initially developed in the 1990s under a collaborative partnership of the National Center for Atmospheric Research (NCAR), the National Centers for Environmental Prediction (NCEP), the Forecast Systems Laboratory (FSL), the

Air Force Weather Agency (AFWA), the Naval Research Laboratory, the University of Oklahoma and the Federal Aviation Administration (FAA). The source code has been made available[1]. The model consists of two dynamical cores: the Advanced Research WRF (ARW) and Nonhydrostatic Mesoscale Model (NMM); the first is commonly used for research and application [SKA 08]. WRF equations are formulated using a terrain-following hydrostatic-pressure vertical coordinate (sigma pressure level). WRF solver currently supports four projections to the sphere: the Lambert conformal, polar stereographic, Mercator and latitude–longitude rojections.

The WRF modeling system includes three components, with pre-processing (known as WPS), main solver (ARW) and post-processing of outputs which can be used for another model (e.g. air quality model) or visualization. The initial conditions for the real-data cases are pre-processed through a separate package called the WRF Preprocessing System (WPS) which takes terrestrial and meteorological data (lateral boundary conditions). Static geographical data such as terrain and land-cover can be taken from the WRF website repository[2]. Lateral meteorology boundary conditions can be taken from the National Center for Environmental Prediction FNL (Final) Operational Global Analysis data which are available on a resolution of 1° (approximately 100 km) for every six hours. The main solver ARW includes two classes of simulation, with ideal initialization and using real data. In this research, we used the real-data which require pre-processing through WPS to generate initial and lateral boundary conditions. The final run is done in a main solver of WRF to generate 3-dimensional (3D) simulated fields of meteorological parameters. This final run is recognized as the most time-consuming process. The system is shown in detail in Figure 18.1.

Multiple physical parameterizations are offered in WRF, included in physics categories, i.e. microphysics, cumulus parameterization, planetary boundary layer (PBL), land surface model (LSM) and radiation. Each parameterization is used to resolve certain specific physical atmospheric processes. For example, water vapor, cloud particle formation is resolved by microphysics, while the effect of sub grid scale clouds is represented by cumulus parameterization schemes. PBL schemes provide flux profile due to eddy transports in the whole atmospheric column. The radiation schemes provide the atmospheric heating profiles and estimation of net radiation for the ground heat budget. The surface layer (SL) schemes are used to calculate the friction velocity and exchange coefficients that enable the estimation of heat, momentum and moisture fluxes by the LSMs.

---

1 http://www2.mmm.ucar.edu/wrf/users/download/get_source.html.
2 http://www2.mmm.ucar.edu/wrf/users/download/get_sources_wps_geog.html.

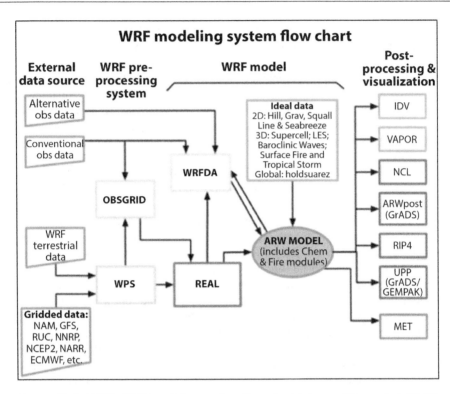

Figure 18.1. *WRF–ARW modeling system flow chart (source: Wang et al. 2016). For a color version of this figure, see www.iste.co.uk/laffly/torus1.zip*

18.2.1.1. *Experimental set-up for performance and scalability of the system*

To assess performance and scalability, we prepared two benchmarking configurations: i) experiment 1 (E1), single domain with a different grid number (constant grid resolution of 18×18 km^2 is presented in Figure 18.2), and ii) experiment 2 (E2), nesting domain, i.e. 3 domains with a resolution of 18, 6 and 2 km respectively (as presented in Figure 18.3). The detailed geographical configuration of E2 WRF experiment is presented in Table 18.1.

For E1, WRF was used to simulate a 6-hour period (approximately 21,600 seconds), from January 1, 2007, 00:00 AM to January 1, 2007, 06:00 AM. For E2, WRF was used to simulate a 5-day period (January 1, 2016, 00:00 AM to January 5, 2016, 00:00 AM) for all cases of grid sizes. For both experiments, we performed simulations using different combinations of number of nodes, N (1, 2 and 4), number of MPI tasks per node (MPN) and number of threads per MPI task, TPM (1, 2, 4, 8 and 16).

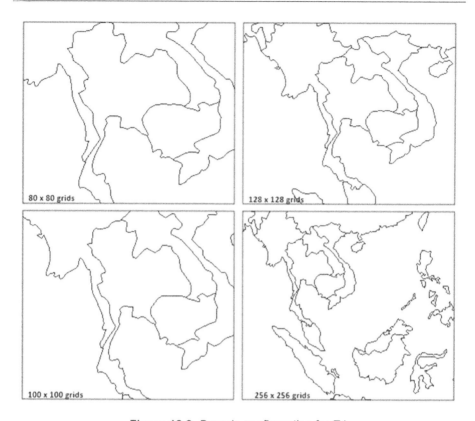

Figure 18.2. *Domain configuration for E1*

We then monitored the following parameters:

– time (T) required to finish each simulation (sum of computation, writing output processing input, and processing boundary conditions);

– simulation speed (S) that is defined as the ratio of the actual period simulated by WRF to the time required to finish simulation;

– total core (TC) that is estimated by the following equation:

$$\text{Total cores} = N \times MPN \times TPM \qquad [18.1]$$

with N, MPN and TPM defined above.

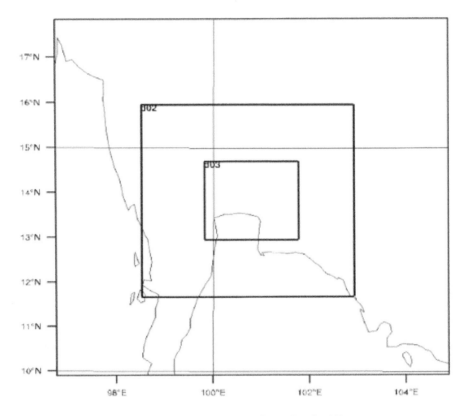

Figure 18.3. *Domain configuration for E2*

The coarsest domain for the E2 experiment comprised 50 × 50 grid cells with a grid resolution of 18 km. The second and the finest domains consisted of 81 × 81 and 96 × 99 grid cells with a grid solution of 6 km and 2 km, respectively (Table 18.1).

Selection of physics options is important as the incorporated physics options would affect the time required for simulation. We selected meteorological physics options, namely microphysics, cumulus, radiation, boundary layer and land surface interaction from previous publications that are suitable for this region [CHO 11, PRA 13]. The WRF experiment E1 (single domain) used the options presented for domain 1 in Table 18.2, while experiment E2 (nesting domain) used all of the options presented in the same table.

Domains	X	Y	Lon	Lat
Domain 1: dx = 18 km				
Number of Dot Points	51	51	–	–
Starting Lower Left i, j of Parent Grid	1	1	–	–
Domain 2: dx = 6 km				
Number of Dot Points	82	82	–	–
Starting Lower Left i, j of Parent Grid	12	12	–	–
LCP of the SW Dot Point (km)	–243	–243	98.5	11.6
LCP of the NE Dot Point (km)	243	243	102.99	16.0
Domain 3: dx = 2 km				
Number of Dot Points	97	100	–	–
Starting Lower left i, j of Parent Grid	24	24	–	–
LCP of the SW Dot Point (km)	–105	–105	99.7	12.8
LCP of the NE Dot Point (km)	87	93	101.5	14.7

Table 18.1. *Geographical configuration of "two-way" nesting domains*

Physics options	Domain 1 (18 km)	Domain 2 (6 km)	Domain 3 (2 km)
Microphysics	WDM6	WSM3	WSM3
Cumulus parameterization	BMJ	BMJ	BMJ
Short-wave radiation	Dudhia	Dudhia	Dudhia
Long-wave radiation	RRTM	RRTM	RRTM
Planetary Boundary Layer	YSU	YSU	YSU
Surface Layer	Monin-Obukhov	Monin-Obukhov	Monin-Obukhov
Land Surface Layer	Noah LSM	5-layer thermal diffusion	5-layer thermal diffusion

Table 18.2. *Physics options selected for the WRF experiment E1 (domain 1) and E2 (all 3 domains)*

The combinations of N, MPN and TPM used in all experiments are presented in Table 18.3. Simulations for each domain were done for all 15 combinations.

No.	N	MPN	TPM
1	1	1	16
2	1	2	8
3	1	4	4
4	1	8	2
5	1	16	1
6	2	1	16
7	2	2	8
8	2	4	4
9	2	8	2
10	2	16	1
11	4	1	16
12	4	2	8
13	4	4	4
14	4	8	2
15	4	16	1

Table 18.3. *Combinations of N, MPN and TPM used in experiments. N = number of node; MPN = number of MPI tasks per node; TMP = number of threads per MPI task*

18.3. Architecture of multicore HPC system

The results we show in this chapter were taken from an initial run on the COKA installed cluster at the University of Ferrara in Italy. The COKA cluster has 5 computing nodes, each node hosting 2 Intel Xeon E5-2630v3 CPUs, 256 GB of memory and 8 dual-gpu NVIDIA K80 boards. The Intel Xeon E5-2630v3 processor embeds an 8-core, each supporting the execution of 2 threads, and 20 MB of L3-cache. It runs at a 2.40 GHz frequency that can be boosted up to 3.20 GHz under specific conditions of workloads. Nodes are interconnected with 56 Gb/s FDR InfiniBand links, and each node hosts 2 Mellanox MT27500 Family [ConnectX-3] HCA, allowing *multirail networking* for a doubled inter-node bandwidth. The two InfiniBand HCAs are connected respectively to the two PCIe root complexes of the two CPU sockets. This allows for a symmetric hardware configuration, where each processor has one local InfiniBand HCA, connected to the same PCIe root complex; so, data messages do not need to traverse the Intel Quick Path inter-socket communication link.

Since processors of this cluster are multi-core, the WRF code has been configured to use both the OpenMP and MPI libraries. In practice, our application launches one or more MPI processes, and each process spawns several threads associated to a physical core of the processor. This allows us to fully exploit all the levels of the parallelism offered by the machine: node-level parallelism is handled through the MPI library, while core-level parallelism is handled through the OpenMP library.

Under the TORUS project, cloud cluster infrastructure (computing node and storage) was installed at the Asian Institute of Technology (AIT), Pathumthani, Thailand. To exploit the running of WRF on cloud, 10 nodes (each consisting of 8 cores) were installed over virtual machine (VM) configuration as part of total 20 × proc Intel Xeon E5 2650 10 cores or 200 cores. This hardware infrastructure has total 640 GB of RAM, 10 nodes, on X6800 multi-node rack of Huawei brand. The system has a hardware infrastructure storage of total 114 TB storage, 6 TB high-speed storage.

18.4. Results

This section will report the results we have measured on the cluster about the performance and scalability of the system. Even though time (T) was recorded in our experiments, the results presented here are mainly focused on the simulation speed (S) of each combination for both E1 and E2.

18.4.1. Results of experiment E1

For each grid-size case, the speed (S) is presented against MPN and TPM as plotted in Figure 18.4. We observe that using a single node, the highest value of S was achieved with 8 MPN and 2 TPM for all grid size configurations. However, this pattern was not seen if we used 2 nodes that seem to be dependent on the grid-size configuration.

In this experiment, using 4 nodes, the optimum performance was achieved when we used 2 MPN and 8 TPM for the grid-size configuration corresponding to 80 × 80 and 100 × 100 cells; however, for the larger number of grid cells, the highest simulation speed was achieved using 8 MPN and 2 TPM (Figure 18.4). Overall, the increase in the number of grids was associated with lower simulation speed. The increase in the number of nodes used in the simulation was associated with increased performance (higher simulation speed). In Table 18.4, we report the simulation speed achieved for a different grid size as a function of the total number of cores (TC) used. TC is defined as the product of N, MPN and TPM as expressed in [18.1]

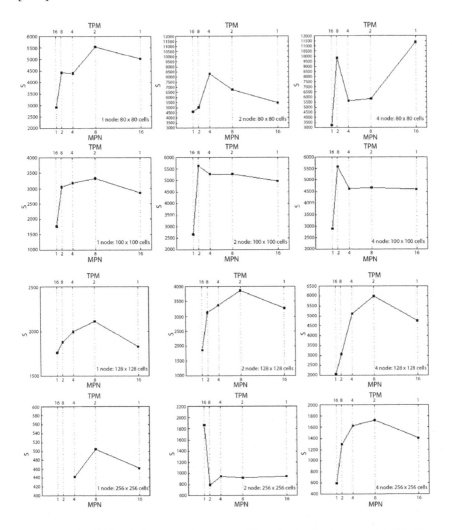

Figure 18.4. *Simulation speed measured for all combinations under E1. The lower horizontal axis reports MPN (the number of MPI task per node), and the upper is the corresponding TPM (the number of threads per MPI task). The vertical axis reports the simulation speed (S)*

Horizontal grid size (number of cells)	Total number of core (TC)	Simulation speed (S)
80 × 80	16	5,553
	32	8,308
	64	11,368
100 × 100	16	3,328
	32	5,640
	64	5,596
128 × 128	16	2,114
	32	3,864
	64	6,000
256 × 256	16	463
	32	1,864
	64	1,728

Table 18.4. *Relationship between grid size, total core and simulation speed for experiment E1*

It was found that the increase in the total number of cores would increase the simulation speed; however, the grid-size configuration would also affect this relationship. For the grid size corresponding to 80 × 80 and 128 × 128 cells, a clear relationship was seen. However, for the grid sizes corresponding to 100 × 100 and 256 × 256 cells, the optimum performance was achieved for the total number of cores of 32 rather than 64, although the difference was not large. This indicated that the WRF domain configuration during the parallel computation, plays an important role in its computation performance.

In Table 18.5, we analyzed the time required for different processes, including the processing input, writing output, processing boundary conditions and simulation and present the results. Computation dominated the share of the total time required, i.e. 89–98% with the average value of 94.3% followed by the output writing of 1.2–8.5% (averaged at 4.3%). Other processes collectively shared only 0.13–4.2% (averaged at 1.38%). It is obvious that the simulation speed is largely affected by the time required for computation which, in turn, is affected by the model configuration.

Process	% of total time		
	Average	Max	Min
Computation	94.30	98.40	89.05
Writing output	4.32	8.47	1.16
Processing input	0.60	1.61	0.10
Processing lateral boundary	0.78	2.68	0.03

Table 18.5. *Share of different processes to the total time required for experiment E1*

18.4.2. *Results of experiment E2*

The relationship between MPN, TPM and S is presented in Figure 18.5 for WRF experiment E2 over 3 domains. It was found that when using a single node, optimum performance (highest S value) was achieved using 8 MPM and 2 TPM. Similar results were seen for all the experiments with 4 nodes. However, a different pattern was observed when we used 2 nodes which had the optimum performance achieved using 4 MPM and 4 TPM. Overall, using 2 nodes would increase performance (1.4 times faster) than only a single node. However, increasing the number of nodes to 4 would only slightly improve the performance (Table 18.6). There is a need to further investigate a bottle neck, especially when we used 2 and 4 nodes.

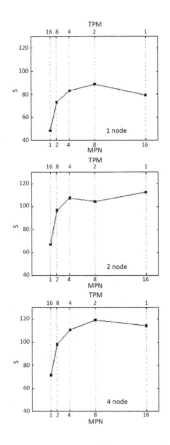

Figure 18.5. *Simulation speed measured for all combinations under experiment E2. The lower horizontal axis reports MPN (the number of MPI task per node) and the upper is TPM (the corresponding number of threads per MPI task). The vertical axis reports the simulation speed (S)*

Configuration*	Number of total core	Simulation speed
1-1-16	16	48
1-2-8	16	73
1-4-4	16	83
1-8-2	16	89
1-16-1	16	79
2-1-16	32	67
2-2-8	32	97
2-4-4	32	108
2-8-2	32	104
2-16-1	32	113
4-1-16	64	72
4-2-8	64	98
4-4-4	64	111
4-8-2	64	119
4-16-1	64	114

Table 18.6. *Relationship between the total number of cores (TC) and the simulation speed (S) based on the results of experiment E2. *Number of node = MPI task per node thread per MPI task*

Similar to experiment E1, we also analyzed the time required for different processes, and the results are presented in Table 18.7. The computation consumed the most, i.e. 98.7–99.6%, of the total computation time with the average of 99.13%, followed by the output writing of 0.32–1.14% with an average of 0.81%. Other processes collectively shared only 0.03–0.1% with an average of 0.06%. As compared to the results of experiment E1, the time required for computation in experiment E2 is larger. This is because in experiment E2, the 2-way nesting simulation was simultaneously applied for all three domains and hence more time was required.

Process	% of total time		
	Average	Max	Min
Processing input	0.05	0.08	0.03
Writing output	0.81	1.14	0.32
Processing lateral boundary	0.01	0.02	0.00
Simulation	99.13	99.64	98.77

Table 18.7. *Share of time consumed for different processes to the total time required for experiment E2*

18.5. Conclusion

WRF model version 3.7 was applied for a tropical convective dominated domain of SEA, using multicore HPC at the University of Ferrara, Italy, for performance and scalability analysis. Single domain with different grid sizes (experiment E1) and nesting domain (experiment E2) configurations were simulated and evaluated in terms of time and simulation speed under different node set-ups, MPI task and thread. E1 results showed that the simulation speed decreased when the number of grid cells in the domain increased, which was expected, and the increase in the number of nodes used in the simulation would increase the simulation speed. In E1, when using a total of 64 cores, the highest speed was obtained for the domains 80×80 and 128×128 cells, and this was better than the results of 16 and 32 cores. E2 results showed the optimum performance when using 4 nodes, 8 MPN and 2 TPM which was only slightly better than using 2 nodes. Overall, the time required for computation contributed the most (89–99%) for both experiments compared to that consumed for input processing and output writing. Simulation speed of nesting domain configuration experiment (E2), when two-way nesting was applied for simultaneous simulation on 3 domains, was 100 times slower than the one-way nesting simulation for single domain (E1); thus, WRF model domain configuration (one-way or two-way nesting) was an important factor for simulation speed, in addition to the computing core configuration.

Future work should be firstly extended to cover a more extensive performance analysis and scalability for ideal cases of WRF simulations, such as hurricane/typhoon and meteorology forecasting. Secondly, similar tests should be conducted for WRF applications to drive air quality dispersion models. Thirdly, simulations with different computing configurations using GP–GPUs need to be conducted to significantly reduce the execution time of most computing intensive kernel routines. Fourthly, GP–GPUs can be used by new and recent programming frameworks such as OpenACC, which would allow reduced execution time of several scientific applications. Lastly, a scalability study needs to be performed with similar WRF benchmarks using the newly installed TORUS cloud cluster at AIT.

18.6. References

[BON 18] BONATI C., CALORE E., D'ELIA M. et al., Portable multi-node LQCD Monte Carlo simulations using OpenACC. International Journal of Modern Physics C, 29(1), doi: 10.1142/S0129183118500109, 2008.

[CAL 16] CALORE E., GABBANA A., KRAUS J. et al., Performance and portability of accelerated lattice Boltzmann applications with OpenACC, Concurrency Computation, 28(12), 3485–3502, doi: 10.1002/cpe.3862, 2016.

[CHU 17] CHU Q., XU Z., CHEN Y. *et al.*, Evaluation of the WRF model with different domain configurations and spin-up time in reproducing a sub-daily extreme rainfall event in Beijing, China, *Hydrology and Earth System Sciences*. Available at: https://doi.org/10.5194/hess-2017-363, 2017.

[HPC 15] HPC AC, WRF 3.7.1: Performance Benchmarking and Profiling. Report, High Performance Computing Advisory Council, 2015.

[MIC 08] MICHALAKES J., HACKER J., LOFT R. *et al.*, WRF nature run. *Journal of Physics: Conference Series*, 125(1), 2008.

[POW 17] POWERS J.G., KLEMP J.B., SKAMAROCK W.C., *et al.*, The Weather Research and Forecasting (WRF) model: Overview, system efforts, and future directions. *Bulletin for the American Meteorological Society*. Available at: https://doi.org/10.1175/BAMS-D-15-00308.1, 2017.

[SKA 08] SKAMAROCK W.C., KLEMP J.B., DUDHIA J. *et al.*, A description of the advanced research WRF version 3. Technical Note, NCAR, Boulder, Colorado, USA, 2008.

List of Authors

Florent DEVIN
EISTI (International School of
Information Processing Science)
Pau
France

Astrid JOURDAN
EISTI (International School of
Information Processing Science)
Pau
France

Dominique LAFFLY
University of Toulouse 2 – Jean Jaurès
France

Yannick LE NIR
EISTI (International School of
Information Processing Science)
Pau
France

Peio LOUBIÈRE
EISTI (International School of
Information Processing Science)
Pau
France

Eleonora LUPPI
University of Ferrara
Italy

Nhat Ha Chi NGUYEN
Asian Institute of Technology
Pathum Thani
Thailand

Thi Kim Oanh NGUYEN
Asian Institute of Technology
Pathum Thani
Thailand

Didin Agustian PERMADI
Asian Institute of Technology
Pathum Thani
Thailand

Hichem SAHLI
Vrije University of Brussels
Belgium

Sebastiano Fabio SCHIFANO
University of Ferrara
Italy

Luca TOMASSETTI
University of Ferrara
Italy

Index

Summary of Volume 2

Chapter 3. Image Quality

Dominique LAFFLY

Chapter 4. Remote Sensing Products

Van Ha PHAM, Viet Hung LUU, Anh PHAN, Dominique LAFFLY,
Quang Hung BUI and Thi Nhat Thanh NGUYEN

Chapter 5. Image Processing in Spark

Yannick LE NIR, Florent DEVIN, Thomas BALDAQUIN, Pierre MESLER LAZENNEC, Ji Young JUNG, Se-Eun KIM, Hyeyoung KWOON, Lennart NILSEN, Yoo Kyung LEE and Dominique LAFFLY

Chapter 6. Satellite Image Processing using Spark on the HUPI Platform

Vincent MORENO and Minh Tu NGUYEN

Chapter 9. Spatial Data Infrastructure

Quang Hung BUI, Quang Thang LUU, Duc Van HA, Tuan Dung PHAM,
Sanya PRASEUTH and Dominique LAFFLY

Summary of Volume 3

Preface

Chapter 1. Introduction to Environmental Management and Services

Thi Kim Oanh NGUYEN, Quoc Tuan LE, Thongchai KANABKAEW, Sukhuma CHITAPORPAN and Truong Ngoc Han LE

Chapter 4. Atmospheric Modeling with Focus on Management of Input/Output Data and Potential of Cloud Computing Applications

Thi Kim Oanh NGUYEN, Nhat Ha Chi NGUYEN, Nguyen Huy LAI and Didin Agustian PERMADI

4.1. Introduction
  4.1.1. Atmospheric modeling
  4.1.2. Roles of modeling in air quality management
  4.1.3. Existing modeling systems
4.2. Model architecture of chemistry transport model
  4.2.1. Conceptual framework and structure
  4.2.2. Data flow and processing
4.3. Output data processing
  4.3.1. Output data processing
  4.3.2. Model performance evaluation
4.4. Potential applications of cloud computing in atmospheric modeling
  4.4.1. Current status of cloud computing applications in atmospheric modeling
  4.4.2. Potential applications of cloud computing in air quality modeling
4.5. Case studies of air pollution modeling in Southeast Asia
  4.5.1. Modeling air quality in Vietnam
  4.5.2. Modeling air quality in the Bangkok Metropolitan Region
  4.5.3. Modeling air quality in the Southeast Asia domain
4.6. Summary and conclusion
4.7. References

Chapter 5. Particulate Matter Concentration Mapping from Satellite Imagery

Thi Nhat Thanh NGUYEN, Viet Hung LUU, Van Ha PHAM, Quang Hung BUI and Thi Kim Oanh NGUYEN

5.1. Introduction
5.2. Relation of aerosol optical thickness, meteorological variables and particulate matter concentration
  5.2.1. Data collection
  5.2.2. Outlier detection
  5.2.3. Data integration
  5.2.4. Correlation analysis
  5.2.5. Validation of satellite-derived AOD and ground-measured AOD
  5.2.6. Relation of particulate matter concentration and meteorological variables
  5.2.7. Relation of particulate matter concentration and satellite-derived AOD

Chapter 6. Comparison and Assessment of Culturable Airborne Microorganism Levels and Related Environmental Factors in Ho Chi Minh City, Vietnam

Tri Quang Hung NGUYEN, Minh Ky NGUYEN and Ngoc Thu Huong HUYNH

Chapter 7. Application of GIS and RS in Planning Environmental Protection Zones in Phu Loc District, Thua Thien Hue Province

Quoc Tuan LE, Trinh Minh Anh NGUYEN, Huy Anh NGUYEN and Truong Ngoc Han LE

Chapter 10. Assessing Impacts of Land Use Change and Climate Change on Water Resources in the La Vi Catchment, Binh Dinh Province

Kim Loi NGUYEN, Le Tan Dat NGUYEN, Hoang Tu LE, Duy Liem NGUYEN, Ngoc Quynh Tram VO, Van Phan LE, Duy Nang NGUYEN, Thi Thanh Thuy NGUYEN, Gia Diep PHAM, Dang Nguyen Dong PHUONG, Thi Hong NGUYEN, Thong Nhat TRAN, Margaret SHANAFIELD and Okke BATELAAN

Conclusion and Future Prospects

Other titles from

in

Computer Engineering

2020

OULHADJ Hamouche, DAACHI Boubaker, MENASRI Riad
Metaheuristics for Robotics
(Optimization Heuristics Set – Volume 2)

SADIQUI Ali
Computer Network Security

2019

BESBES Walid, DHOUIB Diala, WASSAN Niaz, MARREKCHI Emna
Solving Transport Problems: Towards Green Logistics

CLERC Maurice
Iterative Optimizers: Difficulty Measures and Benchmarks

GHLALA Riadh
Analytic SQL in SQL Server 2014/2016

TOUNSI Wiem
Cyber-Vigilance and Digital Trust: Cyber Security in the Era of Cloud Computing and IoT

2017

BENMAMMAR Badr
Concurrent, Real-Time and Distributed Programming in Java

HÉLIODORE Frédéric, NAKIB Amir, ISMAIL Boussaad, OUCHRAA Salma,
SCHMITT Laurent
Metaheuristics for Intelligent Electrical Networks
(Metaheuristics Set – Volume 10)

MA Haiping, SIMON Dan
Evolutionary Computation with Biogeography-based Optimization
(Metaheuristics Set – Volume 8)

PÉTROWSKI Alain, BEN-HAMIDA Sana
Evolutionary Algorithms
(Metaheuristics Set – Volume 9)

PAI G A Vijayalakshmi
Metaheuristics for Portfolio Optimization
(Metaheuristics Set – Volume 11)

2016

BLUM Christian, FESTA Paola
Metaheuristics for String Problems in Bio-informatics
(Metaheuristics Set – Volume 6)

DEROUSSI Laurent
Metaheuristics for Logistics
(Metaheuristics Set – Volume 4)

DHAENENS Clarisse and JOURDAN Laetitia
Metaheuristics for Big Data
(Metaheuristics Set – Volume 5)

LABADIE Nacima, PRINS Christian, PRODHON Caroline
Metaheuristics for Vehicle Routing Problems
(Metaheuristics Set – Volume 3)

LEROY Laure
Eyestrain Reduction in Stereoscopy

LUTTON Evelyne, PERROT Nathalie, TONDA Albert
Evolutionary Algorithms for Food Science and Technology
(Metaheuristics Set – Volume 7)

MAGOULÈS Frédéric, ZHAO Hai-Xiang
Data Mining and Machine Learning in Building Energy Analysis

RIGO Michel
Advanced Graph Theory and Combinatorics

2015

BARBIER Franck, RECOUSSINE Jean-Luc
COBOL Software Modernization: From Principles to Implementation with
the BLU AGE® Method

CHEN Ken
Performance Evaluation by Simulation and Analysis with Applications to
Computer Networks

CLERC Maurice
Guided Randomness in Optimization
(Metaheuristics Set – Volume 1)

DURAND Nicolas, GIANAZZA David, GOTTELAND Jean-Baptiste,
ALLIOT Jean-Marc
Metaheuristics for Air Traffic Management
(Metaheuristics Set – Volume 2)

MAGOULÈS Frédéric, ROUX François-Xavier, HOUZEAUX Guillaume
Parallel Scientific Computing

MUNEESAWANG Paisarn, YAMMEN Suchart
Visual Inspection Technology in the Hard Disk Drive Industry

2014

BOULANGER Jean-Louis
Formal Methods Applied to Industrial Complex Systems

BOULANGER Jean-Louis
Formal Methods Applied to Complex Systems:Implementation of the B Method

GARDI Frédéric, BENOIST Thierry, DARLAY Julien, ESTELLON Bertrand, MEGEL Romain
Mathematical Programming Solver based on Local Search

KRICHEN Saoussen, CHAOUACHI Jouhaina
Graph-related Optimization and Decision Support Systems

LARRIEU Nicolas, VARET Antoine
Rapid Prototyping of Software for Avionics Systems: Model-oriented Approaches for Complex Systems Certification

OUSSALAH Mourad Chabane
Software Architecture 1
Software Architecture 2

PASCHOS Vangelis Th
Combinatorial Optimization – 3-volume series, 2nd Edition
Concepts of Combinatorial Optimization – Volume 1, 2nd Edition
Problems and New Approaches – Volume 2, 2nd Edition
Applications of Combinatorial Optimization – Volume 3, 2nd Edition

QUESNEL Flavien
Scheduling of Large-scale Virtualized Infrastructures: Toward Cooperative Management

RIGO Michel
Formal Languages, Automata and Numeration Systems 1: Introduction to Combinatorics on Words
Formal Languages, Automata and Numeration Systems 2: Applications to Recognizability and Decidability

SAINT-DIZIER Patrick
Musical Rhetoric: Foundations and Annotation Schemes

TOUATI Sid, DE DINECHIN Benoit
Advanced Backend Optimization

2013

ANDRÉ Etienne, SOULAT Romain
The Inverse Method: Parametric Verification of Real-time Embedded Systems

BOULANGER Jean-Louis
Safety Management for Software-based Equipment

DELAHAYE Daniel, PUECHMOREL Stéphane
Modeling and Optimization of Air Traffic

FRANCOPOULO Gil
LMF — Lexical Markup Framework

GHÉDIRA Khaled
Constraint Satisfaction Problems

ROCHANGE Christine, UHRIG Sascha, SAINRAT Pascal
Time-Predictable Architectures

WAHBI Mohamed
Algorithms and Ordering Heuristics for Distributed Constraint Satisfaction Problems

ZELM Martin *et al.*
Enterprise Interoperability

2012

ARBOLEDA Hugo, ROYER Jean-Claude
Model-Driven and Software Product Line Engineering

BLANCHET Gérard, DUPOUY Bertrand
Computer Architecture

BOULANGER Jean-Louis
Industrial Use of Formal Methods: Formal Verification

BOULANGER Jean-Louis
Formal Method: Industrial Use from Model to the Code

CALVARY Gaëlle, DELOT Thierry, SÈDES Florence, TIGLI Jean-Yves
Computer Science and Ambient Intelligence

MAHOUT Vincent
*Assembly Language Programming: ARM Cortex-M3 2.0: Organization,
Innovation and Territory*

MARLET Renaud
Program Specialization

SOTO Maria, SEVAUX Marc, ROSSI André, LAURENT Johann
Memory Allocation Problems in Embedded Systems: Optimization Methods

2011

BICHOT Charles-Edmond, SIARRY Patrick
Graph Partitioning

BOULANGER Jean-Louis
Static Analysis of Software: The Abstract Interpretation

CAFERRA Ricardo
Logic for Computer Science and Artificial Intelligence

HOMES Bernard
Fundamentals of Software Testing

KORDON Fabrice, HADDAD Serge, PAUTET Laurent, PETRUCCI Laure
Distributed Systems: Design and Algorithms

KORDON Fabrice, HADDAD Serge, PAUTET Laurent, PETRUCCI Laure
Models and Analysis in Distributed Systems

LORCA Xavier
Tree-based Graph Partitioning Constraint

TRUCHET Charlotte, ASSAYAG Gerard
Constraint Programming in Music

VICAT-BLANC PRIMET Pascale *et al.*
Computing Networks: From Cluster to Cloud Computing

2010

AUDIBERT Pierre
Mathematics for Informatics and Computer Science

BABAU Jean-Philippe *et al.*
Model Driven Engineering for Distributed Real-Time Embedded Systems

BOULANGER Jean-Louis
Safety of Computer Architectures

MONMARCHE Nicolas *et al.*
Artificial Ants

PANETTO Hervé, BOUDJLIDA Nacer
Interoperability for Enterprise Software and Applications 2010

SIGAUD Olivier *et al.*
Markov Decision Processes in Artificial Intelligence

SOLNON Christine
Ant Colony Optimization and Constraint Programming

AUBRUN Christophe, SIMON Daniel, SONG Ye-Qiong *et al.*
Co-design Approaches for Dependable Networked Control Systems

2009

FOURNIER Jean-Claude
Graph Theory and Applications

GUEDON Jeanpierre
The Mojette Transform / Theory and Applications

JARD Claude, ROUX Olivier
Communicating Embedded Systems / Software and Design

LECOUTRE Christophe
Constraint Networks / Targeting Simplicity for Techniques and Algorithms

2008

BANÂTRE Michel, MARRÓN Pedro José, OLLERO Hannibal, WOLITZ Adam
Cooperating Embedded Systems and Wireless Sensor Networks

MERZ Stephan, NAVET Nicolas
Modeling and Verification of Real-time Systems

PASCHOS Vangelis Th
Combinatorial Optimization and Theoretical Computer Science: Interfaces and Perspectives

WALDNER Jean-Baptiste
Nanocomputers and Swarm Intelligence

2007

BENHAMOU Frédéric, JUSSIEN Narendra, O'SULLIVAN Barry
Trends in Constraint Programming

JUSSIEN Narendra
A TO Z OF SUDOKU

2006

BABAU Jean-Philippe *et al.*
From MDD Concepts to Experiments and Illustrations – DRES 2006

HABRIAS Henri, FRAPPIER Marc
Software Specification Methods

MURAT Cecile, PASCHOS Vangelis Th
Probabilistic Combinatorial Optimization on Graphs

PANETTO Hervé, BOUDJLIDA Nacer
Interoperability for Enterprise Software and Applications 2006 / IFAC-IFIP I-ESA'2006

2005

GÉRARD Sébastien *et al.*
Model Driven Engineering for Distributed Real Time Embedded Systems

PANETTO Hervé
Interoperability of Enterprise Software and Applications 2005

Printed and bound by CPI Group (UK) Ltd, Croydon, CR0 4YY